Corporate Governance: Political and Legal Perspectives

Corporate Governance in the New Global Economy

Series Editors: Kevin Keasey
Leeds Permanent Building Society Professor of Financial Services and Director of the International Institute of Banking and Financial Services, Leeds University Business School, UK
Steve Thompson
Professor of Strategic Management, Nottingham University Business School, UK
Mike Wright
Professor of Financial Studies and Director of the Centre for Management Buy-out Research, Nottingham University Business School, UK

Wherever possible, the articles in these volumes have been reproduced as originally published using facsimile reproduction, inclusive of footnotes and pagination to facilitate ease of reference.

For a list of all Edward Elgar published titles visit our site on the World Wide Web at
www.e-elgar.com

Corporate Governance: Political and Legal Perspectives

Edited by

Mark J. Roe

Berg Professor of Corporate Law
Harvard Law School, USA

CORPORATE GOVERNANCE IN THE NEW GLOBAL ECONOMY

An Elgar Reference Collection
Cheltenham, UK • Northampton, MA, USA

Published by
Edward Elgar Publishing Limited
The Lypiatts
15 Lansdown Road
Cheltenham
Glos GL50 2JA
UK

Edward Elgar Publishing, Inc.
William Pratt House
9 Dewey Court
Northampton
Massachusetts 01060
USA

This book has been printed on demand to keep the title in print.

A catalogue record for this book is available from the British Library

ISBN 978 1 84542 113 7

Printed and bound in Great Britain by Marston Book Services Limited, Didcot

Contents

Acknowledgements

The editor and publishers wish to thank the authors and the following publishers who have kindly given permission for the use of copyright material.

Elsevier for article: Raghuram G. Rajan and Luigi Zingales (2003), 'The Great Reversals: The Politics of Financial Development in the Twentieth Century', *Journal of Financial Economics*, **69**, 5–50.

Georgetown Law Journal for article: Henry Hansmann and Reinier Kraakman (2001), 'The End of History for Corporate Law', *Georgetown Law Journal*, **89**, 439–68.

Journal of Legal Studies and The University of Chicago Law School for article: Paul G. Mahoney (2001), 'The Common Law and Economic Growth: Hayek Might Be Right', *Journal of Legal Studies*, **XXX**, June, 503–25.

Oxford University Press for excerpt: Mark J. Roe (2003), *Political Determinants of Corporate Governance: Political Context, Corporate Impact*, 1–25, 27–37, 199–206, references.

Oxford University Press and University of Chicago Press for excerpt: Mark J. Roe (2004), 'Explaining Western Securities Markets', in Anna Grandori (ed.), *Corporate Governance and Firm Organization: Microfoundations and Structural Forms*, 279–96.

University of Chicago Press for article: Rafael La Porta, Florencio Lopez-de-Silanes, Andrei Shleifer and Robert W. Vishny (1998), 'Law and Finance', *Journal of Political Economy*, **106** (6), 1113–55.

Every effort has been made to trace all the copyright holders but if any have been inadvertently overlooked the publishers will be pleased to make the necessary arrangement at the first opportunity.

In addition the publishers wish to thank the Marshall Library of Economics, Cambridge University and the Library of the University of Warwick for their assistance in obtaining these articles.

Introduction
Political vs. Corporate Institutions as Explaining Western Securities Markets?

Mark J. Roe

The issue to explain in this literature is why some nations have deep securities markets, while others do not. The issue is not just academic, but embedded in the programs of the development agencies: since poorer nations tend to have poorer securities markets, are securities markets a road to wealth? Or are securities markets the results of wealth? The latter was perhaps the older feeling, while the former – securities markets as an instrument toward wealth – is perhaps the newer hope: build a securities market and industry will come.

In recent years two newer theories have emerged to help explain the presence or absence of strong securities markets: in one theory, corporate law propels securities markets, with, as a key corollary, common law systems especially as adept at developing the right corporate law. In the other theory, a nation's politics is more important than its common or civil law origin. Either legal system can construct good corporate law, if its policy wants it. More basic institutions than corporate law get the nation to the level of wealth in which securities markets with ownership separation could play a role. But once those basic institutions – many of them legal institutions available to either legal origin – are in place (property rights, enforceable contracts, low levels of corruption, effective macro policies), corporate law is (relative to getting good contract enforcement and strong property rights) easy. For those nations that have the basic institutional foundations, whether or not a nation has much securities development and ownership separation depends largely on something other than institutional capacity, but, so the second theory runs, depends largely on political currents inside that nation. If politics is supportive of corporate and securities institutions in nations where the basic property and contract institutions are functional, then that nation will get the corporate institutions.

Legal Origins

The Theory

The legal origins theory has been pushed forward most vigorously and most originally by La Porta, Silanes, Shleifer, and Vishny. In a series of articles they make the case that legal protection of minority stockholders is critical to ownership separation, with legal origin (civil law vs. common law) as the critical determinant of that protection (La Porta *et al.*, 1997, 1998, 1999, 2000). (The 1998 article is reproduced as Chapter 2, this volume.) Legal origins matter, their theory runs, because a) common law adeptly protects minority stockholders through common law's fiduciary duties, and b) civil law systems over-regulate. Data show a strong correlation between legal origins and ownership separation, as well as between legal origins and an index of legal protections.

On the former idea – the particular relevance of common law legal systems and their production of corporate law – Cheffins (2000), Coffee (2001), and Roe (2000) argue that the stock exchanges may have been more important initial engines of stockholder protection (however weak that protection was), and Miwa and Ramseyer (2002) and deLong (1991) argue that reputational institutions were key in Japan and the United States at the end of the nineteenth and the beginning of the twentieth centuries. On the latter idea – over-regulation as central – Coffee (2001) argues that civil law systems stifled self-regulatory organizations like stock exchanges. In Chapter 6, this volume, Roe (2004) argues that legal origin does not nicely explain the results: common law nations use civil law-type structures to regulate their corporations (via securities laws, which are heavily codified and primarily enforced by a regulator, not the judge). Equally importantly, he shows, fiduciary duties in the common law nations cover much less than they are usually understood to cover. Other institutions must be in play, he argues.

Bebchuk (1999) frees the corporate law theory from its legal origin specificity. He analyzes how weak minority shareholder protection weakens securities markets. As long as there are significant private benefits of control that a blockholder can garner, then diffuse ownership is unstable. If diffuse ownership should appear in a system that badly protects minority stockholders, then a blockholder will seek to enter the firm, take a block, and begin diverting the private benefits to himself or herself. Accordingly, the blockholder will not give up control if private benefits are high, and if he does, the diffusely owned structure is unstable. He does not theorize on how and why a nation gets good law to protect minority stockholders, but concludes that it is necessary for ownership to separate and for stock markets to develop.

Doubts about the Corporate Law Theory

The legal origins argument is not universally accepted. In one direct critique, Rajan and Zingales (2003, Chapter 3, this volume) present data that stock markets were developing nicely in most of the richer civil law nations at the end of the nineteenth and beginning of the twentieth centuries. While many of the firms that went public had blockholders, and ownership had not yet fully separated (as it had not in the United States), blockholders and dispersed stockholders lived together in the same firms in most civil law countries. Stock market capitalization in France and Germany rivaled that of the United States.

Rajan and Zingales thereby implicitly challenge the over-regulatory theory: in that theory (Coffee, 2001; La Porta, 1997), civil law systems are seen to over-regulate and to undermine private law institutions like stock markets. However, Rajan and Zingales' (2003a) findings suggest otherwise. Whatever 'excessive' regulation of stock exchanges existed in France and Germany, it was not so excessive as to destroy nascent stock markets in those nations. Rather, the trend lines for the nation-by-nation development of western securities markets suggest that the atrophy of civil law stock markets was a mid-twentieth-century phenomenon, rather than one tied to longstanding legal origins or the base level of regulation. Some nations' over-regulation may indeed have been sub-optimal, but it was not so excessive as to kill their nascent securities markets before World War I. It may well have been the political *sturm und drang* of the European early twentieth century that set securities markets back, and not its civil law mode of making law (Roe, 2005). The world wars had varying effects on the world's richest nations, and those varying effects – in destroying institutions and affecting post-war politics – nicely predict the strength of late-twentieth-century securities markets.

Other modern data also call into question the legal origins thesis: data that measure private benefits vary considerably from nation to nation, even among civil law nations (very high, as expected, in Italy, but low in Germany and Scandinavia; indeed at levels about that of the UK and the US) (Dyck and Zingales, 2004; Nenova, 2003; Franks and Mayer, 2001 (Germany)).

Roe (2004) in the last item in this volume offers an alternative conceptual account of legal origins. The common law system is 'low' in regulation; the civil law system is 'high'. The common law acts through judges interpreting in context via fiduciary duties; the civil law system operates through stiff codes and regulations. However, the principal protection for minority stockholders in the United States comes, Roe argues, through the securities laws and the SEC, which are *regulatory* institutions, not common law institutions. Roe argues that the base-line legal technology of *either* legal origin is not well suited to deal with securities markets; even if civil law would tend to over-regulate, common law would under-regulate. Each must adapt and the question he sees as primary, once a nation is rich enough to conceivably build securities markets, is whether the political will to do so is there.

Moreover, argues Roe (2002, 2003, 2004, 2005), vast portions of the corporate structure are effectively not regulated directly, and sometimes only weakly and indirectly, by corporate law. The American business judgment rule effectively has corporate law active in ferreting out thievery, but *not* in directly attacking mismanagement, but if managers mismanage the firm for stockholders, then ownership will tend not to separate and securities markets will tend to be weak. The institutions that keep managers aligned with shareholders are not primarily corporate law institutions.

Property Rights

For transitional and third-world nations especially, what is at stake might not be corporate law in particular, but the weakness of property rights in general. Mahoney (2001, Chapter 4, this volume) traces out the relationship – cf. Milhaupt (1998) (the state as retaining control rights over firms) and Gordon (2004) (the state as actor).

Let me offer a related account, one that builds on those cited in the prior paragraph, but that is not precisely theirs. If property rights are secure, then the economy will grow and large organizations will develop. Large organizations will then demand a good foundation of contract and even stronger property law. When we detect weak corporate law in the third-world and transitional nations, we are not, in this view of the institutional structure, detecting the primary basis for the weakness of securities markets and ownership separation. Rather we are detecting weak economies with little need yet for large business organizations. Weak corporate law is (simply?) derivative of those nations' weak property rights and ineffective contract law, not their weak corporate law. Corporate law would be the dessert, but they do not (yet) have the basic nutrition.

Once nations have developed strong property and contract institutions, they can grow, and some do. Once they grow and become richer, some will have the political will to develop diffuse ownership (more on that below). Those that do will get the corporate law that they need, as corporate law is a (relatively) 'simple', or at least not revolutionary, variant of its foundation of good property and contract law. Either this relatively 'simple' variant can develop through corporate law or, more often, through semi-private, self-regulatory organizations (Mahoney, 1997; Roe, 2001; Coffee, 2001). Today nations need not even have the developmental capacity; they can copy what works elsewhere, if they have both a) the foundational institutions and b) the political will to do so.

Thus, there are two separate questions to ask, and neither depends *solely*, or even primarily, on legal origins and the quality of corporate law. *First*, are property rights (and contract rights) sufficiently well protected that firms will grow and organizations become complex? If *no*, then corporate law is irrelevant (or its weakness just reflects the weakness of contract and property law). One strain in the current literature, while it lacks this precise emphasis, focuses on institutional quality, with that quality coming from sources other than legal origin (Acemoglu, Johnson and Robinson, 2002; Berkowitz, Pistor and Richard, 2003). (But cf. Beck, Demirgüç and Levine, 2003.)

If *yes*, then *second*, are political configurations favorable in the nation that has large organizations to securities markets and ownership separation? If *yes* to the second question, then that nation is probably not going to have much trouble building good corporate and securities law if it wishes to build it. In this vision, corporate law quality is not irrelevant, but a) it only comes into play in rich nations, once property rights are sufficiently strong, and b) once property is sufficiently strong, i) corporate law should not be hard to build and ii) political trends can undermine even good corporate law. Corporate law is an 'assist', not the primary determinant in either the poor or the rich setting.

Peace as Predicate

Roe (1994, 2003) presents two complementary theories on how politics can 'determine' the degree of ownership and the strength of securities markets in a nation that a) has a strong enough base of property and contract rights and b) is rich enough to have large firms. Some of this material is in this volume's first chapter.

First, 'populism' has propelled diffuse ownership by weakening financial institutions' role in large American firms and generally making financial control of large organizations harder (see Roe, 1990, 1994; Jensen, 1993). Second, social democratic, and closely related corporatist, polities have tended to hold back European securities market development and ownership separation.

The latter, the social democratic demeaning of securities markets and ownership separation, has occurred through two channels. The first channel has been inside the firm: managers in separated firms would not be as loyal to shareholders in social democratic polities as they would be in more conservative polities. Labor can make greater claims on the firm's cash flows, and there are, or have been, greater pressures emanating from the government in some nations, and less pressure in other nations, to expand employment to avoid down-sizing, etc. In some nations managers in diffusely owned firms would be more susceptible than in others to pressure to act in ways detrimental to shareholders. Even if the appropriate corporate law institutions were in place in those nations, the institutions would not be used if the difference in value to shareholders between close ownership (which keeps the managers from wandering too far from shareholder value) and diffuse ownership is too great. Roe (2001, 2002, 2003) shows data consistent with this.

The second channel is that social democratic polities have been less willing to provide the infrastructure that makes managers loyal to dispersed stockholders. They are sometimes less interested in transparency, usually stop hostile takeovers, and typically castigate high incentive pay even when it is functional. Insider trading has been seen as the wealthy maneuvering against the wealthy, an issue of limited public concern. These polities have generally not provided the pro-shareholder tools. In this view it is not so much that their legal origins have disabled them from providing the shareholder tools, but that their polities have had little interest in further fostering capitalist institutions. Securities markets in several of these nations were developing nicely at the end of the nineteenth and early twentieth century, including France and Germany, and most of the rest of the European civil law nations (Rajan and Zingales, 2003a). At that time those nations were conservative. The institutional structure was haphazard, the stock exchanges not modern, and so on, but then again the parallel organizations in the United States were also weak, at times corrupt (Coffee, 2001; Rock, 2001), and were not developed properly until later in the twentieth century.

The peace-as-predicate political perspective has a parallel in the property rights literature. Long ago Harold Demsetz organized thinking about property rights vs. the commons around the simple idea that 'the emergence of new property rights [read, for us: corporate law rights] takes place in response to the desires of the interacting persons [read, for us: dominant and diffuse stockholders] [to] adjust[] to new benefit-cost possibilities' (Demsetz, 1967, at p. 350). Where the benefits to dominant and diffuse shareholders of dispersion are limited (because rights to corporate cash flows and other benefits have not been strictly defined between shareholders and labor), then there has been little demand to define the rights of shareholders well (even when that institutional possibility is not especially costly, as it has not been in nations where the foundation of good property and contract rights has been laid down), because the benefits of doing so just are not there for the interacting parties, the diffuse and dominant shareholders.

The interesting question then is, if a nation has the basic institutional capacity, why does the demand not arise to develop corporate institutions? Roe (2001, 2003a) offers labor politics as an answer. Perotti and Von Thadden (2003) offer an analogous human capital explanation: if the median voter has few financial assets and high human capital, then that voter will demand a low risk corporate environment (cf. Pagano and Volpin, 2002). Rajan and Zingales (2003a, b) look at trade, protectionism, and incumbents who wish to protect their positions. In each view, the strength or weakness of corporate law is derivative of other, mostly political, currents in society.

Overall, a nation that impedes financial institutional involvement in large firms but promotes profit-making tends to get diffuse ownership. A nation that supports (or does not impede) financial involvement in large firms but that denigrates profit-making and shareholder wealth-maximizing institutions tends to get close ownership. (There is no clear, empirically confirmed welfare economics result. A common economics and corporate law perspective sees ownership separation as progress, and clearly separation gives some more capital-raising opportunities. However, it is seen by some to be ambiguous in welfare terms (see, e.g., Blair and Stout, 1999), and certainly many European assumptions have been, at least until recently, that pro-labor and go-slow is better (but cf. Hansmann and Kraakman, 2001, who detect change).)

Hansmann and Kraakman (2001) provide Chapter 5 in this volume. While they do not directly dispute either the corporate law or the political theory, their analysis provides a quite different perspective and, in effect, a challenge to both the legal and the political theories. The first challenge is in their claim that corporate law and corporate structures around the world have several deep similarities, such as limited liability and centralized management. They have these similarities because that is what works, and the shareholder-centered model has become so obviously more successful than its competitors that it will become the standard model around the world, if it has not already done so (cf. Salmon, 2002 for an analogous general analysis of national bench-marking). If law must change to accommodate the future, it will. Interest groups and incumbents impede reform, as emphasized by Bebchuk and Roe (2004) and Rajan and Zingales (2003a, 2003b), but the impediments will give way to the power of ideas that work, as key players, especially policymakers, in each nation see that progress and wealth depend on their adopting a shareholder-centered model for corporate law.

References

Acemoglu, D., Johnson, S. and Robinson, J.A. (2002), 'Reversal of Fortune: Geography and Institutions in the Making of the Modern World Income Distribution', *Quarterly Journal of Economics*, November, 1231.

Bebchuk, L.A. (1999), 'A Rent-Protection Theory of Corporate Ownership and Control', Cambridge, Mass.: Harvard Law and Economics Working Paper (Discussion Paper No. 260).

Bebchuk, L.A. and Roe, M.J. (2004), 'A Theory of Path Dependence in Corporate Ownership and Governance', in J.N. Gordon and M.J. Roe (eds), *Convergence and Persistence in Corporate Governance*, Cambridge: Cambridge University Press.

Becht, M. and Röell, A. (1999), 'Blockholdings in Europe: An International Comparison', *European Economic Review*, **43**, 1049–56.

Beck, T., Demirgüç, A. and Levine, R. (2003), 'Law, endowments, and finance', *Journal of Financial Economics*, **70**, 137.

Berkowitz, D., Pistor, K. and Richard, J.-F. (2003), 'Economic Development, Legality, and the Transplant Effect', *European Economic Review*, **47**, 165.

Black, B.S. (2000), 'The Core Institutions That Support Strong Securities Markets', *Business Lawyer*, **55**, 1565–607.

Black, B.S. and Kraakman, R. (1996), 'A Self-Enforcing Model of Corporate Law', *Harvard Law Review*, **109**, 1911–82.

Blair, M. and Stout, L. (1999), 'A Team Production Theory of Corporate Law', *Virginia Law Review*, **85**, 247.

Cheffins, B.R. (2000), 'Does Law Matter?: The Separation of Ownership and Control in the United Kingdom', *Journal of Legal Studies*, **30**, 459.

Coffee, J.C. (1999), 'The Future as History: The Prospects for Global Convergence in Corporate Governance and Its Implications', *Northwestern University Law Review*, **93**, 641–707.

Coffee, J.C. (2001), 'The Rise of Dispersed Ownership: Theories of Law and the State in the Separation of Ownership and Control', *Yale Law Journal*, **111**, 1–82.

DeLong, J.B. (1991), 'Did J.P. Morgan's Men Add Value?', in P. Temin (ed.), *Inside the Business Enterprise: Historical Perspectives on the Use of Information*, Chicago: University of Chicago Press.

Demsetz, H. (1967), 'Toward a Theory of Property Rights', *American Economic Review Papers & Proceedings*, **57**, 347.

Dyck, A. and Zingales, L. (2001), 'Private Benefits of Control: An International Comparison', *Journal of Finance*, **59**, 537.

Edwards, J. and Nibler, M. (2000), 'Corporate Governance in Germany: The Role of Banks and Ownership Concentration', *Economic Policy*, **15**, 239–67.

Edwards, J.S. and Weichenrieder, A.J. (1999), 'Ownership Concentration and Share Valuation: Evidence from Germany' (Working paper).

Franks, J. and Mayer, C. (2001), 'Ownership and Control of German Corporations', *Review of Financial Studies*, **14**, 943.

Gordon, J.G. (2004), 'The International Relations Wedge in the Corporate Convergence Debate', in J.G. Gordon and M.J. Roe (eds), *Convergence and Persistence in Corporate Governance*, Cambridge: Cambridge University Press.

Hansmann, H. and Kraakman, R. (2001), 'The End of History for Corporate Law', *Georgetown Law Journal*, **89**, 439.

Jensen, M. (1993), 'The Modern Industrial Revolution, Exit, and the Failure of Internal Control Systems', *Journal of Finance*, **48**, 831.

La Porta, R. (1997), 'Legal Determinants of External Finance', *Journal of Finance*, **52**, 1131–55.

La Porta, R. (1998), 'Law and Finance', *Journal of Political Economy*, **106**, 1113–50.

La Porta, R., Lopez-de-Silanes, F. and Shleifer, A. (1999), 'Corporate Ownership Around the World', *Journal of Finance*, **54**, 471–517.

La Porta, R. and Vishny, R. (2000), 'Investor Protection and Corporate Governance', *Journal of Financial Economics*, **58**, 3–27.

Mahoney, P.G. (1997), 'The Exchange as Regulator', *Virginia Law Review*, **83**, 1453.

Mahoney, P.G. (2001), 'The Common Law and Economic Growth: Hayek Might Be Right', *Journal of Legal Studies*, **30**, 503.

Milhaupt, C. (1998), 'Property Rights in Firms', *Virginia Law Review*, **84**, 1145.

Miwa, Y. and Ramseyer, J.M. (2002), 'The Value of Prominent Directors: Corporate Governance and Bank Access in Transitional Japan', *Journal of Legal Studies*, **31**, 273.

Modigliani, F. and Perotti, E. (1998), *Security Versus Bank Finance: The Importance of a Proper Enforcement of Legal Rules*, Cambridge, Mass.: MIT Sloan School of Management.

Modigliani, F. and Perotti, E. (1997), 'Protection of Minority Interest and the Development of Security Markets', *Managerial and Decision Economics*, **18**, 519–28.

Ncnova, T. (2003), 'The Value of Corporate Votes and Control Benefits: A Cross-Country Analysis', *Journal of Financial Economics*, **68**, 325.

Nestor, S. (2000), 'Corporate Governance Trends in the OECD Area: Where Do We Go From Here?', Paris: OECD. Working paper.

OECD (1999), *Ad hoc Task Force, Principle of Corporate Governance*, Paris: OECD.

Pagano, M. and Volpin, P.F. (2002), 'The Political Economy of Finance', *Oxford Review of Economic Policy*, **17**, 502.

Perotti, E.C. and von Thadden, E.-L. (2003), 'The Political Economy of Bank and Market Dominance', SSRN working paper.

Pistor, K. (2001), 'Law as a Determinant for Equity Market Development: The Experience of Transition Companies', in P. Murrell (ed.), *Assessing the Value of Law in Transition Economies*, Ann Arbor: University of Michigan Press.

Rajan, R.G. and Zingales, L. (2003a), 'The Great Reversals: The Politics of Financial Development in the Twentieth Century', *Journal of Financial Economics*, **69**, 5.

Rajan, R.G. and Zingales, L. (2003b), *Saving Capitalism from the Capitalists*, New York: Crown Business.

Rock, E.B. (2001), 'Encountering the Scarlet Woman of Wall Street: Speculative Comments at the End of the Century', *Theoretical Inquires in Law*, **2**, 1.

Roe, M.J. (1994), *Strong Managers, Weak Owners: The Political Roots of American Corporate Finance*, Princeton, N.J.: Princeton University Press.

Roe, M.J. (2000), 'Political Preconditions to Separating Ownership from Corporate Control', *Stanford Law Review*, **53**, 539–606.

Roe, M.J. (2001), 'Rents and Their Corporate Consequences', *Stanford Law Review*, **53**, 1463–94.

Roe, M.J. (2002), 'Corporate Law's Limits', *Journal of Legal Studies*, **31**, 233.

Roe, M.J. (2003), *Political Determinants of Corporate Governance*, Oxford: Oxford University Press.

Roe, M.J. (2004), 'Corporate Law and Politics in Explaining Western Securities Markets', in Anna Grandori (ed.), *Corporate Governance and Firm Organization*, Oxford: Oxford University Press.

Roe, M.J. (2005), 'Legal Origin and Stock Markets in the Twentieth Century', Harvard Law School Working paper.

Salmon, P. (2002), 'Decentralization and Supranationality: The Case of the European Union', in E. Ahman and V. Tanzi (eds), *Managing Fiscal Decentralization*, New York: Routledge.

Vagts, D. (2002), 'Comparative Corporate Law – The New Wave', in R. Schweitzer and U. Gasser (eds), *Festschrift for Jean-Nicolas Druey*, Zurich: Schulthess.

[1]

Introduction

Before a nation can produce, it must achieve social peace. Factories that fail to produce because of internal turmoil or external upheaval are less valuable than those that produce smoothly. If conflict is expected, investors invest reluctantly, or not at all, and the factory is not built. Or investors search for the organizational form that minimizes the chances and costs of conflict. Dampening turmoil, or insulating the firm from it, can be a strong force in shaping firms' ownership and governance. Perhaps secondary in the United States, these considerations have historically often been primary in other nations.

Social peace has been reached in different nations by differing means, some of which have then been embedded in business firms, in corporate ownership patterns, and in corporate governance structures. The ways to achieve and maintain social peace vary, and that variety explains quite a bit of why corporate governance structures vary around the world.

Politics can affect a firm in many ways: it can determine who owns it, how big it can grow, what it can produce profitably, how it raises capital, who has the capital to invest, how managers or employees see themselves and one another, and how authority is distributed inside the firm. For concreteness I focus on one key variable: the degree to which ownership separates from control. This is in itself a key aspect of the modern corporation, and emphasizing it gives us the discipline of dealing with a single variable, one for which finance theory is well developed and about which data can be had to test, probe, and better understand how the firm's political environment affects it. Ownership will be our primary focus, but it reflects the bigger claim, that much of the firm's structure is affected, sometimes determined, by its political environment, and if we fail to scrutinize the political impact on a firm, we are unlikely to get the full story.

The large publicly held, diffusely owned firm dominates business in the United States despite its infirmities, namely the frequently fragile relations between stockholders and managers. Managers' agendas can differ from shareholders'; and tying managers' actions tightly to shareholders' goals has been central to American corporate governance. But in other economically advanced nations ownership is not diffuse but concentrated. The problem to explain is why ownership of large

2 INTRODUCTION

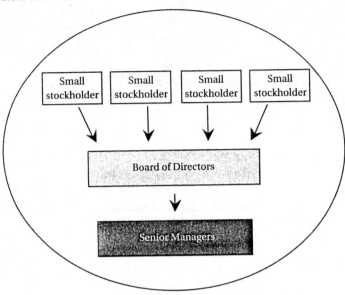

Fig. 1. Diffuse ownership

firms in the United States is diffuse, as depicted in Figure 1, while in so much of the rest of the wealthy West fewer firms go public at all, and of those that do, the firm's ownership is typically concentrated not diffuse, with a dominant stockholder as depicted in Figure 2. Although the American institutional investor has in recent years made the American stockholder less remote than it once was, even today ownership is much less concentrated in the United States than it is in the other nations in the wealthy West. It has been concentrated elsewhere in the wealthy West in no small measure because the delicate threads that tie managers to distant shareholders in the public firm fray easily in common political environments, such as those in the continental European social democracies.

Social democracies press managers to stabilize employment, to forgo some profit-maximizing but risky opportunities for the firm, and to use up capital in place rather than to downsize when markets no longer are aligned with the firm's production capabilities. Managers must have discretion in the diffusely-owned public firm, and how they use that discretion is crucial to stockholders, in that managers' actions produce the firm's profits. Social democratic pressures induce managers to stray further than otherwise from their shareholders' profit-maximizing goals: managers with discretion there are pushed away from being aligned with shareholders' typical profit-oriented goals. Moreover, the modern means that align managers with diffuse stockholders in the United States—incentive compensation, transparent accounting (whose recent failures highlight both its importance and its fragility), hostile takeovers, and strong shareholder-wealth maximization norms—have been weaker and sometimes denigrated by continental social democracies.

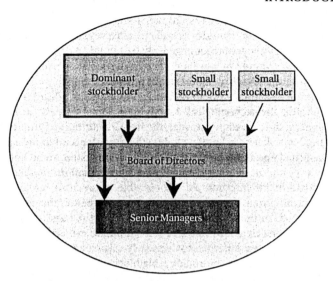

Fig. 2. Dominant stockholder in public firm

Hence, public firms there, all else equal, have had higher managerial agency costs, and large-block shareholding has persisted as shareholders' best remaining way to control those costs. Indeed, when we line up the world's richest nations on a left-right political continuum and then line them up on a close-to-diffuse ownership continuum, the two correlate powerfully.

True, the effects on total social welfare are ambiguous; social democracies may enhance total social welfare, but if they do, they do so with fewer public firms than less socially responsive nations. We thus uncover not only a political explanation for ownership concentration in Europe, but also a crucial political prerequisite to the rise of the public firm in the United States, namely the weakness of social democratic pressures on the American business firm.

* * *

That corporate governance structures around the world have differed is hardly contested. The very fact that many people talk today, at the beginning of the twenty-first century, about corporate convergence due to globalization tells us that people believe that corporate structures have sharply varied. The task here is to better explain why they varied. The thesis here is straightforward: prevailing explanations—based on the level of economic and technological development, on differing economic tasks, on random variation, and on the quality of technical corporate law—while important and not to be discarded, are incomplete. One big explanation is absent from the literature, namely that how social conflict has been settled powerfully affects how firms are owned and how authority is divided.

4 INTRODUCTION

Politics at times directly requires boardrooms and ownership structures to be a certain way. At other times it induces reactions, as, say, owners seek to mitigate political effects or employees react negatively to a political or economic result. At other times politics simply raises the costs of a particular structure, making that more costly structure less likely to arise and prosper.

No single explanation is going to dominate the others at all times: the level of economic wealth, the technological demands for large size, the institutions of capital-gathering, the prevailing tax rules, the legal institutions of the large firm are all important. My task here is hardly to refute the importance of these explanations for the rise of the large firm and the separation of ownership from control, but to focus on a deep, important, and missing political explanation.

I focus on two major corporate differences: the degree of separation of owner-ship from control, primarily and, secondarily, the degree of labor influence. The two are connected. In the United States ownership of the largest firms has been diffuse for quite some time; on the European continent, ownership has been con-centrated, with even the largest firms privately-owned or, if their stock traded publicly, with a single owner controlling a big block of stock. In the United States, labor participates rarely in the core institutions of the firm's governance at the top, rarely owns significant stock directly, and even more rarely participates on the board. In France, a dynamic family and entrepreneurial sector challenged a government-dominated sector; public policy favored employees with jobs in place, and diffusely-owned firms were rare. In Germany labor still takes half of the seats of the supervisory board, in the most explicit manifestation of a political determinant of corporate governance. In Italy in the decades ending the twentieth century there were few public firms, social conflict in the largest firms spilled over into politics when the communist party in Italy was strong, and nominally con-servative governments both denigrated the profit-oriented culture needed to make large firms' managers function well for shareholders and built up small businesses at the expense of large ones to deny fertile fields to the communist unions. In Japan, the firm was typically run at the top by a large board of insiders assured of lifetime employment. Banks have also been shareholders, and their loans induced them not to seek to maximize their wealth as shareholders. Some of these structures arose and prospered in Japan during times of intense social conflict. Similarly, the incidence of hostile takeovers, proxy fights, and incentive compensation mechan-isms varies greatly around the world; sometimes used not at all, sometimes becoming central to corporate governance.

Those are nation-by-nation specifics. But we can generalize into a theory with predictions. Social democracies favor employees with jobs in place. They wedge open the gap between shareholders and managers by pressing managers to expand, to avoid downsizing, and to go slow in taking risks that would affect the work place. These are just the kinds of managerial agency costs that have been common at times in the large American firm: American managers when not strongly tied to shareholders' interests have *also* tended to expand, avoid, and go slow, despite the weaker political pressures here on managers to expand, avoid, and go slow. Moreover, social democracies denigrate the modern pro-shareholder tools—such as incentive compensation, hostile takeovers, shareholder wealth maximization norms, etc.—because it is *not* their policy to promote purely shareholder values.

* * *

Non-political explanations abound for why some nations have concentrated ownership and some do not. Different levels of economic development, technology, culture, or tax and legal structures have all been invoked. Specific structures in one nation or another influence the ownership result: Germany's tax rules favored block ownership. Italy's weak courts made complex corporate legal structures hard to maintain. French statist institutions weakened securities markets. British pension funds facilitated diffuse ownership. Banks in Germany, and incumbents more generally, have tried to block securities market development.

Each local institutional structure surely explains some variation. And for some nations at some times a specific structure could explain much variation. But each local explanation is compatible with there *also* being a political explanation that runs across national boundaries. No *one* single explanation determines ownership and corporate governance.

And each local explanation fails to fully explain the ownership and governance results around the world, leading us to need more to explain the differences. For example, while many developing nations have weak securities markets, there are also several wealthy nations in the West whose securities markets are shallow. Differences in the quality of technical institutions surely explain some of the variation, especially when we compare the wealthy West with the developing East. But too many rich nations have very good institutional structures and strong institutions—corporate, legal, and otherwise—but *nevertheless* have concentrated ownership. Something else is at work promoting concentration and impeding diffusion, and to understand why securities markets and ownership separation do or do not develop, we need to find a better explanation.

We can do so, with a powerful political story, by relating a nation's macro-politics to the firm's micro-structure. Begin by abstracting the firm into three basic parts: ownership, management, and employment. Social conflict, often among owners, managers, and employees, leads to political settlements—indeed, for a nation to be one of the world's richest, social conflict must somehow have been kept from getting out of hand—and these settlements can determine the structure of one of these pieces of the firm.

By determining one of the three basic pieces, politics can thereby often determine the others as well, because the pieces fit together—like pieces of a jigsaw puzzle—as complements. That is, some politically required employment pieces fit well with only a few types of management pieces. Hence, politics could, say, determine a particular labor structure, which might call forth only one type of ownership or management structure. For example, German codetermination—by which labor takes half of the board seats—demands concentrated ownership, because shareholders would do poorly if they failed to meet the boardroom's labor block with their own block. Which came first is not important to the analysis. (And, since concentrated ownership came first, the political complementarity between labor

6 INTRODUCTION

voice and ownership concentration has not been seen clearly.) But once one institution is locked into place, the other is called forth, and *neither* can change easily
without the other changing as well. Co-ordinating change of multiple institutions
simultaneously is hard, and that is one major reason why many of the differing
corporate structures around the world have thus far persisted, resisting full convergence despite the post-war convergence of living standards and productivity.

I proceed in this book by telling a few quick stories for national systems and
then, in this book's mid-section, I generalize the inquiry. Social democracy fits
badly with the diffusely owned public firm. Social democracies fray the ties
between shareholders and managers, and ownership thereby seeks a better way to
control management, with the best alternative in a social democracy being a
concentrated ownership structure. The correlation between a nation's political
orientation and its corporate ownership structure is powerful.

Other economic and political elements fit together as well. One can see two
packages of industrial organization, democratic macro-politics and corporate
ownership structure. One has weakly competitive markets fitting with social democratic politics and concentrated ownership. The other matches fiercely competitive markets, conservative almost *laissez-faire* politics, and diffuse ownership.
Many of the social democracies have had weakly competitive product markets.
Weak product markets weaken one important constraint on managerial agency
costs, making diffuse ownership more costly for shareholders. This tends to induce
more concentrated ownership, all else equal.

Moreover, contests over how to split the monopoly corporate profits can spill
over into democratic politics in ways that are harder to politicize if competitive
markets limit the firm to competitive profits: the cupboard is too easily bare,
leaving less to contest. Globalization, for example, is said to press firms to do less
for employees. Part of the globalization pressure we see around the world is due to
the shrinking of local monopolies as product market competition intensifies. True,
employees may do better overall when globalization improves their welfare as
consumers even if it squeezes them as employees. But the corporate governance
implication here is that globalization presses firms to match pay closely to productivity: managers have less discretion over wages than when they faced less
competitive product markets. That shrinking of local monopolies weakens stakeholder pressures on the firm's managers—because there is less available over
which managers have discretion to share—and as those internal pressures to share
diminish, this source of the demand for concentrated ownership might diminish
as well, opening the way for a nation to develop deeper and wider securities markets.

While we examine the rest of the developed world in this book's mid-section, the
theory here is one about the United States as well. And that is where we shall
conclude: there was a powerful political pre-condition to ownership separating
from control in the United States, to the rise and persistent dominance of the
American large public firm with diffuse ownership, and to the eventual disap-
pearance of block and family ownership, namely *the absence in the U.S. of a strong
social democracy*. Where social democracy was strong, the public firm was unstable,
weak, and unable to dominate without difficulty; where social democracy was

weak, ownership diffusion of the large firm could, if other economic and institutional conditions prevailed, begin.

* * *

The argument here is not normative: it is *not* that strong social democracies do not deliver the goods in a utilitarian sense. There is tension between large diffusely-owned firms and strong social democratic polities, and, hence, one might, by showing this relationship, be taken to suggest that this strain of politics short-changes its citizens. But that is not the argument. Indeed, one might intuitively think the contrary: by providing *more* for a *wider* base of people, those governments may achieve a utilitarian goal of the greatest good for the greatest number more effectively than other polities.

But I do not evaluate this utilitarian possibility—that these arrangements could be more than just a second-best accommodation but a first-best result—one way or the other. Moreover, the argument I present suggests the possibility of *several* roads to utilitarian goals: peace is predicate to production. If substantial social peace is achieved in different ways in different nations, then the historical routes were several to achieve a modern economy.

* * *

Today's policy-makers have reasons to come to grips with these political reflections inside the large firm. International agencies seek to change corporate governance systems in developing and transition nations. But corporate governance is not just mechanical rules and basic institutional capacities (such as good corporate law, good courts, and so on). The corporation ties, sometimes tightly, to national politics, and plunking down modern (usually read as American) rules and business institutions would be unlikely to produce the reformers' desired results if the institutions badly match the politics. The mechanical rules and institutions could be the same, but if politics sharply differs, so might the corporate results.

True, reformers can change business practices and legal rules more easily than they can change a nation's deep political and social structure. So, if one approaches corporate governance from a law reform perspective, it usually is correct to analyse the business firm as it has conventionally been analysed, as an economic, financial, and technological organization: we, or the reform agencies, assume the political and social predicates of the society as given, and look at the 'marginal' institutions susceptible of immediate change. If one seeks to improve business results, it is best to focus first on what can be changed and not what, at least in the short run, will resist change. No need to examine political bedrock, if drilling through it in the short run is impossible.

Yet we cannot always avoid examining it: if the mechanical institutions just do not mesh with the underlying political foundations, fixing the mechanics will be harder than the reformers anticipate. And if our goal is to explain which institutions prevailed in the wealthy West, we cannot avoid looking at the firm's political environment.

* * *

8 INTRODUCTION

The task here lies across several disciplines, including law, political science, and economics. And the methodologies needed are several as well—the logical analysis of incentives and institutions from law and economics, the statistics and modeling (simple though they may be here) of financial economics, and the historical/political scrutiny of comparative politics. I do not purport to be sufficiently expert to catch every nuance in each field or method, but I hope that by combining them, we gain deeper insights.

* * *

A road map for this book: in Part I, I set out the general theory that peace must precede production and how the terms of peace can affect corporate governance. I also set out the core differences in corporate governance around the world.

In Part II, I set out the theory that social democracy and the diffusely owned firm are in tension. I link a nation's political orientation to the micro-structure of the firm, by showing how social democracies press managers to coalesce with employees, not with distant shareholders, and how the means that tie managers to shareholders in American public firms fray in strong social democracies. Owners must consequently seek other means to control managers, and the best alternative is close ownership or block ownership of the equity. Whether life is better for more people is hard to know, but public firms would be fewer and ownership separation narrower.

In Part III, I test the political hypothesis with a simple statistical inquiry: if we array nations on a left-to-right political scale, and then array them on a highly-concentrated to highly diffuse ownership scale, the two scales correlate powerfully. The political explanation, in statistical terms, does as well, or better, at explaining variation in ownership concentration in the world's richest nations as do competing theories, such as a currently-popular one based on the strength of technical corporate law.

In Part IV, I narrate relationships between social politics and corporate governance in seven of the world's richer nations. France has a long history of statist economic policy. Before the First World War, when the overall tenor of its statism was *conservative*, securities markets were developing strongly; in modern times its leftward bent precluded sharp ownership separation. German codetermination is the clearest institutional manifestation of the social democratic thesis. Labor takes half of the board seats in large firms, inducing shareholders to be better off with a counter-coalition. Italy for a quarter of a century had a communist party on the verge of political power; ownership concentration helped to make deals stick inside the big firms and facilitated a counter-coalition inside the firm and inside the polity. Japanese lifetime employment is another way to achieve social peace. Japanese firms' insider-dominated boards and their history of strong bank-creditor influence—both being risk-avoiding players—fit with lifetime employment. Sweden also exemplifies the thesis: the world's first social democracy, it had strong minority stock issuance, but very little ownership separation. The United Kingdom's securities markets first developed during its first strong *laissez-faire* period and seemed to stagnate mid-century when its political economy changed. And the United States has had one of the world's weakest social democratic influences and one of its strongest securities markets, with much ownership separation.

In Part V, I deepen the inquiry by examining the direction of causality. In the first four Parts I take politics as given and examine its consequences for the firm. In Part V, I inquire into how corporate and economic structures can induce political backlash. Not all efficient structures are politically stable. Some structures induce political backlash, inducing corporate structures to bend to survive, or to crack and fail. I offer some generalized instances of each and show some corporate governance implications. I also in Part V link the political story to product markets: there are complementary fits of ownership structure, politics, and industrial organization. One can in theory take the same agency cost-driven political story of Part I and, by beginning with the severity of market-place product competition, derive the same corporate governance (and, surprisingly, political) results. Separation fits with conservative democratic politics and fierce product market competition. Some of the social tensions around the world today are due to one piece of the package changing quickly without the others yet changing as quickly.

In Part VI, I discuss the fit between the political theory and a leading academic theory, that the quality of technical corporate law determines whether securities markets will arise, whether ownership will separate from control, and whether the modern corporation will prosper. The theory has been used convincingly to explain why we see weak corporate structures in transition and developing nations, less convincingly to explain why concentrated ownership persists in continental Europe, and probably incorrectly to explain why ownership separated from control in the United States. Surely, when an economically weak society lacks regularity—a gap that may be manifested by weak or poorly enforced corporate law—that lack of regularity and economic strength precludes complex institutions like securities markets and diffusely owned public firms. But the converse is not true: when we see ownership concentration we cannot be sure whether distant stockholders fear the rapacity of insiders—who could, if corporate law is weak, divert value to themselves—or the disloyalty of managers, who might fail to get good shareholder profits. Corporate law deals with rapacity and self-dealing, *not* with managerial mistake. But the latter can impede diffuse ownership as easily as the first, and via America's elaborate business judgment rule the latter *is immune from corporate law inquiry*. Indeed, even in nations with good legal structures generally and, by measurement, good shareholder protection—such as in Germany and Scandinavia—ownership *did not* separate from control. Something more than just weak corporate law impeded securities markets from flourishing in such nations. The political theory I offer here tells us what that something else was.

The analysis in Part VI is quite relevant to today's policy-making corporate bodies, such as the international agencies that are promoting corporate governance institutions in Third World and transition nations that would mimic American institutions. Their goals are worthy, but even if they succeed in building the mechanical institutions they are after, the corporate structures might persist if the nations' underlying politics is not conducive to the policy-makers' goals.

10   INTRODUCTION

In Part VII I unify two political theories: a democratic polity does not easily accept powerful pro-shareholder institutions. In the United States, this unease once manifested itself in a populism that historically kept financial institutions small, denied them strong stock-based portfolios, and took away their authority to act directly inside the firm. In more modern times, this popular force manifested itself in laws that dampened hostile takeovers in many states, without eliminating them. By taming the strongest shareholder institutions such as concentrated financial power, the American polity more willingly, albeit perhaps grudgingly, accepted other pro-shareholder institutions. In Europe, this political force sought to tame capital directly, by constricting its range of motion in the firm: employees with jobs got both protection from being laid off and voice inside the firm, pro-shareholder institutions were denigrated, and owners reacted to maximize their value in that kind of polity. If one fails to understand these political impulses, one cannot fully understand the world's, or any single nation's, corporate governance institutions.

POLITICAL CONFLICT AND THE CORPORATION

The corporation is an economic and legal institution and its determinants are usually seen as economic and legal as well, with its principal economic determinants arising from the needs of the engineers for large-scale production, of the financiers for diversification, and of the managers for discretion. These determinants are central, but so are the political predicates to large-scale production, which are rarely examined.

The critical political predicate is simple: sufficient social peace inside the corporation so that it can produce and sell its products. Many means of making social peace diminish shareholder wealth. But the specifics are many, and different nations have reduced social conflict differently, often adopting institutions that affect the structure of the large-scale firm. Japan achieved industrial peace after the Second World War with promises of lifetime employment to many employees. Germany built labor codetermination into its boardrooms. France had a strong state voice in the corporation, a voice that typically has taken labor's side when there was conflict. The United States had little of these, because it had little of the same kind of industrial conflict; but historically similar forces fragmented finance, thereby hastening the development of the diffusely held public firm (because American politics precluded strong financial institutions, thus pushing finance more heavily into other channels).

We can generalize. One persistent contrast in corporate ownership around the world is concentrated versus diffuse ownership. In many continental European nations, families or financial institutions have owned the largest business firms. In the United States for quite some time, and more recently in Great Britain, stock ownership is more diffuse. Some nations achieved economic peace by becoming social democracies, where the state regularly sided with employees. In such social democracies, the diffusely-owned public firm did not fit well with the political institutions. For diffuse ownership to prevail, managers must be tied to shareholders, but social democracies did not allow these ties to be tight. When the ties cannot be tight, the public firm is unstable, unlikely to arise, and unlikely to dominate and spread further if it had already arisen.

12 POLITICAL CONFLICT AND THE CORPORATION

More abstractly: pure shareholder wealth maximization fits poorly with a modern democracy. Everywhere democracies put distance between strong shareholder control and the day-to-day operation of the firm, shielding employees from tight shareholder control. But the means and degree differ around the world. Some nations fragment financial institutions, lower shareholder voice, and keep the ownership interests distant from the firm; others allow ownership interests to be close to the firm, but reduce the range of their activities inside the firm. How a nation settles social conflict and distances shareholders from the firm's day-to-day operation— how a nation achieves social peace—can thereafter deeply affect that nation's institutions of corporate governance.

Peace as Predicate

Before a nation can produce, it must achieve social peace. The proposition is obvious, but has thus far not been widely used to understand corporate institutions. To build large enterprises, particularly those in which ownership separates from control, a society must achieve not only key economic, legal, and technological pre-conditions, but political pre-conditions as well, namely, a particular kind of social peace, one in which managers if freed from direct shareholder control would still be largely loyal to distant, non-controlling shareholders. Some ways by which modern societies achieved social peace made it harder for the public firm to emerge and prosper, because they made a diffusely owned firm's managers less loyal to shareholders. Hence, public firms were less valuable to shareholders in those environments. And hence there were fewer of them.

1.1. The Political Foundations to the Firm
1.2. Variety and Persistence in Distancing Shareholders from Employees

1.1. THE POLITICAL FOUNDATIONS TO THE FIRM

The large-scale public firm is typically seen as a purely economic institution, one that solves the economic problem of mobilizing capital from financiers and of organizing large-scale production by managers. Its economic and technical pre-conditions are well-recognized—a transparent accounting system, a good legal system, technologies that are best effectuated via large-scale organization, a cadre of trained managers, a capacity to mobilize finance, etc.

Recognized less well, or not at all, are two political foundations to the public corporation: first, before serious economic activity can take place, social and economic conflict must be minimized, and the ways modern societies have minimized it can affect, and have affected the structure of the modern corporation. All societies have put distance between shareholders and the firm, but they have done so differently, and these differences often determined the institutions of corporate governance.

14   POLITICAL CONFLICT AND THE CORPORATION

Second, under one modern and widespread political condition, ownership could not easily separate from control, and the truly public firm could not dominate business. Strong social democracies pressed firms to favor employees over invested capital, but shareholders resisted this, and their best way to resist was often to build or to keep concentrated, and often private, ownership. Moreover, social democracies also frayed the kinds of ties that today bind managers to diffuse shareholders in the American public firm and, with the ties between the two frayed, shareholders had another reason to concentrate their ownership.

Strong social democracies and the public firm have mixed badly. This oil-and-water-mix not only strongly explains why ownership and control have not yet widely separated in European social democracies but also identifies a critical pre-condition to the rise and dominance of the public firm in the United States, namely a political environment that did not tie managers to employees, one that more easily permitted tying managers to shareholders, a political environment not present in every advanced industrial nation.

1.2. VARIETY AND PERSISTENCE IN DISTANCING SHAREHOLDERS FROM EMPLOYEES

The ways to produce social peace in the corporate context are many. All have the common effect of distancing shareholders from the day-to-day operation of the firm. Employees can be guaranteed representation on the firm's board of directors, a solution that still prevails in Germany. Or, some of them may be guaranteed lifetime employment, a solution that benefited large firms' core employees in Japan. Or, the largest industrial firms can be run by the government, and then run in a way that favors incumbent employees, a result common until recently in France. Or, key visible purveyors of shareholder wealth—large, private, salient financial institutions—could attract political attention, and the polity could then fragment them or deny them authority either to own stock or to play a major role in industry, a result historically common in the United States. Or, a social democracy could through rules and norms limit the actions that firms can take *vis-à-vis* incumbent employees.

Dismissing these institutions as inefficient is too easy, especially for a market-oriented American analyst. Understanding them is harder. One can begin by understanding the obvious, that politics can affect, and even disrupt, markets. Voters may see market arrangements as unfair, leading them to lash back and disrupt otherwise efficient arrangements. To quell this backlash, legal and insti-tutional structures may arise and survive, despite that they could not withstand a normal efficiency critique. They may be politically necessary for production, and, were they absent, the social turmoil might be economically unbearable. The prospect of a severe backlash, one that would destroy efficient institutions and drive a society into impoverished turmoil, or of co-optation, in which politicians strategically temper otherwise efficient rules and institutions to finesse away a more destructive backlash, complicates a standard efficiency analysis.

PEACE AS PREDICATE   15

This kind of backlash is usually ignored in American law and economics inquiries, often I believe for good reason. Its absence in American analysis is not so much due to logic, but to American exceptionalism: this kind of backlash and this need to temper social conflict have been much less severe historically in the U.S. than in the other rich nations, as we shall examine later in Chapter 16. But ignoring it can leave the analysis of why an institution looks the way it does incomplete. Its absence in American analyses opens up two gaps in understanding corporate institutions: first, in nations where stronger means of settling social conflict were needed, we must understand these stronger means and their consequences in order to understand their corporate institutions. Second, in the United States, we must understand that several of our institutions—including, I shall argue in Part III, the diffuse ownership of the public firm itself—rest on the relative absence of such severe social conflict.

The Wealthy West's Differing Corporate Governance Structures

What are the major differences in corporate ownership and governance in the developed nations? Differences can be categorized roughly into those affecting ownership, those affecting management, and those affecting employment. One major corporate governance difference to explain is the degree of block ownership and the extent of ownership separation. Another is the degree of managerial control over day-to-day operations. Yet another is the degree of labor influence on the firm. There is reason to think that each can affect the others. Determining one can affect, or determine, the others.

2.1. Diffuse versus Block Ownership
2.2. Managerial Compensation and Labor influence
2.3. Can a Nations's Size, Development Level, or Corporate Legal Institutions
      Alone Explain the Differences?

2.1. DIFFUSE VERSUS BLOCK OWNERSHIP

In the United States for quite some time distant, diffuse stockholders have owned the largest firms. In contrast, in continental Europe even the largest firms have been closely held, because many never went public, and big blockholders persisted even in those that did. In Germany at the end of the twentieth century, nearly every large firm still had a large blockholder, usually from a family, but for some firms from a bank, insurance company, or another corporation.[1] In France, the family sector in recent decades was large, growing, and highly competitive.[2] In Italy family firms still persist and there are few fully public firms.[3] Firms in continental Europe are owned less by diffuse stock markets and more

---

[1] Julian Franks and Colin Mayer, 'Ownership and Control of German Corporations', 14 *Rev. Fin. Stud.* 943, 944 (2001).

[2] Paul Windolf, 'The Governance Structure of Large French Corporations', in *Corporate Governance Today* 705 (1998) (Columbia Sloan Project on Corporate Governance).

[3] Alessandro Portolano, 'The decision to adopt defensive tactics', 20 *Int'l Rev. L & Econ.* 425, 427 (2000); cf. Eugenio Ruggiero, *Italy*, in *The Legal Basis of Corporate Governance in Publicly Held Corporations: A Comparative Approach* 79, 82, (ed. by Arthur R. Pinto and Gustavo Visentini 1998) (declining number of listings in 1990s on Italy's leading stock exchange).

by concentrated blockholders than in the United States, with the blocks usually owned by families or, particularly in Germany, financial institutions. Some of this is an artifact of the Post-Second World War family-founders of some large firms. But ownership concentration has persisted longer than a generation, and thus far *even* when a family sells out, it typically sells to another, new blockholder, *not* to dispersed stockholders via, say, an initial public offer followed by a relentless sell-off of the family's holdings.[4] Perhaps family-owners will someday prefer this American-style method of exit, but thus far they have not had that opportunity, even in many of the world's wealthier nations.

A few ownership contrasts: in the twenty firms in Germany that have just over $500 million in stock market capitalization (to keep the size comparison across borders constant), *eighteen* have blockholders owning 20 per cent or more of the stock. In France and Italy, *every* one of these mid-sized firms has a 20 per cent + blockholder. In Sweden, eighteen do. In the United States, only *two* do.[5] In Germany, financial institutions have fifty ownership blocks of 5 per cent or more of the stock in the 100 largest German firms;[6] in the United States such institutional blocks are few, at about zero.

One could make the case that the difference is becoming more one of degree than of kind. Not only are large European firms seeking capital from new sources, but institutional investors in the United States are no longer the 100-share individuals of the standard model. They own bigger slices of a company's stock. They are informed about corporate governance trends. And some of them are informed enough about a firm's operations and business to give serious feedback to directors and managers.

But differences remain even today. The data shows that even the new American institutional investors tend to own smaller blocks of stock than institutions, families, and individuals outside the United States.[7] And the European firms may be seeking new sources of capital, but their ownership has not yet diffused as widely as has that of American firms.

2.2. MANAGERIAL COMPENSATION AND LABOR INFLUENCE

Management and managerial control structures tend to differ as well. In the United States, powerful incentive pay goes to American managers, directors are often outsiders, and takeovers and proxy fights occur often enough that they affect managerial motivation. Incentive compensation, takeovers, and proxy fights have all historically been less important in continental Europe and Japan.

---

[4] Franks and Mayer, supra, note 1 at 955. [5] Table 2.1.

[6] 13 *Monopolkommission Hauptgutachten* 1998/1999, *Wettbewerbspolitik in Netzstrukturen* 251–56 (2000); *Monopolkommission Hauptgutachten* 1996/1997, *Marktoffnung Umfassend Verwirklichen* 187–92 (1998). [7] See Tables 2.1 and 6.1.

18 POLITICAL CONFLICT AND THE CORPORATION

Labor's role also differs. In Germany labor participates directly in the core governance institutions: as is well known, the largest German firms must have half of the board members from labor. Sometimes labor's effect on the core governance institutions is indirect: in Japan, lifetime employment is a basic institution in the largest firms, and corporate governance structures have had to adapt to this. Two adaptations are the inside-board and the prevalence of shareholder-creditors. Each suppresses pure shareholder goals. And in France and Italy, corporate governance structures have had to adapt to the power of labor in the political arena, usually inducing the firms to be smaller and private, or, if large and public but not government-owned, at least with a concentrated ownership block.

And in the United States, in contrast, labor rarely participates in the board or in high-level management. Labor markets are fluid and employment flexible. Labor's absence and the fluid labor market permit corporate governance institutions that the United States could not have developed easily had its labor market been fixed and rigid.

2.3. CAN A NATION'S SIZE, DEVELOPMENT LEVEL, OR CORPORATE LEGAL INSTITUTIONS ALONE EXPLAIN THE DIFFERENCES?

Analysts might once have dismissed the contrast in ownership as a function of economic development. Right after the Second World War, American business and living standards were so far ahead that this alone might have explained the different ownership structures then. But standards of living have converged in the past half-century, yet the ownership structures have not. Our primary task will be to explain why. True, corporate ownership and governance structures change more slowly than the outside environment, but this lag, although important, is not the only basis for differences.

And analysts might once have dismissed the contrasting ownership structures as due to size, in that firms in the United States were larger, and one might then have thought that only the largest firms become truly public firms. Even today, the largest American firms tend to be much larger than the largest firms in Europe and Japan. But we now know enough to reject size as explaining the ownership differences. Even among *similarly sized* large firms around the world today, the public firm is *still* more widespread in the United States than in continental Europe. These differences thus far have persisted, despite converging living standards and business technology.

Technical corporate law institutions, especially those that protect distant minority stockholders from the rapacity of controlling insiders, could in theory be determinative. If outside stockholders do not feel protected, they will not invest. But although the technical institutions are important, building them is not rocket science for societies that already have some of them, like courts that can enforce a contract or regulators who are effective. When the political conditions for stock

Table 2.1. *Ownership Separation:*
Portion of Mid-Sized Firms without a 20
per cent Blockholder in 1995 (From
the 20 Public Firms with a Capitalization
just over $500 Million)[8]

Austria	0.00
Italy	0.00
France	0.00
Germany	0.10
Netherlands	0.10
Sweden	0.10
Belgium	0.20
Finland	0.20
Norway	0.20
Australia	0.30
Denmark	0.30
Japan	0.30
Switzerland	0.50
Canada	0.60
United Kingdom	0.60
United States	0.90

markets and diffuse ownership are there in an economically-ripe rich nation, supporting institutions should not be that hard to build so that ownership can separate.
That is, they can be built, if the political will to build them is there. In modern
times, in the modern rich democracies, that lack of political will is manifested in
social democracy. And in fact, in some nations the technical institutions *are* there
in rudimentary form, as we shall see in Part VI, Corporate Law's Limits. But if the
political configuration was not conducive to separation, ownership still did not
separate from control.

Academic theorists and policymakers have recently turned to technical corporate law as the foundation for ownership separation. But suffice it to say for now
that corporate law's scope is too narrow to be critically central to organizing an
economy: American corporate law, for example, often seen as exemplary nowadays,
leaves a huge surface area of corporate action untouched: the American business
judgment rule has judges *refusing* to review and regulate managers' unconflicted
acts. Managerial mistakes, disloyalty to shareholders (as long as the managers'
hands are not in the cookie jar), over-investment, under-investment, and so on,
are just *not* subject to corporate law review. And these possibilities of systematic
managerial mistake can easily destabilize diffuse ownership. More on this gap—
and how the political theory explains much of what is going on in this gap—below,
in Part VI, Corporate Law's Limits. So, our working hypothesis is that political

[8] Adapted from Rafael La Porta, Florencio Lopez-de-Silanes, and Andrei Shleifer, 'Corporate
Ownership Around the World', 54 *J. Fin.* 471, 492 (1999).

20 POLITICAL CONFLICT AND THE CORPORATION

differences explain much here. Some of these differences arose nation-by-nation, and some of these differences can be generalized and tested across the developed world: social democracies fit badly with the diffusely-owned public firm, and one would predict fewer public firms in the stronger social democracies.

* * *

The public firm is not a *necessary*, inevitable organizational evolution. It has important strengths, as well as critical weaknesses. The strengths are that it provides a means of raising (or for many firms, holding) capital beyond that which a single family or small group of individuals could handle: it facilitates economies of scale and scope. It helps to separate the second or third generation after a firm's founding from control of the firm, an important task when that second or third generation lacks the skill or interest to run the firm. And, conversely, it lets managers with administrative talent but little capital run the firm. And that specialization has its capital market correlate: it enables owners uninterested in managing to diversify and gain liquidity.

These advantages are commonly known. Emphasized less often is the interaction between capital markets and product markets. The possibility of easy separation and easy raising of equity capital facilitates product market competition in one important dimension: an incumbent can often find itself facing a competitor who can compete more quickly and more effectively because it has good access to equity markets. Securities markets just by providing a means of quickly raising capital and the possibility of separation can enhance product market competition. The possibility of an entrepreneur eventually exiting via a public offering of his or her stock can motivate new players to enter and compete. A potential competitor, especially if an individual, is more likely to jump in if it knows it can exit if successful. Selling out via the stock market and full separation is an important means of exit, one that helps motivate players to enter. It's probably an underrated reason why public firms can promote economic well-being.

The public firm's principal weakness on which we will focus is the frequently fragile ties between managers and shareholders. A firm's capabilities may become misaligned with its product market, but it might respond slowly because managers are used to the old routines. The managerial agents may react too slowly for shareholders' tastes. Or managers may be unwilling to take astute risks that shareholders would consider good bets, because managers might not want to rock the boat while diversified shareholders want to maximize value. Or managers may build empires for prestige and power. All of these are the costs to shareholders of running their firm through managerial agents. If owners, potential and actual, worry too much that their managerial agents will not do shareholders' bidding, then founding owners are reluctant to sell, distant investors are reluctant to buy, and ownership does not separate from control.

A General Theory

One way to achieve social peace is for labor to get a strong voice inside the firm. When labor influence is high, the pressure increases on managers to be less loyal to shareholders.[1] This amplified labor voice can come via codetermination, via lifetime employment, or via state action that favors employees when conflict arises.

3.1. Owners, Managers, and Employees
3.2. Codetermination and Lifetime Employment
3.3. Positive and Normative Theory
3.4. Efficiency Implications?
3.5. Social Democracy

3.1. OWNERS, MANAGERS, AND EMPLOYEES

The firm can be abstracted into three simple, broad parts: ownership, management, and employment. Much that is important can be said by keeping the firm's abstract parts simplified. Keeping them simple lets us see how they must fit together and what forces can upset their fit.

Owners, usually from the richest strata in the society, cannot be seen to have acquired their wealth too unjustly; otherwise neither managers nor employees will work well for the owners. Managers must be motivated to do their jobs. They cannot run their firms into the ground or divert its wealth to themselves; otherwise owners will not invest and employees will be too uncertain of long-term prospects to work hard for the firm that would soon be run into the ground. And employees must be motivated to work and be unable to appropriate owners' investments; otherwise owners will not invest. Nor can the employees be positioned to prevent managers from running the firm; otherwise managers cannot effectively induce the firm to produce.

---

[1] Mark J. Roe, *Strong Managers, Weak Owners: The Political Roots of American Corporate Finance* (1994). See infra, Chapter 27, 'Populism and Socialism in Corporate Governance', in Part VI: 'Unifying Two Political Theories'.

22   POLITICAL CONFLICT AND THE CORPORATION

These conflicts inside the firm either map onto broader social conflicts in a society, or can spill over from firms into political and social conflict. If the society cannot minimize these conflicts, it cannot produce. One or another of these inputs could withdraw, or sulk, denying the firm a critical input.

Politics often determines the structure of one of these broad parts of the firm. And by determining one part, politics could thereby determine the others, because sometimes only a few forms of the others fit well with the fixed institution.

3.2. CODETERMINATION AND LIFETIME EMPLOYMENT

A few brief examples, to be detailed in Part II: Germany settled upon codetermination, with labor getting half of the seats on the boards of large firms. This brought about labor peace, but then the other pieces, management and ownership, reacted. For managers to have the freedom that they either needed or wanted, German boards were kept, or made, weaker than they otherwise would have been. Powerful boards, one common tool of owners elsewhere, were not available to German owners. But owners must oversee managers from time-to-time. Block ownership provides owners such a means when boards are weak and, hence, codetermination may explain why block ownership persists in Germany.

Similarly, one way for owners to motivate senior managers is via stock options and other incentive compensation that tie them more directly to stockholders. Even if owners do not monitor managers regularly, stock-based incentive compensation can make managers think like owners. But that kind of incentive compensation may not fit well with a codetermined board, one that is leery of compensating managers highly and uncomfortable with seeing managers tied more tightly to owners. More generally, high managerial compensation, whether of the incentive variety or not, might make managers more loyal to shareholders but it can in some environments exacerbate tensions inside the firm, tensions that can reduce the firm's productivity. A cost-benefit trade-off (better motivated managers, but more demoralized employees) could make distant owners pay a price whichever way they go.

In Japan, social conflict not too different from that in Germany led to a social compact with many large firms promising lifetime employment to their core employees. Lifetime employment helped to bring about social peace, but it is not always the best way to motivate employees. Internal promotional tournaments developed, with the last tournament having favored managerial employees promoted to a large board of other honored insiders.

3.3. POSITIVE AND NORMATIVE THEORY

The argument here is positive not normative. My point is not that societies short-change themselves when they demean one organizational form or another (although they may), but that before production can roll, social peace must be achieved. To achieve it, compromises must be made, politics must become stable, social conflict minimized. The forces that stabilize a society inevitably affect the corporation, sometimes directly, sometimes indirectly.

In a sense, one cannot normatively criticize on utilitarian grounds a means of achieving peace if, were that peace not attained, the alternative of turmoil would have been worse. (Nor should one think that the United States has always been immune to the need to settle such conflict. It has not been. It just settled what conflict it had differently, historically by keeping financial intermediaries small and without a sustained powerful voice inside the large firms.)

3.4. EFFICIENCY IMPLICATIONS?

Any efficiency implications here are attenuated. While right now these economies are not performing as well as the American, the contrary was so in the 1980s, especially if we contrasted Germany and Japan with the United States. Differing corporate governance structures generate differing advantages and disadvantages. Sometimes these net out to zero, sometimes these favor one economy over another when the production task is geared to the type of corporate governance they have. Perhaps one system is overall better and will in the long-run dominate, or perhaps a system that could mix and match would be better overall, by allowing for more variety and competition.

Relative efficiency is not the main story here. What is striking is that the corporate governance systems historically have been national, without a strong mix in each nation. The United States has had diffuse ownership, Germany has had bank voice and family ownership, Japan has had bank blocks in the largest firms, France and Italy still have few fully public firms, etc. The fact that variation has tended to be national, and not across industries or tailored to specific firms inside a nation, makes one think that key explanations are likely to be national as well.

3.5. SOCIAL DEMOCRACY

Social peace in many nations has been an ongoing issue in the post-Second World War world. In social democracies, employees were often systematically protected from actions that owners (and managers) might otherwise have liked to take. Lay-offs have been harder than they might otherwise have been, the range of managerial discretion on the shop floor more limited than it was elsewhere, and unemployment benefits were high and easy to obtain. Social peace in strong social democracies also disfavored the core means by which owners tie managers to ownership interests—high incentive compensation via stock options, shareholder wealth maximization norms, and hostile takeovers. Social peace in the strongest social democracies demeaned high incentive compensation (at least if publicly

24 POLITICAL CONFLICT AND THE CORPORATION

known) because the resulting envy would have weakened employee motivation, weakened or obliterated shareholder wealth maximization norms, or made hostile takeovers illegal or easy to disrupt by those whom such takeovers would have hurt. Social democracies thereby made diffuse ownership harder for the owners, who would have found that managers were harder to monitor, motivate, and keep loyal; and owners accordingly were more likely than otherwise to own big blocks of stock in private or near-private companies.

I treat politics as fixed, for the most part, so that we can analyze political differences carefully. But although treating it as fixed is plausible—basic politics often only changes slowly—it is just a useful working assumption. Later, principally in Chapter 21, Political Change in Continental Europe, I discuss political change, especially the modern political shift to the right (and toward greater acceptance of markets) in Europe, and how it could be affecting corporate governance and ownership.

* * *

Social democracy is not a precise term. I use it in part due to want of a better term. In social democracies—nations committed to private property but whose governments play a large role in the economy, emphasize distributional considerations, and favor employees over capital-owners when the two conflict[2]— public policy emphasizes managers' natural agenda and demeans shareholders' natural agenda. Perhaps a better operational phrase than social democracy would be the less-common 'stakeholder society', or simply a nation in which employee pressures are strong. Italy, for example, is not usually thought of as a strong social democracy—it does not have a cradle-to-grave state support system as has Sweden nor a socially supportive state bureaucracy as France has nor a corporate-law mandated corporate compromise as German codetermination reflects—but stakeholder pressures are high in Italy, and those pressures would affect shareholder interests in large firms, were there many of them.

So we use the phrase social democracy, recognizing its limits. It describes those nations in which the pressure on the firm for low-risk expansion is high, the pressure to avoid risky organizational change is substantial, and the tools that would induce managers to work in favor of invested capital—such as high incentive compensation, hostile takeovers, transparent accounting, and acculturation to shareholder-wealth maximization norms—are weak. Life may well be better for more people in the strongest social democracies, but the internal structure of public firms must necessarily be weaker for shareholders.

* * *

[2] See Adam Przeworski, 'Socialism and Social Democracy', in *The Oxford Companion to Politics of the World* 832, 835 (ed. by Joel Krieger *et al.*, 1993) (social democracies seek 'to implement "functional socialism", even if ownership of productive resources remains private'); S.C. Stimson, 'Social Democracy', in 4 *The New Palgrave: A Dictionary of Economics* 395, 396 (ed. by John Eatwell, Murray Milgate, and Peter Newman, 1987) (European social democracy seeks not to end private ownership, but to improve material conditions for the many).

I next in Part II illustrate how social democracy could affect corporate governance structures. We could instead have begun illustrating the thesis with, say, Japanese lifetime employment and traced its effects on the large Japanese firm. Or we could have begun with the effects of a French élite that aimed to reduce lay-offs and downsizings inside large firms. Or we could have begun with Italy's 1969 'hot autumn', as they called it—of militant labor actions, strikes, factory occupations, and mass demonstrations—and then thought through how revolutionary pressures could have affected ownership structures there.

We could have started elsewhere, but we begin with German codetermination because it vividly shows social democracy affecting corporate governance. The others would also illustrate how political pressures can affect the firm's ownership and governance, but codetermination paints that picture more quickly, more starkly, and more clearly.

SOCIAL CONFLICT AND THE INSTITUTIONS OF CORPORATE GOVERNANCE

Here we illustrate the peace-as-predicate principle.

Social conflict led Germany to seek a 'middle way' between unbridled capitalism and strong socialism. Inside the large business firm, employees got half the seats in the boardroom. This affected corporate governance directly, by giving German firms a distinctive employee voice in the boardroom. And social conflict affected corporate governance indirectly but powerfully, because managers and shareholders preferred that the boardroom not become powerful and well informed. Board meetings historically were infrequent, information flow to the board poor, and the board often too big and unwieldy to be effective. Instead, out-of-the-boardroom shareholder caucuses and meetings between managers and large shareholders substituted for effective boards. Moreover, diffuse ownership would have ended these informal channels of shareholder control and information flow. Diffuse stockholders would have had to choose between strengthening the board (and hence further empowering the board's employee-half) or keeping it weak and thus living with sub-standard (by current world criteria) boardroom governance. Strong labor voice, one can plausibly speculate, called forth concentrated ownership.

This effect has been more general. Social democracies demeaned shareholder primacy, pushing firms to stabilize employment, to expand whether or not expansion was profitable for shareholders, and to avoid change that would disrupt the quality of the work place. These democratic goals map right to the typical goals of unconstrained managers, typically labelled as agency costs. Social democratic pressures increased managerial agency costs for shareholders and thus decreased the firm's value to diffuse shareholders. Owners presumably sought alternatives that reduced those agency costs, such as close ownership.

Because these social democratic pressures were weaker in the United States, managerial agency costs were smaller here. Despite being smaller, institutions still arose to tie managers to shareholders, institutions such as shareholder wealth maximization norms, transparent accounting, high incentive compensation, and hostile takeovers. Each can fall short, as recent American corporate failures like

28   SOCIAL CONFLICT AND CORPORATE GOVERNANCE

Enron and WorldCom show. But overall each tool narrows the gap between American managers and shareholders. And each gap-reducing tool has tended to be weakened, often deliberately so, in the world's stronger social democracies.

Social democracies pressured firms in ways that increased managerial agency costs to shareholders, thereby widening the gap between managers and any diffuse shareholders. Moreover, social democracies weakened the tools that in the United States closed up much of the American firms' smaller gap between the firm and its diffuse shareholders.

Social Democracies and Agency Costs: Raising the Stakes

Social democracies raised agency costs for shareholders in the public firm, and shareholders' natural reaction would have been to use an alternative organizational form that kept those costs down. German codetermination—by which labor gets one-half of the supervisory board of Germany's largest firms—is an explicit manifestation of social democracy, one that well illustrates the effects on corporate organization of social democracy. We first look at social democracy's effects through codetermination, by imagining the dilemma that a family-owned firm faced when considering whether to take their firm public. Then we generalize by looking at social democracy's effects on agency costs and ownership structure without codetermination. The formal social-democratic institution of codetermination is not needed for social democracy to affect the public firm's internal workings, but the formal institution boldly illustrates the political effects.

4.1. Social Democracy's Effects through Codetermination
4.2. Social Democracy's Effects without Codetermination
4.3. General Effects: Favoring Employees over Shareholders
4.4. Direct Effects: Softening Change and Raising Agency Costs
4.5. Indirect Effects: Rigid Labor Markets as Raising Agency Costs

4.1. SOCIAL DEMOCRACY'S EFFECTS THROUGH CODETERMINATION

Germany's long ideological and political encounter with codetermination began just after the First World War when revolutionary leaders established workers' councils (counterparts to the better-known soviets arising elsewhere), which evolved into employee representation on the supervisory council of the larger firms.[1] After

---

[1] Charles S. Maier, *Recasting Bourgeois Europe: Stabilization in France, Germany, and Italy in the Decade After World War I* 59–60, 138, 141–44 (1975).

30   SOCIAL CONFLICT AND CORPORATE GOVERNANCE

the Second World War, labor leaders sought to be represented on the boards, partly to convince the Allies not to dismantle Germany's coal and steel industry, by asserting that they, labor, would constrain the wartime industrialists via positions on the firms' supervisory boards. From this 'deal' came full-parity codetermination of labor and shareholders in the coal and steel industry. Later political events expanded this codetermination to one-third of the supervisory boards of most other industrial firms, and in 1976 to one-half of the boards of Germany's larger firms.[2]

Codetermination also had its capitalist promoters, who sought a 'middle way' between the raw capitalism of the market-place and the extreme socialism of state ownership. Industrial leaders sought to co-opt revolutionary ideals,[3] and reformers 'envisioned a gradual dissolution of central state authority and the growth of works councils and industrial self-government. . . . [W]orkers and entrepreneurs of a given industry could [and should] be seated at the same table to hammer out common policy. . . .'[4]

Business and political leaders such as Walter Rathenau promoted this idea of a corporate middle way between raw market-place capitalism and socialism,[5] and the institution of codetermination has grown into one that many Germans have been proud of.[6]

Consider how codetermination affects agency costs, and thereby should have affected German corporate ownership structure and securities markets, by imagining how a successful family firm, thinking about making an initial public offering and in time withdrawing from managing and owning the company, might have reacted to codetermination. Their supervisory board was never strong. It has met for the statutory minimum of twice annually.[7] The meetings in the 1990s, when we imagine the family owners inquiring whether or not to go public, are formal, without serious give and take. The accounting reports that the board gets are not very good. The reports are given to the board at the very beginning of a

---

[2] Katharina Pistor, 'Codetermination: A Sociopolitical Model with Governance Externalities', in *Employees and Corporate Governance* 163, 167–69 (ed. by Margaret M. Blair and Mark J. Roe, 1999).   [3] Charles S. Maier, *In Search of Stability* 165 (1987).

[4] Maier, supra, note 1, at 12.

[5] Maier, supra, note 1, at 142. More precisely, Rathenau sought to make business property something intermediate between a private possession and a socialized asset. Maier, supra, note 3, at 40 (1987); Walter Rathenau, *Die Neue Wirtschaft* (1918); Walter Rathenau, *Vom Aktienwesen* (1922). Rathenau, a leading thinker and political leader, was from the family that founded Germany's leading electrical company; he ran wartime production and later became Germany's foreign minister.

[6] See Jean-Marie Colombani, Eric Le Boucher, and Arnaud Leparmentier, [Interview with] Gerhard Schröder, *'Je ne pense plus souhaitable une société sans inégalités'*, *Le Monde*, 20 Nov. 1999, at 3 (quoting German Chancellor Schröder's belief that, in contrast to the American model, Germany's 'is founded on the participation of workers not just in our prosperity but also in decision-making, notably via codetermination').

[7] Until recently, German boards needed to meet only twice annually, and they often kept to the limit. Well-publicized corporate governance failures in a few public firms induced business pressures and legal changes that pushed supervisory boards to meet three or four times a year. Compare Aktiengesellschaft § 110, in Hannes Schneider and Martin Heidenhain, *The German Stock Corporation Act* 115 (2000) (four) with Uwe Huffer, *Aktiengesetz* § 110, at 440 (1995) (two). See Thomas J. André, Jr, 'Some Reflections on German Corporate Governance: A Glimpse at German Supervisory Boards', 70 *Tul. L. Rev.* 1819, 1825 n.21 (1996).

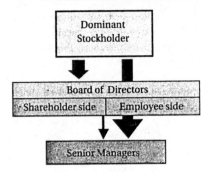

Fig. 4.1. German firm's dominant stockholder, by-passing the codetermined board

semiannual meeting, and are then whisked away at its end. The board has not been a serious monitoring mechanism inside the firm. This until recently has been the typical picture painted of the German boardroom.[8]

Board-level monitoring has not thus far been critical to the firm for two reasons. First, many family owners have also been the firm's managers; hence, the disjunction between ownership and management was weaker than in the fully public firm, and managerial agency costs were lower. Second, even if the family did not manage the firm directly but instead hired professional managers, the family members met regularly with managers to review results and performance, as illustrated in Figure 4.1. In effect, the monitoring role of an active board was fulfilled apart from the supervisory board, whose meetings were stale, formal, and ineffective.

The family may have considered moving more of the monitoring into the boardroom, partly to get ready for a public offering, partly to formalize the informal monthly meetings with managers. But they decided not to move it inside the boardroom because they preferred not to give more information and authority to the labor members of the supervisory board. (Codetermination requirements, which are based on the number of employees, apply to both public and private firms. But the private company's owners can by-pass the board more easily than diffuse shareholders of the public company can.)

The family is hoping to leave the firm. They want to sell their stock and diversify their investments. The firm has been returning $50 million in earnings to them annually, and they accord a capitalization rate of ten to those earnings, valuing the firm at $500 million.

The underwriters with whom they speak confirm that the firm would be worth $500 million if the average annual earnings of $50 million were expected to persist. But the underwriters, hoping to sell the stock to potential diffuse public

---

[8] See Pistor, supra, note, 2, at 191; see also Jeremy Edwards and Klaus Fischer, *Banks, Finance and Investment in Germany* 213 (1994) ('Supervisory boards . . . receive relatively little detailed information about the firm's operations.'); Wulf von Schimmelmann, 'Unternehmenskontrolle in Deutschland', in *Finanzmärkte* 7 (ed. by Bernhard Gahlen, Helmut Hesse, and Hans Jürgen Ramser, 1997); Florian Schilling, 'Der Aufsichtsrat ist für die Katz', *Frankfurter Allgemeine Zeitung*, 27 Aug. 1994, at 11 (German survey of business leaders concludes that the supervisory board is weak and that, as a result of codetermination, it avoids controversial topics).

32 SOCIAL CONFLICT AND CORPORATE GOVERNANCE

stockholders, say that they fear the earnings will not persist if the board remains weak, meeting only twice annually and receiving such poor information. Eventually there will be an external crisis in the firm's markets, or an internal one in the firm's organization, and a weak, poorly informed board is likely to respond more slowly and less effectively than a stronger one. Eventually current managers will retire or be unable to manage the firm well, and a weak board will resolve a succession crisis less effectively than a strong one. Thus far, the underwriters say, the family fulfilled the role that a strong board would play. But if the family leaves, the firm will at times be rudderless.

The underwriters consider this potential lack of direction when they value the firm, estimating that over time earnings will be $40 million, rather than $50 million, if the board is weak and ineffective. They accord those earnings the same capitalization rate of ten, valuing the firm at $400 million, not $500 million.

The family and underwriters then consider strengthening the board, by changing the by-laws to have the board meet monthly, by improving the information flow to the board, by adopting transparent, understandable accounting with statements going to the board well before the meetings, by instilling in the board an ethic of involvement, and by building aggressive audit, executive, and compensation committees. These improvements to the board, the family tells the underwriters, will improve monitoring and reduce the weak board problems. As a result the expected earnings should be re-pegged to $50 million, and the firm should be valued at the original $500 million in the initial public offer, not $400 million. (Up to here the story would not be much different in the United States prior to an initial public offering.)

The underwriters though respond that, yes, the board will be better. But, they ask, in whose interest will the board run the firm? With the supervisory board codetermined, a charged-up board would tilt more to labor when labor's and shareholders' interests conflict than does a purely shareholder-dominated board. Managers would be monitored more, but not necessarily more in shareholders' interests. The enhanced board would create value, but some of that value would go to labor, not to stockholders. The underwriters conclude that the firm would indeed be worth $500 million, but $100 million of that value would they believe go to labor.

These numbers are not out of line with current empirical work on the effect of the 1976 codetermination law, which expanded labor's representation from one-third of the supervisory boards of large firms to one-half. The data available suggest that the increase had a 10 to 20 per cent negative effect on shareholder value.[9]

But the family wants to keep that $100 million. How can they keep it? They can revisit whether they should sell out completely. They may decide to keep the firm

[9] Felix R. FitzRoy and Kornelius Kraft, 'Economic Effects of Codetermination', 95 *Scandinavian J. Econ.* 365, 374 n.6 (1993) (the 1976 change resulted in a productivity loss of '13%–14% of value added'); Frank A. Schmid and Frank Seger, 'Arbeitnehmermitbestimmung, Allokation von Entscheidungsrechten und Shareholder Value', 5 *Zeitschrift für Betriebswirtschaft* 453 (1998); Gary Gorton and Frank A. Schmid, 'Class Struggle Inside the Firm: A Study of German Codetermination' 25 (National Bureau of Economic Research Working Paper, Oct. 2000) (codetermination reduces market-to-book ratio of equity by 27%). Contra Theodor Baums and Bernd Frick, 'The Market Value of the Codetermined Firm', in *Employees and Corporate Governance*, supra, note 2, at 206, 232

private and to re-examine whether they can find an heir who will run it. Or they may hire professional managers to run the firm, if they have not done so already. Or they may sell the firm, but sell it not to diffuse stockholders who will discount the price because they would fear agency costs, but to another dominant owner, who need not discount the price because he or she can overcome those costs. Such block sales are common in Germany.[10] To keep that $100 million difference, the family does *not* launch an initial public offer; as a consequence, there is one less public firm in Germany and one less family interested in seeing Germany develop a strong securities market.

Hence, German social democracy, institutionalized in corporate governance via codetermination, plausibly induces this firm to stay private, so as to avoid the costs to shareholders of an enhanced labor voice inside the firm. Social democracy in the form of supervisory board codetermination mixes badly with the public firm.

4.2. SOCIAL DEMOCRACY'S EFFECTS WITHOUT CODETERMINATION

Codetermination illustrates the thesis crisply, but social democracy even without codetermination has the same effect in inducing concentrated ownership. Social democracy's pressure on the public firm persists even if we remove the formal institution of German supervisory board codetermination. Social democracies press firms and managers from many sides to favor employees with jobs in place.

A simple countervailing coalition image helps to explain why ownership concentration has persisted so long. If employees are favored through private organization, formal representation, or state action, owners will be induced, all else equal, to coalesce to reduce their internal conflicts and face employees more cohesively.

4.3. GENERAL EFFECTS: FAVORING EMPLOYEES OVER SHAREHOLDERS

The effects political pressures can have on the firm can be seen by thinking through the consequences to shareholders of increased managerial agency costs.

Recall the basic agency costs to shareholders: unconstrained managers, unlike shareholders, prefer to expand their firms for more satisfaction, power, prestige, and pay. Managers want to avoid many profit-maximizing risks that would risk

(finding no financial loss to stockholders from court decisions extending codetermination rights); see also Bernd Frick, Gerhard Speckbacher, and Paul Wentges, 'Arbeitnehmermitbestimmung und moderne Theorie der Unternehmung', *Zeitschrift für Betriebswirtschaft* 745–63 (1999) (critiquing studies that showed codetermination as negatively affecting stock price).

[10] See Julian Franks and Colin Mayer, 'Ownership and Control of German Corporations', 14 *Rev. Fin. Stud.* 943, 955 (2001).

34   SOCIAL CONFLICT AND CORPORATE GOVERNANCE

their careers. Managers prefer to use up capital in place rather than to restructure a firm, because restructuring is painful. And managers may be more willing to tolerate slack than would shareholders.

These basic agency costs are well understood. But less well discerned is that these managerial tendencies fit well with employees' goals, and that a second basic corporate governance problem for employees and capital providers has been the persistent tension between invested capital and current employees, a tension muted in the United States, but historically not muted everywhere else. Employees *also* are averse to risks to the firm, as their human capital is tied up in the firm and they are not fully diversified. Employees *also* prefer that the firm expand, not downsize, because expanding often yields them promotion opportunities, while downsizing risks leaving them unemployed. (Likewise, institutional creditors, who loomed larger in European firms than in their American counterparts, preferred to avoid risk and to maintain stability. And incompletely diversified family stockholders, the last key player in large continental European firms, also preferred stability more strongly than diversified American public firm stockholders. The key risk-avoiding pieces all fit together in continental Europe.)

On a simple level, employees prefer higher wages, and shareholders prefer lower wages (at the same level of productivity). Because wages are not precisely determined, managers hold some discretion in setting wages,[11] and weakly monitored managers ordinarily would not fight as strongly for shareholders as would strongly monitored managers. Even in the United States, slight differences in shareholder control of managers affect wage rates, with less-monitored managers in states where anti-takeover laws are strong conceding higher salaries to employees than similar managers in states where anti-takeover laws are weak.[12] On a more complex level, American managers of firms in declining industries tended in the 1980s to use up their equity capital before shrinking their firms unless corporate governance controls induced them not to use up equity first;[13] this is the strategy that incumbent employees would prefer.

Even today in the United States these stakeholder effects, although much weaker than the pressures abroad, can be detected. Delaware law seems to have increased a firm's value in 1990s data,[14] and the reason seems to be its more expansive takeover law. Although Delaware law is moderately anti-takeover, it obstructs the offeror less than other states do. This extra room for offering companies to maneuver may account for the noticeable increase in value in Delaware firms in the 1990s, of about 2 to 5 per cent over similar firms incorporated elsewhere. Although stakeholder pressure is weaker in American states than it was in most

[11] Lloyd G. Reynolds, *The Structure of Labor Markets: Wages and Labor Mobility in Theory and Practice* 156 (1951); Richard A. Lester, 'A Range Theory of Wage Differentials', 5 *Indus. & Lab. Rel. Rev.* 483, 500 (1952).

[12] Marianne Bertrand and Sendhil Mullainathan, 'Is There Discretion in Wage Setting? A Test Using Takeover Legislation', 30 *Rand J. Econ.* 535, 537 (1999).

[13] Cf. Michael C. Jensen, 'Agency Costs of Free Cash Flow, Corporate Finance, and Takeovers', 76 *Am. Econ. Rev.* 323, 324–25 (1986).

[14] Robert Daines, 'Does Delaware Law Improve Firm Value?' 62 *J. Fin. Econ.* 525 (2001).

continental European nations, such pressure in Delaware was even weaker than that in its sister states.[15] Weaker stakeholder pressure—Delaware is small and the weight of the local bar and other professionals is heavier than more traditional stakeholder interest groups—translated into less pressure to impede takeovers.

4.4. DIRECT EFFECTS: SOFTENING CHANGE AND RAISING AGENCY COSTS

Social democracies historically favored incumbent employees. They favored them directly by insisting that firms not lay off employees; when managers are not tied tightly to shareholders, they would not strongly resist such pressures. Managers in the social democratic environment would usually not be paid much for defying the authorities, would prefer the result themselves anyway, and would suffer by taking the heat if they resisted. Hence, agency costs have been higher, as government policy wedged open the gap between managers and employees on one side and shareholders on the other.

True, such governments also sought to stabilize employment in firms *with* dominant stockholders. But dominant stockholders, with their own money on the line, can oftentimes resist the government's actions more vigorously or more surreptitiously. And, next seen, strong owners could avoid getting the firm into a position where those costs from government pressure would be high.

4.5. INDIRECT EFFECTS: RIGID LABOR MARKETS AS RAISING AGENCY COSTS

Even when social democratic employment policies affect diffusely-held and closely-held firms equally, they still affect ownership structure and should still induce close ownership by dominant stockholders.

Social democratic policies often make it hard to lay off workers, even during economic adversity.[16] True, *when* the firm actually faces adversity and seeks to downsize, each ownership structure, whether concentrated or diffuse, faces similar constraints. Hence, one might mistakenly conclude that social democracies should not affect the choice between ownership structures. But dominant stockholders would be more averse to expanding *ex ante* where labor markets were rigid than where employment rules were looser.

[15] Mark J. Roe, 'Takeover Politics', in *The Deal Decade* 321 (ed. by Margaret Blair 1993).

[16] 'Des réactions politiques et syndicales sévères', *Le Monde*, 11 Sept. 1999, at 16 (leader of the governing French party says '[i]t's unacceptable that a large firm can decide to reduce employment . . . simply to enhance shareholder profits').

36   SOCIAL CONFLICT AND CORPORATE GOVERNANCE

Unconstrained managers often prefer to expand their firms, as is well developed in the managerial literature. Since they gain prestige, pay, and power as the firm expands, but do not always pay the price if expansion turns out to be unprofitable, they tend (unless constrained) to expand, and their firms' value to stockholders would deteriorate. When initial owners and potential investors anticipate this risk, stock diffuses into public markets less in social democracies than in more conservative nations, because in a social democracy the stock would be worth less to diffuse stockholders than to close owners.

Competitive capital, product, and labor markets can grind away at these political efforts. Thus political constraints were easier for the political players to implement when European international product and capital markets were less integrated than they are today, back when polities and economies were more or less coextensive with a single nation.

Social democratic government policies wedged open the gap between shareholders and employees by creating laws and a social climate that made it harder for managers to downsize when technology demanded it, or harder for managers to take risks with the enterprise when markets warranted it from the shareholders' perspective. They gave employees more rights to resist change.[17] They constructed nationwide bargaining platforms that favored employees, platforms in which employees coalesced and so shareholders sought to lower their own 'coalition costs', seeking to be more effective by acting cohesively. To be cohesive, shareholders needed to be identifiable—not anonymous, diffuse, and distant.

Such societies also often saw managers and employees as allied with one another, but opposed to distant institutional shareholders, who, because they merely seek financial gain, must be constrained.[18] Consider, for example, this passage from a book by a manager and public figure, a book well known in European business circles: 'Is the firm a simple piece of merchandise...? Or is it...a community *in which the stockholders' power is balanced by managerial power, which is in turn...co-opted...by the employees...?*'[19] Managers, already disposed for their own reasons to expand unnecessarily, to go slow when revamping the firm, to avoid risk, and to refuse to downsize, felt pressured to slow down further and faced social opprobrium if they moved too quickly. Managers who excessively expanded their enterprises in a strong social democracy would

---

[17] Gerhard Schröder, when minister of Lower Saxony—he is now, in 2001, the German Prime Minister—had a steel mill nationalized rather than see it taken over by a foreign firm, because he did not want a restructuring that would affect the German employees. Arnaud Leparmentier, 'L'Allemagne industrielle de nouveau conquérante', *Le Monde*, 28 Nov. 1998, at 1.

[18] Frédéric Lemaître, 'Le succès de l'actionnariat salarié bouleverse le capitalisme français', *Le Monde—Enterprises*, 2 Mar. 1999, at 15; see also Alain Faujas, 'Français, Allemands et Italiens n'attendent rien de bon des entreprises', *Le Monde—Economie*, 1 June 1999, at IV ('60% [of the French] feel that government regulation and taxes handicap French firms, but [they applaud this result] as 51% also say the State must more severely control firms to prevent them from degrading social conditions'); id. (a majority in each of Germany, Italy, and France believe 'the firms' interests and the people's interest are not the same', while in Britain a majority thought the contrary).

[19] Michel Albert, *Capitalisme contre Capitalisme* 19 (1991) (translated from the French) (emphasis added).

especially burden their shareholders, since reversing a mistaken expansion is hard in a social democracy. The agency cost issue is not that managers there are lazy, less effective, or more prone to error, but that they are pushed away from dependably acting for shareholders.

Strong social democracies raised the pressures on managers to abandon their shareholders and side with employees to do what managers want to do all along: expand, avoid risk, and avoid rapid change.

Strong social democracies, in short, raised managerial agency costs.

Populism and Socialism in Corporate Governance

American-style populism and European-style social democracy are differing sides of the same political coin. The polity pays up to affect corporate governance institutions. The deep structure of the political goal has been similar—reining in capital—but the means and degree have differed. And these differences have deeply affected corporate governance, militating toward differing ownership and governance structures.

Democratic polities have a hard time reconciling themselves with pure, strong shareholder values. Democracy usually wedges open gaps between shareholders and the firm, although the means of wedging the two apart, and the size of any gap, differ from nation to nation. Pure shareholder voice can be muffled in some nations, by, say, suppressing one breed of shareholder, such as the powerful financial institution with a strong say inside the industrial firm. American-style populism did this. Or the range and force of capital can be constricted, by rules, norms, or labor structures that preclude shareholders from rapidly laying off employees or quickly changing the nature of the work place. Continental-European-style social democracy did this. Or a society can set up informal constraints so that a wide class of employees cannot be fired during the core of the working life. Post-war Japan did this.

Each political impulse calls forth distinctive corporate ownership structures: once financial institutions are suppressed, then as long as capital is otherwise free to tie managers to shareholders, the diffusely-held public firm prospers. Once labor is strongly protected and capital is restricted from acting too negatively on labor, that tends to call forth fewer diffuse-held public firms, especially if the means that would make managers loyal to shareholders are denigrated.

In each case what is at work is a democratic polity's reluctance to facilitate strong, unmodulated shareholder voice.

* * *

200 UNIFYING TWO POLITICAL THEORIES

The goal here has not been to show some gross inefficiency in one corporate governance system or another. Concentrated ownership looked good in the 1980s, when German and Japanese industry seemed to out-compete several American industrial sectors. Diffuse ownership looks good now, as it is associated with advanced technologies and rapid adaptation. Lost in the debate is the possibility that each has some advantages, for some industries, for some firms, for some periods of the firms' life cycle. Politics by skewing firms to one type of ownership and governance system probably denies each some variety in organizational form.

* * *

Capital movement is fluid and can be channeled. Capital, corporate structure, and financial flows attract political attention, and the political result deeply affects the organization of the large firm. In the United States, populist politics historically suppressed powerful financial institutions and their voice inside the large firm.[1] This suppression especially affected the structure of the very largest firms, because the largest American firms were (and for the most part still are) too large for even the richest American families to take and retain long-term big blocks; for many of the biggest firms, only financial institutions could.[2] Complementary pro-shareholder institutions developed to support distant shareholding in public firms, both in those public firms that were very large and in those that were merely large, and hence the public firm dominates in the United States.[3] In contrast, modern European social democratic politics pressed on invested capital, and weakened or barred those complementary institutions that support the public firm. Hence, close ownership, both family and institutional, has thus far persisted in Europe.

[1] Mark J. Roe, *Strong Managers, Weak Owners: The Political Roots of American Corporate Finance* 1–101 (1994).

[2] A look at the Forbes list of richest Americans quickly tells us why: the richest for the most part already have big blocks in a single firm (Gates in Microsoft; Dell in Dell). For them to take a big block of stock in another firm, they would have to give up the block they have. In effect the 'supply' of very rich people is small in relation to the supply of very large firms.

[3] Roe, supra, note 1, at 7–8.

Conclusion

Political conditions affect whether the large public firm can arise and prosper, and whether ownership can easily separate from control. In the United States these conditions have been in place for quite some time; in contrast, modern continental social democracies historically mixed badly with the American-style public firm.

The American-style public corporation is a fragile contraption, filled with contradictions, easy to destabilize and destroy. Although it dominates American business, due to its counter-balancing ability to agglomerate capital and efficiently spread private risk, it needs multiple preconditions to arise, survive, and prosper. One powerful precondition is that shareholders if they disperse can remain assured of managerial loyalty, an assurance that a social democracy reduces, or destroys.

True, the benefits with which the public firm is associated—innovation, competition, and high technology, for example—might be obtained without ownership separation and public firms. Innovation, competition, and efficient production can be reached in different organizations. Nations that deny themselves one organizational form do not condemn themselves to economic backwardness, but leave themselves without one tool in the organizational toolkit. Public firms and the capacity to go public can motivate entry, can enhance product market competition, and can democratize the appearance of business. But all these can be accomplished otherwise, although perhaps occasionally at higher technical cost. (And, similarly, nations that overly fragment institutional shareholding and financial voice inside the corporate boardroom deny themselves a different tool.)

Moreover, this is hardly a reason to criticize social democracies. What gets lost in shareholder tools may be gained on the shop floor; net efficiency effects may be zero. And the solidarity and equality in these nations may make more citizens happier, and those societies may in the long run be more stable and productive than they would be otherwise. Many European players, even managerial players, believe this to be so.[1] Citizens in nations with a yearning for stability, perhaps one created by gloomy destructive histories, may get special value from the stability of a social democracy.

---

[1] Michel Albert, *Capitalisme contre capitalisme* 169–92 (1991).

202   CONCLUSION

But productivity effects and the *overall* value of a social democracy are not the principal lines of thought here. The story here is not the normative one of which is better, but the positive one of why we see corporate differences that cannot be fully explained without looking at a society's political foundations. The key point is that for a nation to create public firms and deep securities markets it needs more than just the right legal institutions; rather, it faces a problem that goes to the core of that society's social and political organization. As such, reformers have thus far often found technical solutions frustrating or impossible to implement; and, even if implemented, the technical reforms have sometimes had little effect unless and until the underlying political reality changed. One may see little demand for the institutions that support securities markets until a social democracy has softened enough to lay the political foundation for making public firms viable. That softening may have happened in Europe during the past decade; in the United States that social democracy never existed.

Capital markets and institutions, managerial markets and institutions, and labor markets and institutions interrelate. Some types fit well together, complementing one other, and some do not. Politics can determine one type of the three and thereby indirectly determine the other two, because sometimes only a restricted set of the others fits the one that politics determined. America's historical antipathy to private institutional power over-emphasized one kind of capital market, and thereby affected the managerial institutions of the public firm.[2] European politics affected labor institutions and these in turn affected managerial institutions and capital structure. Had American labor institutions differed—had the United States been more of a social democracy—the public firm would have had a harder time in the United States and may have evolved as a minor rather than a major American business institution.

So, to restate, the fewer public firms and historically shallower security markets in France, Germany, and the rest of continental Europe have often been seen as technical results, as deriving from the inability to build the needed *institutional* prerequisites. Accounting needs to be transparent. Culture that leads the upper middle class in Europe to avoid owning stocks and that calls forth too few entrepreneurs is blamed. Securities laws need revamping; insider traders must be jailed when discovered. And, most recently, analysts have discovered minority stockholder protection as a fundamental prerequisite to public firms and deep securities markets.

Some technical problems are important, others are surmountable. France and Germany have built good bureaucracies, staffed by capable and motivated professionals. If securities laws determine the differences in securities markets, then one wonders why and how 'technical' law could be the difference here, because France and Germany are often better than the United States at drafting and implementing comprehensive statutory schemes and then building government agencies to enforce them.

---

[2] Mark J. Roe, *Strong Managers, Weak Owners: The Political Roots of American Corporate Finance* xiii–xvi, 283–87 (1994).

Technical institutions that support the large public firm are useful, but for the world's wealthier democracies, their construction is hardly rocket science. Several already have them. When the political will is there, they usually can get built. The lack of political will in modern times in the rich democracies is manifested in social democracy. And in some nations the technical institutions are there, but if the political configuration is not conducive, ownership does not separate from control. Visions of what makes for a good society differ, and those differing visions lead to differing corporate organization.

If the wealthier democratic nations do not build the corporate stockholder protections often, or if securities markets do not flourish even when they do, then other explanations must account for their inaction. *The demand for those institutions might be low, because other institutions—namely, social democracy itself— render public firms less valuable to diffuse shareholders.* When blocks persist, one cannot tell a priori whether distant stockholders fear dominant stockholders or fear high managerial agency costs in public firms. If they fear high managerial agency costs, blockholding would tend to persist as that nation's shareholders' best way to control managerial agency costs.

This result is not merely technical, arising just from the accidents of which technical institutions a society has built. And, hence, no change will be purely technical either. The result maps back to a society's political condition: social democracies raised the managerial agency costs to shareholders in the public firm. They exacerbated managerial tendencies to expand unprofitably, to avoid risk at all costs, and to avoid biting the bullet and forcing organizational change when markets and technologies shifted. In each case incumbent employees often preferred that these changes not go forward; incumbent employees have had a strong political voice in social democracies; and owners and managers have had a rougher time bringing about organizational change in the social democracies.

Political differences among the world's rich democracies explain much about their corporate differences. Social democracies wedged open the gap between shareholders and managers in public firms, by raising agency costs higher and reducing the efficacy of the techniques that would control them. This wedge has been small in the United States, and we have thereby uncovered the critical precondition to the separation of ownership from control and, hence, of the rise and persistence of the dominant form of business organization in the United States: namely the historical absence of a strong social democracy.

* * *

Corporate governance can be analyzed solely in terms of the inner workings of the corporation: the mechanical requirements for the board of directors, the degree to which minority stockholders are protected from insider machinations, the degree to which incentive-compatible compensation is implemented, the quality of specialized committees, the quality of securities law disclosure and insider-trading enforcement, etc.

The fragile ties between managers and diffuse shareholders are all too easy to sever. Not all societies favor shareholders. Some fray the ties between managers and shareholders, because they dislike many ways that managers act for share-holders. Such societies can induce unconstrained managers to expand firms even when not profitable to do so, to go slow in downsizing when the firm is misaligned with its product market, and to shy away from profitable risks that could disrupt the work place. If they push managers to expand, go slow, and avoid risk, then diffuse shareholders will find their stock less valuable than if the firm could find a way to avoid these pressures. Diffuse stockholders will be fewer than in societies without such pressures. And if the modern tools that align managers with share-holders in the United States are also denigrated—incentive compensation, hostile takeovers, shareholder primacy norms, and transparency—then diffuse stock-holders have a doubled-up reason to be wary.

The corporation is part of a larger society. One recalls Pierre Trudeau's comment about what it was like for Canada to be right next to the United States, which I mentioned in this book's Introduction. It is like sleeping next to an elephant, Trudeau said. Even if the elephant is benign, even if it is paying little attention to you, slight movements during the elephant's sleep could have a very large effect.

For corporate governance, the elephants are labor markets, politics, and capital and product markets. Small changes in any, and especially small changes in polit-ical results, can make for big changes in how corporate governance looks.

Or to use another metaphor: if one wants to understand the flow of the world's waters in rivers, bays, and oceans, then attending to viscosity, rainfall, erosion, and so on is important. Some of these one can control; some one cannot. But one cannot fully understand the water's movements without understanding the huge gravitational pull of the moon, and the concomitant tidal effects. The moon's pull is unseen, unchangeable by humans, but powerful. For corporate governance the moon's pull comes from politics.

ACKNOWLEDGEMENTS

For a conference I organized as part of Columbia Law School's Sloan Project on corporate governance in March 1997, I invited two dozen corporate law scholars to pick a country, speculate on what was missing from corporate governance analysis in that country, and consider how that reflected on corporate governance elsewhere. I chose Germany and speculated how codetermination could fit with weak boardrooms and concentrated ownership. That sketch eventually became the core of Chapter 4 of this book. This book expands on that assertion, with a view that the formal institution is not needed to yield similar effects. Politics affects corporate governance.

Two deans, David Leebron and Robert Clark, and two foundations, Sloan at Columbia and Olin at Harvard, supported this research. Several colleagues read the underlying articles. I thanked them then, and I thank them here again. Several, including Lucian Bebchuk, Ronald Gilson (my co-author of the article on Japanese lifetime employment), Victor Goldberg, and Jeffrey Gordon, commented on more than one of the underlying articles. Victor Brudney, Gérard Hertig, Michelle Jewett, Mark Ramseyer, and Detlev Vagts read and critiqued the entire manuscript, Margaret Blair, Einer Elhauge, Howell Jackson and Lorenzo Stanghellini parts of it.

David Musson from Oxford University Press and Colin Mayer from Oxford's Business School gave me the opportunity to collect these thoughts in the Clarendon Lectures on Management in May 1999. The book focuses on, and expands upon, the second of the three lectures.

Portions of this book draw on these prior articles:

1. 'Political Preconditions to Separating Ownership from Control', 53 *Stanford Law Review* 539 (2000).
2. 'Rents and their Corporate Consequences', 53 *Stanford Law Review* 1463 (2001).
3. 'Corporate Law's Limits, 31 *Journal of Legal Studies* 233 (2002).
4. 'The Shareholder Wealth Maximization Norm and Industrial Organization', 149 *University of Pennsylvania Law Review* 2063 (2001).
5. 'The Political Economy of Japanese Lifetime Employment', in *Employees and Corporate Governance* (with Ronald Gilson) (Margaret M. Blair & Mark J. Roe, eds, 1999).
6. 'Lifetime Employment: Labor Peace and the Evolution of Japanese Corporate Governance', 99 *Columbia Law Review* 508 (1999) (with Ronald Gilson).

206   ACKNOWLEDGEMENTS

7. 'German Securities Markets and German Codetermination', 98 *Columbia Business Law Review* 167 (1998).

8. 'Backlash', 98 *Columbia Law Review* 217 (1998).

9. 'From Antitrust to Corporate Governance: The Corporation and the Law', 1959–1995, in *The American Corporation Today*, 102–27 (Carl Kaysen, ed., 1996).

Books, Manuscripts, and Journal Articles

Albert, Michel. *Capitalisme contre Capitalisme.* Paris: Editions du Seuil, 1991.

André, Thomas J. 'Some Reflections on German Corporate Governance: A Glimpse at German Supervisory Boards'. 70 *Tulane Law Review* 1819 (1996).

Baums, Theodor and Bernd Frick. 'The Market Value of the Codetermined Firm'. In *Employees and Corporate Governance*, edited by Margaret M. Blair and Mark J. Roe, at 206. Washington, DC: Brookings Institution, 1999.

Bertrand, Marianne and Sendhil Mullainathan. 'Is There Discretion in Wage Setting? A Test Using Takeover Legislation'. 30 *Rand Journal of Economics* 535 (1999).

Daines, Robert. 'Does Delaware Law Improve Firm Value?' 62 *Journal of Financial Economics* 525 (2001).

Edwards, Jeremy and Klaus Fischer. *Banks, Finance and Investment in Germany.* Cambridge, UK.; New York: Cambridge University Press, 1994.

FitzRoy, Felix R. and Kornelius Kraft. 'Economic Effects of Codetermination'. 95 *Scandinavian Journal of Economics* 365 (1993).

Franks, Julian and Colin Mayer. 'Ownership and Control of German Corporations'. 14 *Review of Financial Studies* 943 (2001).

Frick, Bernd, Gerhard Speckbacker and Paul Wentges. 'Arbeitnehmermitbestimmung und moderne Theorie der Unternehmung'. 69 *Zeitschrift für Betriebswirtschaft* 745 (1999).

Gorton, Gary and Frank A. Schmid. 'Class Struggle Inside the Firm: A Study of German Codetermination'. Cambridge, Mass.: National Bureau of Economic Research, October 2000. (Working Paper No. 7945).

Jensen, Michael C. 'Agency Costs of Free Cash Flow, Corporate Finance, and Takeovers'. 76 *American Economic Review* 323 (1986).

La Porta, Rafael, Florencio Lopez-de-Silanes, and Andrei Shleifer. 'Corporate Ownership Around the World'. 54 *Journal of Finance* 471 (1999).

Maier, Charles S. *Recasting Bourgeois Europe: Stabilization in France, Germany and Italy in the Decade After World War I.* Princeton University Press, 1975.

Pinto, Arthur R. and Gustavo Visentini (eds.) *The Legal Basis of Corporate Governance in Publicly Held Corporations: A Comparative Approach.* The Hague; Boston: Kluwer Law International, 1998.

Pistor, Katharina. 'Codetermination: A Sociopolitical Model with Governance Externalities'. In *Employees and Corporate Governance*, edited by Margaret M. Blair and Mark J. Roe, 163. Washington, DC: Brookings Institution Press, 1999.

Portolano, Alessandro. 'The Decision to Adopt Defensive Tactics in Italy'. 20 *International Review of Law and Economics* 425 (2000).

Przeworski, Adam. 'Socialism and Social Democracy'. In *The Oxford Companion to Politics of the World*, edited by Joel Krieger, *et al.*, at 832. New York: Oxford University Press, 1993.

Rathenau, Walther. *Die Neue Wirtschaft.* Berlin: S. Fischer, 1918.

Reynolds, Lloyd George. *The Structure of Labor Markets: Wages and Labor Mobility in Theory and Practice*. New York: Harper, 1951.

Roe, Mark J. *Strong Managers, Weak Owners: The Political Roots of American Corporate Finance*. Princeton, NJ: Princeton University Press, 1994.

—— 'Takeover Politics'. In *The Deal Decade: What Takeovers and Leveraged Buyouts Mean for Corporate Governance*, edited by Margaret M. Blair, at 321. Washington, DC: Brookings Institution, 1993.

Schimmelmann, Wulf von. 'Unternehmenskontrolle in Deutschland'. In *Finanzmärkte*, edited by Bernard Gahlen, Helmut Hesse, and Hans Jürgen Ramser, 7. Tübingen: Mohr Siebeck, 1997.

Schmid, Frank A. and Frank Seger. 'Arbeitnehmermitbestimmung, Allokation von Entscheidungsrechten und Shareholder Value'. 5 *Zeitschrift für Betriebswirtschat* 453 (1998).

Stimson, S. C. 'Social Democracy'. In *The New Palgrave: A Dictionary of Economics*, edited by John Eatwell, Murray Milgate, and Peter Newman, 395. Vol. 4. London: Macmillan, 1987.

Newspaper and Magazine Articles

Colombani, Jean Marie, Eric Le Boucher, and Arnaud Leparmentier. '[Interview with] Gerhard Schröder, [Chancelier de la République Fédérale d'Allemagne:] Je ne pense plus souhaitable une société sans inégalités'. *Le Monde* (Paris), 20 November 1999, 3.

Faujas, Alain. 'Français, Allemands et Italiens n'attendent rien de bon des entreprises'. *Le Monde–Economie* (Paris), 1 June 1999, IV.

Lemaître, Frédéric. 'Le succès de l'actionnariat salarié bouleverse le capitalisme français'. *Le Monde–Entreprises* (Paris), 2 March 1999.

Leparmentier, Arnaud. 'L'Allemagne industrielle de nouveau conquérante'. *Le Monde* (Paris), 28 November 1998, 1.

Schilling, Florian. 'Der Aufsichtsrat ist für die Katz'. *Frankfurter Allgemeine Zeitung*, 27 August 1994, 11.

[2]

Law and Finance

Rafael La Porta, Florencio Lopez-de-Silanes, and Andrei Shleifer
Harvard University

Robert W. Vishny
University of Chicago

This paper examines legal rules covering protection of corporate shareholders and creditors, the origin of these rules, and the quality of their enforcement in 49 countries. The results show that common-law countries generally have the strongest, and French-civil-law countries the weakest, legal protections of investors, with German- and Scandinavian-civil-law countries located in the middle. We also find that concentration of ownership of shares in the largest public companies is negatively related to investor protections, consistent with the hypothesis that small, diversified shareholders are unlikely to be important in countries that fail to protect their rights.

I. Overview of the Issues

In the traditional finance of Modigliani and Miller (1958), securities are recognized by their cash flows. For example, debt has a fixed promised stream of interest payments, whereas equity entitles its

We are grateful to Mark Chen, Steven Friedman, Magdalena Lopez-Morton, and Katya Zhuravskaya for excellent research assistance; to Robert Barro, Eric Berglof, Bernard Black, Bertyl G. Bylund, Francesco DeNozza, Yoshikata Fukui, Edward Glaeser, Zvi Griliches, Oliver Hart, Martin Hellwig, James Hines, Louis Kaplow, Raghu Rajan, Roberta Romano, Rolf Skog, Eddy Wymeersch, Luigi Zingales, and three anonymous referees for comments; and to the National Science Foundation for financial support of this research. Documentation of the data on legal rules presented in this paper is available from the authors on request.

[*Journal of Political Economy*, 1998, vol. 106, no. 6]

owner to receive dividends. Recent financial research has shown that this is far from the whole story and that the defining feature of various securities is the rights that they bring to their owners (Hart 1995). Thus shares typically give their owners the right to vote for directors of companies, whereas debt entitles creditors to the power, for example, to repossess collateral when the company fails to make promised payments.

The rights attached to securities become critical when managers of companies act in their own interest. These rights give investors the power to extract from managers the returns on their investment. Shareholders receive dividends *because* they can vote out the directors who do not pay them, and creditors are paid *because* they have the power to repossess collateral. Without these rights, investors would not be able to get paid, and therefore firms would find it harder to raise external finance.

But the view that securities are inherently characterized by some intrinsic rights is incomplete as well. It ignores the fact that these rights depend on the legal rules of the jurisdictions in which securities are issued. Does being a shareholder in France give an investor the same privileges as being a shareholder in the United States, India, or Mexico? Would a secured creditor in Germany fare as well when the borrower defaults as one in Sri Lanka or Italy, with the value of the collateral assumed the same in all cases? Law and the quality of its enforcement are potentially important determinants of what rights security holders have and how well these rights are protected. Since the protection investors receive determines their readiness to finance firms, corporate finance may critically turn on these legal rules and their enforcement.

The differences in legal protections of investors might help explain why firms are financed and owned so differently in different countries. Why do Italian companies rarely go public (Pagano, Panetta, and Zingales 1998)? Why does Germany have such a small stock market but also maintain very large and powerful banks (Edwards and Fischer 1994)? Why is the voting premium—the price of shares with high voting rights relative to that of shares with low voting rights—small in Sweden and the United States, and much larger in Italy and Israel (Levy 1983; Rydquist 1987; Zingales 1994, 1995)? Indeed, why were Russian stocks nearly worthless immediately after privatization—by some estimates 100 times cheaper than Western stocks backed by comparable assets—and why did Russian companies have virtually no access to external finance (Boycko, Shleifer, and Vishny 1993)? Why is ownership of large American and British companies so widely dispersed (Berle and Means 1932)? The content of legal rules in different countries may shed light on these corporate governance puzzles.

In recent years, economists and legal scholars have begun to examine theoretically the costs and benefits of alternative legal rules regarding investor rights (e.g., Grossman and Hart 1988; Harris and Raviv 1988; Gromb 1993; Bebchuk 1994). The trouble is, there have been no systematic data available on what the legal rules pertaining to corporate governance are around the world, how well these rules are enforced in different countries, and what effect these rules have. There is no systematic knowledge, for example, of whether different countries actually do have substantially different rules that might explain differences in their financing patterns. Comparative *statistical* analysis of the legal underpinnings of corporate finance—and commerce more generally—remains uncharted territory.

In this paper, we attempt to explore this territory. We examine empirically how laws protecting investors differ across 49 countries, how the quality of enforcement of these laws varies, and whether these variations matter for corporate ownership patterns around the world.

Our starting point is the recognition that laws in different countries are typically not written from scratch, but rather transplanted— voluntarily or otherwise—from a few legal families or traditions (Watson 1974). In general, *commercial* laws come from two broad traditions: common law, which is English in origin, and civil law, which derives from Roman law. Within the civil tradition, there are only three major families that modern commercial laws originate from: French, German, and Scandinavian. The French and the German civil traditions, as well as the common-law tradition, have spread around the world through a combination of conquest, imperialism, outright borrowing, and more subtle imitation. The resulting laws reflect both the influence of their families and the revisions specific to individual countries. As a result of this spread of legal families and the subsequent evolution of the laws, we can compare both the individual legal rules and whole legal families across a large number of countries.

To this end, we have assembled a data set covering legal rules pertaining to the rights of investors, and to the quality of enforcement of these rules, in 49 countries that have publicly traded companies. For shareholders, some of the rules we examine cover voting powers, ease of participation in corporate voting, and legal protections against expropriation by management. For creditors, some of these rules cover the respect for security of the loan, the ability to grab assets in case of a loan default, and the inability of management to seek protection from creditors unilaterally. In effect, these rules measure the ease with which investors can exercise their powers against management. We also consider measures of the quality of enforcement of legal rules in different countries and of the quality of their accounting systems.

We show that laws vary a lot across countries, in part because of differences in legal origin. Civil laws give investors weaker legal rights than common laws do, independent of the level of per capita income. Common-law countries give both shareholders and creditors—relatively speaking—the strongest, and French-civil-law countries the weakest, protection. German-civil-law and Scandinavian countries generally fall between the other two. The quality of law enforcement is the highest in Scandinavian and German-civil-law countries, next highest in common-law countries, and again the lowest in French-civil-law countries.

Having shown that law and its enforcement vary across countries and legal families, we ask how the countries with poor laws or enforcement cope with this problem. Do these countries have other, *substitute,* mechanisms of corporate governance? These adaptive mechanisms may in fact be incorporated into the law, or they may lie outside the law. One potential adaptation to fewer laws is strong enforcement of laws, but as we pointed out above, this does not appear to be the case empirically. Another adaptation, sometimes referred to as "bright-line" rules, is to legally introduce mandatory standards of retention and distribution of capital to investors, which limit the opportunities for managerial expropriation. We find that only French-civil-law countries have mandatory dividends, and German-civil-law countries are the most likely to have legal reserve requirements of all the legal families.

A further response to the lack of legal protections that we examine is a high ownership concentration. Some concentration of ownership of a firm's shares is typically efficient to provide managers with incentives to work and large investors with incentives to monitor the managers (Jensen and Meckling 1976; Shleifer and Vishny 1986). However, some dispersion of ownership is also desirable to diversify risk. As argued by Shleifer and Vishny (1997) and explained further in Section VI, a very high ownership concentration may be a reflection of poor investor protection. We examine ownership concentration in the largest publicly traded companies in our sample countries and find a strong negative correlation between concentration of ownership, as measured by the combined stake of the three largest shareholders, and the quality of legal protection of investors. Poor investor protection in French-civil-law countries is associated with extremely concentrated ownership. The data on ownership concentration thus support the idea that legal systems matter for corporate governance and that firms have to adapt to the limitations of the legal systems that they operate in.

Section II of the paper describes the countries and their laws. Sections III and IV then compare shareholder and creditor rights, respectively, in different countries and different legal traditions. Section V compares the quality of law enforcement and accounting standards in different countries and legal traditions. Section VI focuses on ownership. Section VII presents concluding remarks.

II. Countries, Legal Families, and Legal Rules

Countries

Most studies of corporate governance focus on one or a few wealthy economies (see, e.g., Berglof and Perotti 1994; Kaplan and Minton 1994; Rajan and Zingales 1995; Gorton and Schmidt 1996). However, corporate governance in all of the three economies that scholars typically focus on—the United States, Germany, and Japan—is quite effective. To understand better the role of legal protection of investors, we need to examine a larger sample of countries. To this end, we have assembled as comprehensive a sample as possible of countries that have some nonfinancial firms traded on their stock exchanges. The sample covers 49 countries from Europe, North and South America, Africa, Asia, and Australia. There are no socialist or "transition" economies in the sample. A country is selected for inclusion if, on the basis of the WorldScope sample of 15,900 firms from 33 countries and the Moody's International sample of 15,100 non-U.S. firms from 92 countries, that country had at least five domestic nonfinancial publicly traded firms with no government ownership in 1993. We restrict attention to countries that have publicly traded firms since our primary focus is on protecting investor rights, and without public shareholders a discussion of investor rights would be limited. Having at least five nonfinancial private firms is also essential for construction of ownership data.

Legal Families

Comparative legal scholars agree that, even though no two nations' laws are exactly alike, some national legal systems are sufficiently similar in certain critical respects to permit classification of national legal systems into major families of law. Although there is no unanimity among legal scholars on how to define legal families, among the criteria often used for this purpose are the following: (1) historical background and development of the legal system, (2) theories and hierarchies of sources of law, (3) the working methodology of jurists within the legal systems, (4) the characteristics of legal concepts employed by the system, (5) the legal institutions of the system, and (6) the divisions of law employed within a system. [Glendon, Gordon, and Osakwe 1994, pp. 4–5]

On the basis of this approach, scholars identify two broad legal traditions that pertain to matters discussed in this paper: civil law and common law.[1]

The civil, or Romano-Germanic, legal tradition is the oldest, the most influential, and the most widely distributed around the world. It originates in Roman law, uses statutes and comprehensive codes as a primary means of ordering legal material, and relies heavily on legal scholars to ascertain and formulate its rules (Merryman 1969). Legal scholars typically identify three currently common families of laws within the civil-law tradition: French, German, and Scandinavian. The French Commercial Code was written under Napoleon in 1807 and brought by his armies to Belgium, the Netherlands, part of Poland, Italy, and western regions of Germany. In the colonial era, France extended its legal influence to the Near East and Northern and sub-Saharan Africa, Indochina, Oceania, and French Caribbean islands. French legal influence has been significant as well in Luxembourg, Portugal, Spain, some of the Swiss cantons, and Italy (Glendon et al. 1994). When the Spanish and Portuguese empires in Latin America dissolved in the nineteenth century, it was mainly the French civil law that the lawmakers of the new nations looked to for inspiration. Our sample contains 21 countries with laws in the French civil tradition.

The German Commercial Code was written in 1897 after Bismarck's unification of Germany, and perhaps because it was produced several decades later, was not as widely adopted as the French code. It had an important influence on the legal theory and doctrine in Austria, Czechoslovakia, Greece, Hungary, Italy, Switzerland, Yugoslavia, Japan, and Korea. Taiwan's laws came from China, which

[1] The religious traditions, such as Jewish law, Canon law, Hindu law, and Muslim law, appear to be less relevant in matters of investor protection. "Thus the Arabian countries unquestionably belong to Islamic law as far as family and inheritance law is concerned, just as India belongs to Hindu law, but economic law of these countries (including commercial law and the law of contract and tort) is heavily impressed by the legal thinking of the colonial and mandatory powers—the Common Law in the case of India, French law in the case of most of the Arab States" (Zweigert and Kotz 1987, p. 66). We focus on the principal secular legal traditions in this study.

borrowed heavily from the German code during its modernization. We have six countries from this family in our sample.

The Scandinavian family is usually viewed as part of the civil-law tradition, although its law is less derivative of Roman law than the French and German families (Zweigert and Kotz 1987). Although Nordic countries had civil codes as far back as the eighteenth century, these codes are not used anymore. Most writers describe the Scandinavian laws as similar to each other but "distinct" from others, so we keep the four Nordic countries in our sample as a separate family.

The common-law family includes the law of England and those laws modeled on English law. The common law is formed by judges who have to resolve specific disputes. Precedents from judicial decisions, as opposed to contributions by scholars, shape common law. Common law has spread to the British colonies, including the United States, Canada, Australia, India, and many other countries. There are 18 common-law countries in our sample.

To classify countries into legal families, we rely principally on Reynolds and Flores (1989). In most cases, such classification is uncontroversial. In a few cases, while the basic origin of laws is clear, laws have been amended over time to incorporate influences from other families. For example, Ecuador, a French-civil-law country, revised its company law in 1977 to incorporate some common-law rules; Thailand's first laws were based on common law but since received enormous French influence; and Italy is a French-civil-law country with some German influence. Most important for our study, after World War II, the American occupying army "Americanized" some Japanese laws, particularly in the company law area, although their basic German-civil-law structure remained. In these and several other cases, we classify a country on the basis of the origin of the initial laws it adopted rather than on the revisions.[2] In the United States, states have their own laws. We generally rely on Delaware law because a significant fraction of large U.S. companies are incorporated in Delaware. In Canada, our data come from Ontario laws, even though Quebec has a system based on French civil law.

---

[2] The European Community is currently attempting to harmonize West European laws, including those pertaining to corporate governance, by issuing directives (Andenas and Kenyon-Slade 1993; Werlauff 1993). Several countries have changed parts of their laws to adhere to E.C. directives. However, in most instances, the directives are not mandatory, and the countries are given some time to change their laws. Moreover, the E.C. directives accommodate a great deal of diversity among countries. As of 1993–94—the point in time for which we examine the legal rules of the countries in our sample—E.C. harmonization has not generally affected the legal rules that we focus on. The one area in which the E.C. impact has been large, namely mergers and acquisitions, is not an area that we examine in this paper (see below).

Legal Rules

We look only at laws pertaining to investor protection, and specifically only at company and bankruptcy/reorganization laws. Company laws exist in all countries and are concerned with (1) the legal relations between corporate insiders (members of the corporation, i.e., shareholders and directors) and the corporation itself and (2) the legal relations between the corporation and certain outsiders, particularly creditors. Bankruptcy/reorganization laws apply more generally than just to companies but deal specifically with procedures that unfold in the case of failure to pay back debt. All these laws are part of the commercial codes in civil-law countries and exist as separate laws, mainly in the form of acts, in common-law countries.

There are several conspicuous omissions from the data set. First, this paper says little about merger and takeover rules, except indirectly by looking at voting mechanisms. These rules are spread between company laws, antitrust laws, security laws, stock exchange regulations, and sometimes banking regulations as well. Moreover, these rules have changed significantly in Europe as part of E.C. legal harmonization. Until recently, takeovers have been an important governance tool in only a few common-law countries, although the situation may change.[3]

Second, this paper also says little about disclosure rules, which again come from many sources—including company laws, security laws, and stock exchange regulations—and are also intended for harmonization across the European Community. We do, however, look at the quality of accounting standards, which to a large extent is a consequence of disclosure rules.

Third, in this paper we do not use any information from regulations imposed by security exchanges. One instance in which this is relevant is exchange-imposed restrictions on the voting rights for the shares that companies can issue if these shares are to be traded on the exchange.

Finally, a potentially important set of rules that we do not deal with here is banking and financial institution regulations, which might take the form of restricting bank ownership, for example. Much has been made of these regulations in the United States by Roe (1994).

---

[3] Several readers have pointed to the U.S. state antitakeover laws as evidence of an anti–minority shareholder position in the U.S. legal system that our data do not capture. Even with all these antitakeover laws, the United States and the United Kingdom still have by far the most takeovers of any country in the world, so their laws are evidently not nearly as antitakeover as those elsewhere.

An inspection of company and bankruptcy laws suggests numerous potentially measurable differences among countries. Here we focus only on some of the most basic rules that observers of corporate governance around the world (e.g., American Bar Association 1989, 1993; White 1993; Institutional Shareholder Services 1994; Investor Responsibility Research Center 1994, 1995; Vishny 1994) believe to be critical to the quality of shareholder and creditor legal rights. Moreover, we focus on variables that prima facie are interpretable as either pro-investor or pro-management since this is the dimension along which we are trying to assess countries and legal families. There are obvious differences in rules between countries, such as, for example, tier structures of boards of directors, that we do not examine because we cannot ascertain which of these rules are more sympathetic to shareholders. Investor rights, as well as the other variables we use in this paper, are summarized in table 1. We discuss individual variables in more detail in the sections in which they are analyzed and present all the data on individual rights that we use in the paper in the relevant tables.

Some Conceptual Issues

Our goal is to establish whether laws pertaining to investor protection differ across countries and whether these differences have consequences for corporate finance. This research design immediately poses some conceptual problems. To begin, some scholars, such as Easterbrook and Fischel (1991), are skeptical that legal rules are binding in most instances, since often firms can opt out of these rules in their corporate charters, which effectively serve as contracts between entrepreneurs and investors. Indeed, in many countries, firms can opt out of some of the rules we examine. As a practical matter, however, it may be costly for firms to opt out of standard legal rules since investors might have difficulty accepting nonstandard contracts and, more important, judges might fail to understand or enforce them. The question of whether legal rules matter is fundamentally empirical: if opting out were cheap and simple, we would not find that legal rules matter for patterns of corporate ownership and finance.

A closely related question is whether more restrictive rules, which reduce the choices available to company founders, are necessarily more protective of shareholders than the alternative of greater flexibility. In an environment of perfect judicial enforcement, the benefits of flexibility probably outweigh the risks when entrepreneurs use nonstandard corporate charters to take advantage of investors, since investors can appeal to a court when they are expropriated in an

TABLE 1
VARIABLES

Variable	Description	Sources
Origin	Identifies the legal origin of the company law or commercial code of each country. Equals one if the origin is English common law, two if the origin is the French commercial code, three if the origin is the German commercial code, and four if the origin is Scandinavian civil law	Reynolds and Flores (1989)
One share—one vote	Equals one if the company law or commercial code of the country requires that ordinary shares carry one vote per share, and zero otherwise. Equivalently, this variable equals one when the law prohibits the existence of both multiple-voting and nonvoting ordinary shares and does not allow firms to set a maximum number of votes per shareholder irrespective of the number of shares owned, and zero otherwise	Company law or commercial code
Proxy by mail allowed	Equals one if the company law or commercial code allows shareholders to mail their proxy vote to the firm, and zero otherwise	Company law or commercial code
Shares not blocked before meeting	Equals one if the company law or commercial code does not allow firms to require that shareholders deposit their shares prior to a general shareholders meeting, thus preventing them from selling those shares for a number of days, and zero otherwise	Company law or commercial code
Cumulative voting or proportional representation	Equals one if the company law or commercial code allows shareholders to cast all their votes for one candidate standing for election to the board of directors (cumulative voting) or if the company law or commercial code allows a mechanism of proportional representation in the board by which minority interests may name a proportional number of directors to the board, and zero otherwise	Company law or commercial code
Oppressed minorities mechanism	Equals one if the company law or commercial code grants minority shareholders either a judicial venue to challenge the decisions of management or of the assembly or the right to step out of the company by requiring the company to purchase their shares when they object to certain fundamental changes, such as mergers, asset dispositions, and changes in the articles of incorporation. The variable equals zero otherwise. Minority shareholders are defined as those shareholders who own 10 percent of share capital or less	Company law or commercial code

Variable	Description	Source
Preemptive rights	Equals one when the company law or commercial code grants shareholders the first opportunity to buy new issues of stock, and this right can be waived only by a shareholders' vote; equals zero otherwise	Company law or commercial code
Percentage of share capital to call an extraordinary shareholders' meeting	The minimum percentage of ownership of share capital that entitles a shareholder to call for an extraordinary shareholders' meeting; it ranges from 1 to 33 percent	Company law or commercial code
Antidirector rights	An index aggregating the shareholder rights we labeled as "antidirector rights." The index is formed by adding 1 when (1) the country allows shareholders to mail their proxy vote to the firm, (2) shareholders are not required to deposit their shares prior to the general shareholders' meeting, (3) cumulative voting or proportional representation of minorities in the board of directors is allowed, (4) an oppressed minorities mechanism is in place, (5) the minimum percentage of share capital that entitles a shareholder to call for an extraordinary shareholders' meeting is less than or equal to 10 percent (the sample median), or (6) shareholders have preemptive rights that can be waived only by a shareholders' vote. The index ranges from zero to six	Company law or commercial code
Mandatory dividend	Equals the percentage of net income that the company law or commercial code requires firms to distribute as dividends among ordinary stockholders. It takes a value of zero for countries without such a restriction	Company law or commercial code
Restrictions for going into reorganization	Equals one if the reorganization procedure imposes restrictions, such as creditors' consent, to file for reorganization; equals zero if there are no such restrictions	Bankruptcy and reorganization laws
No automatic stay on secured assets	Equals one if the reorganization procedure does not impose an automatic stay on the assets of the firm on filing the reorganization petition. Automatic stay prevents secured creditors from gaining possession of their security. It equals zero if such a restriction does exist in the law	Bankruptcy and reorganization laws
Secured creditors first	Equals one if secured creditors are ranked first in the distribution of the proceeds that result from the disposition of the assets of a bankrupt firm. Equals zero if nonsecured creditors, such as the government and workers, are given absolute priority	Bankruptcy and reorganization laws
Management does not stay	Equals one when an official appointed by the court, or by the creditors, is responsible for the operation of the business during reorganization. Equivalently, this variable equals one if the debtor does not keep the administration of its property pending the resolution of the reorganization process. Equals zero otherwise	Bankruptcy and reorganization laws

continued overleaf

TABLE 1 (*Continued*)

Variable	Description	Sources
Creditor rights	An index aggregating different creditor rights. The index is formed by adding 1 when (1) the country imposes restrictions, such as creditors' consent or minimum dividends to file for reorganization; (2) secured creditors are able to gain possession of their security once the reorganization petition has been approved (no automatic stay); (3) secured creditors are ranked first in the distribution of the proceeds that result from the disposition of the assets of a bankrupt firm; and (4) the debtor does not retain the administration of its property pending the resolution of the reorganization. The index ranges from zero to four	Bankruptcy and reorganization laws
Legal reserve	The minimum percentage of total share capital mandated by corporate law to avoid the dissolution of an existing firm. It takes a value of zero for countries without such a restriction	Company law or commercial code
Efficiency of judicial system	Assessment of the "efficiency and integrity of the legal environment as it affects business, particularly foreign firms", produced by the country risk rating agency Business International Corp. It "may be taken to represent investors' assessments of conditions in the country in question." Average between 1980 and 1983 Scale from zero to 10; with lower scores, lower efficiency levels	Business International Corp.
Rule of law	Assessment of the law and order tradition in the country produced by the country risk rating agency International Country Risk (ICR). Average of the months of April and October of the monthly index between 1982 and 1995. Scale from zero to 10, with lower scores for less tradition for law and order (we changed the scale from its original range going from zero to six)	International Country Risk guide
Corruption	ICR's assessment of the corruption in government. Lower scores indicate that "high government officials are likely to demand special payments" and "illegal payments are generally expected throughout lower levels of government", in the form of "bribes connected with import and export licenses, exchange controls, tax assessment, policy protection, or loans." Average of the months of April and October of the monthly index between 1982 and 1995. Scale from zero to 10, with lower scores for higher levels of corruption (we changed the scale from its original range going from zero to six)	International Country Risk guide

Risk of expropriation	ICR's assessment of the risk of "outright confiscation" or "forced nationalization." Average of the months of April and October of the monthly index between 1982 and 1995. Scale from zero to 10, with lower scores for higher risks	International Country Risk guide
Repudiation of contracts by government	ICR's assessment of the "risk of a modification in a contract taking the form of a repudiation, postponement, or scaling down" due to "budget cutbacks, indigenization pressure, a change in government, or a change in government economic and social priorities." Average of the months of April and October of the monthly index between 1982 and 1995. Scale from zero to 10, with lower scores for higher risks	International Country Risk guide
Accounting standards	Index created by examining and rating companies' 1990 annual reports on their inclusion or omission of 90 items. These items fall into seven categories (general information, income statements, balance sheets, funds flow statement, accounting standards, stock data, and special items). A minimum of three companies in each country were studied. The companies represent a cross section of various industry groups; industrial companies represented 70 percent, and financial companies represented the remaining 30 percent	International accounting and auditing trends, Center for International Financial Analysis and Research
Ownership, 10 largest private firms	The average percentage of common shares owned by the three largest shareholders in the 10 largest nonfinancial, privately owned domestic firms in a given country. A firm is considered privately owned if the state is not a known shareholder in it	Moodys International, CIFAR, EXTEL, WorldScope, 20-Fs, Price-Waterhouse, and various country sources
GNP and GNP per capita	Gross national product and gross national product per capita in constant dollars of 1994	World Bank and International Monetary Fund
Gini coefficient	Gini coefficient for income inequality in each country. When the 1990 coefficient is not available, we use the most recent available	Deininger and Squire (1996); World Bank (1993a, 1993b)

unanticipated way. However, with imperfect enforcement, simple, restrictive, bright-line rules, which require only a minimal effort from the judicial system to enforce, may be superior (Hay, Shleifer, and Vishny 1996). Again, the question does not have a clear theoretical answer, and the issue of how legal rules affect corporate finance is ultimately empirical.

Even if we were to find that legal rules matter, it would be possible to argue that these rules endogenously adjust to economic reality, and hence the differences in rules and outcomes simply reflect the differences in some other, exogenous, conditions across countries. Perhaps some countries chose to have only bank finance of firms for political reasons and then adjusted their laws accordingly to protect banks and discourage shareholders. Some individual rules are probably endogenous. However, this is where our focus on the legal origin becomes crucial. Countries typically adopted their legal systems involuntarily (through conquest or colonization). Even when they chose a legal system freely, as in the case of former Spanish colonies, the crucial consideration was language and the broad political stance of the law rather than the treatment of investor protections. The legal family can therefore be treated as exogenous to a country's structure of corporate ownership and finance. If we find that legal rules differ substantially across legal families and that financing and ownership patterns do as well, we have a strong case that legal families, as expressed in the legal rules, actually cause outcomes.

III. Shareholder Rights

We begin by considering shareholder rights from company laws. The rights measures in this section are refined versions of those presented in our working paper (La Porta et al. 1996).[4]

Because shareholders exercise their power by voting for directors and on major corporate issues, experts focus on voting procedures in evaluating shareholder rights. They include voting rights attached to shares, rights that support the voting mechanism against interference by the insiders, and what we call remedial rights. To begin, investors may be better protected when dividend rights are tightly linked to voting rights, that is, when companies in a country are subject to one-share–one-vote rules (Grossman and Hart 1988; Har-

---

[4] We made two significant changes: we redefined the cumulative voting variable to also cover the right of minority shareholders for proportional representation, and we added a variable on preemptive rights of minority shareholders to buy new issues of stock (see below). In this and the following sections, all dummies have been defined so that 1 means more protective.

ris and Raviv 1988).[5] When votes are tied to dividends, insiders cannot have substantial control of the company without having substantial ownership of its cash flows, which moderates their taste for (costly) diversion of cash flows relative to payment of dividends. There are many ways out of the one-share–one-vote principle that laws in different countries accommodate. Companies can issue nonvoting shares, low- and high-voting shares, founders' shares with extremely high voting rights, or shares whose votes increase when they are held longer, as in France. Companies can also restrict the total number of votes that any given shareholder can exercise at a shareholders' meeting, regardless of how many votes he or she controls. We say that a country has one share–one vote if none of these practices is allowed by law. In our sample, only 11 countries impose genuine one-share–one-vote rules.

The next six rights, which we refer to as antidirector rights, measure how strongly the legal system favors minority shareholders against managers or dominant shareholders in the corporate decision-making process, including the voting process. First, in some countries, shareholders must show up in person or send an authorized representative to a shareholders' meeting to be able to vote. In other countries, in contrast, they can mail their proxy vote directly to the firm, which both enables them to see the relevant proxy information and makes it easier to cast their votes. In Japan, for example, annual shareholder meetings are concentrated overwhelmingly on a single day in late June, and voting by mail is not allowed for some shareholders, which makes it difficult for shareholders to exercise their votes.

Second, in some countries, law requires that shareholders deposit their shares with the company or a financial intermediary several days prior to a shareholder meeting. The shares are then kept in custody until a few days after the meeting. This practice prevents shareholders from selling their shares for several days around the time of the meeting and keeps from voting shareholders who do not bother to go through this exercise.

Third, a few countries allow cumulative voting for directors, and a few have mechanisms of proportional representation on the board, by which minority interests may name a proportional number of directors. The effect of either rule, in principle, is to give more power for minority shareholders to put their representatives on boards of directors.

---

[5] One of the E.C. directives recommends the adoption of one-share–one-vote rules throughout the Community. It does not appear that this directive is being incorporated into national laws too rapidly.

Fourth, some countries give minority shareholders legal mechanisms against perceived oppression by directors (in addition to outright fraud, which is illegal everywhere). These mechanisms may include the right to challenge the directors' decisions in court (as in the American derivative suit) or the right to force the company to repurchase shares of the minority shareholders who object to certain fundamental decisions of the management or of the assembly of shareholders, such as mergers or asset sales.

Fifth, some countries grant shareholders a preemptive right to buy new issues of stock, which can be waived only by a shareholder vote. This right is intended to protect shareholders from dilution, whereby shares are issued to favored investors at below-market prices.

Sixth, we look at the percentage of share capital needed to call an extraordinary shareholders' meeting.[6] Presumably, the higher this percentage is, the harder it is for minority shareholders to organize a meeting to challenge or oust the management. This percentage varies around the world from 3 percent in Japan to 33 percent of share capital in Mexico.

For each of the first five antidirector rights measures, a country gets a score of 1 if it protects minority shareholders according to this measure and a score of 0 otherwise. We also give each country a 1 if the percentage of share capital needed to call an extraordinary shareholder meeting is at or below the world median of 10 percent. Finally, we add up these six antidirector rights scores into an aggregate score, which ranges from 0 for Belgium to 5 for Canada and the United States, for example.

The last shareholder rights measure, which we treat differently from others, is the right to a mandatory dividend. In some countries, companies are mandated by law to pay out a certain fraction of their declared earnings as dividends. Because earnings can be misrepresented within the limits allowed by the accounting system, this measure is not as restrictive as it looks. The mandatory dividend right may be a legal substitute for the weakness of other protections of minority shareholders.

Table 2 presents the data on shareholder rights. The values of all variables are listed by country, and countries are organized by legal origin. Columns in table 2 correspond to particular legal provisions concerning shareholder rights, and the values in the tables are dum-

---

[6] For the United States, our reliance on Delaware presents a problem since the state leaves up to corporations the percentage of shares needed to call an extraordinary shareholder meeting. We use 10 percent for the United States because the majority of U.S. states (27) use this number.

mies equal to one if the country has shareholder protections in that particular area. Table 2 also presents equality of means tests for all the variables by origin.

An examination of world means of the variables in table 2 suggests that relatively few countries have legal rules favoring outside shareholders. Only 22 percent of the countries have one share–one vote, only 27 percent allow cumulative voting or give minorities a right of proportional board representation, only 18 percent allow voting by mail, only 53 percent have some oppressed minorities mechanism, and only 53 percent give minority shareholders a preemptive right to buy new shares.

The other clear result in table 2 is that, for many variables, the origin of laws matters. The means of shareholder rights variables are statistically significantly different between legal families. The two variables in which most legal families are similar are one share–one vote, which is an uncommon restriction everywhere (and never happens in Scandinavia, which is therefore different), and cumulative voting/proportional representation, which is also uncommon everywhere (and again never happens in Scandinavia). For the other variables, the differences in shareholder rights between legal origins are more substantial.

Specifically, two major findings emerge from table 2. First, along a variety of dimensions, common-law countries afford the best legal protections to shareholders. They most frequently (39 percent) allow shareholders to vote by mail, they never block shares for shareholder meetings, they have the highest (94 percent) incidence of laws protecting oppressed minorities, and they generally require relatively little share capital (9 percent) to call an extraordinary shareholder meeting. The only dimension on which common-law countries are not especially protective is the preemptive right to new share issues (44 percent). Still, the common-law countries have the highest average antidirector rights score (4.00) of all legal families. Many of the differences between common-law and civil-law countries are statistically significant. In short, relative to the rest of the world, common-law countries have a package of laws most protective of shareholders.

Second, along a broad range of dimensions, French-civil-law countries afford the worst legal protections to shareholders. Although they look average on one share–one vote (29 percent) and cumulative voting (19 percent) and better than average on preemptive rights (62 percent), they have the lowest (5 percent) incidence of allowing voting by mail, a low (57 percent, though not as low as German-civil-law countries) incidence of not blocking shares for shareholder meetings, a low (29 percent, though not as low as Nor-

TABLE 2

SHAREHOLDER RIGHTS AROUND THE WORLD

Country	One Share–One Vote	Proxy by Mail Allowed	Shares Not Blocked before Meeting	Cumulative Voting/Proportional Representation	Oppressed Minority	Preemptive Right to New Issues	Percentage of Share Capital to Call an Extraordinary Shareholder Meeting	Antidirector Rights	Mandatory Dividend
A. Shareholder Rights (1 = Investor Protection Is in the Law)									
Australia	0	1	1	0	1	0	.05[a]	4	.00
Canada	0	1	1	1	1	0	.05	5	.00
Hong Kong	0	1	1	0	1	1	.10	5	.00
India	0	0	1	1	1	1	.10	5	.00
Ireland	0	0	1	0	1	1	.10	4	.00
Israel	0	0	1	0	1	0	.10	3	.00
Kenya	1	0	1	0	1	1	.10	3	.00
Malaysia	0	1	1	0	1	0	.10	4	.00
New Zealand	0	0	1	0	1	0	.05	4	.00
Nigeria	1	0	1	0	1	1	.10	3	.00
Pakistan	1	0	1	0	1	1	.10	5	.00
Singapore	1	1	1	0	1	1	.10	4	.00
South Africa	0	0	1	0	1	0	.05	5	.00
Sri Lanka	0	0	1	1	1	1	.10	3	.00
Thailand	0	1	1	1	0	0	.20[b]	2	.00
United Kingdom	0	1	1	0	1	1	.10	5	.00
United States	0	1	1	1	1	0	.10	5	.00
Zimbabwe	0	0	1	0	1	1	.05	3	.00
English-origin average	**.17**	**.39**	**1.00**	**.28**	**.94**	**.44**	**.09**	**4.00**	**.00**
Argentina	0	0	0	1	1	1	.05	4	.00
Belgium	0	0	0	0	0	0	.20	0	.00
Brazil	1	0	1	0	1	0	.05	3	.50
Chile	1	0	1	1	1	1	.10	5	.30
Colombia	0	0	1	1	0	1	.25	3	.50
Ecuador	0	0	1	0	0	1	.25	2	.50
Egypt	0	0	0	0	0	0	.10	2	.00
France	0	1	0	0	0	1	.10	3	.00
Greece	1	0	0	0	0	1	.05	2	.35

Indonesia	0	0	1	0	0	0	.10	2	.00
Italy	0	0	0	0	0	1	.20	1	.00
Jordan	1	0	1	0	0	0	.25	1	.00
Mexico	0	0	0	0	0	1	.33	1	.00
Netherlands	1	0	0	1	1	1	.10	2	.00
Peru	0	0	1	1	1	0	.20	3	.00
Philippines	0	0	1	1	0	1	open	3	.00
Portugal	0	0	0	0	1	1	.05	3	.00
Spain	0	0	0	1	0	0	.05	4	.00
Turkey	1	0	1	0	1	1	.10	2	.20
Uruguay	0	0	0	0	0	0	.20	2	.00
Venezuela	0	0	1	0	0	0	.20	1	.00
French-origin average	**.29**	**.05**	**.57**	**.29**	**.29**	**.62**	**.15**	**2.33**	**.11**
Austria	0	0	0	0	0	1	.05	2	.00
Germany	0	0	0	0	0	0	.05	1	.00
Japan	1	0	1	1	1	1	.03	4	.00
South Korea	1	0	0	1	1	0	.05	2	.00
Switzerland	0	0	0	0	0	0	.10	3	.00
Taiwan	0	0	0	0	1	0	.03	3	.00
German-origin average	**.33**	**.00**	**.17**	**.33**	**.50**	**.33**	**.05**	**2.33**	**.00**
Denmark	0	0	1	0	0	0	.10	2	.00
Finland	0	0	1	0	0	1	.10	3	.00
Norway	0	1	1	0	0	1	.10[b]	4	.00
Sweden	0	0	1	0	0	1	.10	3	.00
Scandinavian-origin average	**.00**	**.25**	**1.00**	**.00**	**.00**	**.75**	**.10**	**3.00**	**.00**
Sample average	**.22**	**.18**	**.71**	**.27**	**.53**	**.53**	**.11**	**3.00**	**.05**

B. Tests of Means (t-Statistics)

Common vs. civil law	-.72	3.03*	4.97*	.15	5.59*	-.91	1.48	5.00*	-2.55**
English vs. French origin	-.87	2.82*	3.87*	-.05	5.45*	-1.08	-2.53**	4.73*	-2.67**
English vs. German origin	-.85	3.29*	5.00*	.00	2.83*	.46	-2.54**	3.59*	.00
English vs. Scandinavian origin	1.84***	.50	.00	2.55**	17.00*	-1.09	-1.00	1.91***	.00
French vs. German origin	-.22	1.00	-1.78***	-.22	-.96	1.23	2.64**	.00	2.67**
French vs. Scandinavian origin	2.83**	-1.37	-3.87*	2.82**	2.83	-.48	2.43**	-1.06	2.67**
German vs. Scandinavian origin	1.58	-1.00	-5.00*	1.58	2.23***	-1.27	-4.62*	-1.08	.00

NOTE.—Variables are defined in table 1.
[a] As a percentage of votes.
[b] As a percentage of the number of shares.
* Significant at the 1 percent level.
** Significant at the 5 percent level.
*** Significant at the 10 percent level.

dic countries) incidence of laws protecting oppressed minorities, and the highest (15 percent) percentage of share capital needed to call an extraordinary shareholders' meeting. The aggregate antidirector rights score is the lowest (2.33) for the French-civil-law countries. The difference in this score between French civil law and common law is large and statistically significant. It is interesting to note that France itself, except for allowing proxy voting by mail and having a preemptive right to new share issues, does not have strong legal protections of shareholders. These results suggest that shareholders in the two most widely spread legal regimes—common law and French civil law—operate in very different legal environments.

The German-civil-law countries are not particularly protective of shareholders either. They have a relatively high frequency of one-share–one-vote rules (because of East Asia), require few votes to call an extraordinary meeting, and offer preemptive rights in a third of the cases. But they usually block shares before shareholder meetings, never allow voting by mail, and have oppressed minority mechanisms in only half of the countries. The average antidirector score for this family is 2.33, exactly the same as that for the French family. In Scandinavia, no country has oppressed minority protections, a one-share–one-vote restriction, or a cumulative voting/proportional representation mechanism, and only Norway allows voting by mail. At the same time, no country blocks shares before a shareholder meeting, and three out of four give shareholders preemptive rights. The average Scandinavian antidirector rights score is 3.

The one remedial measure in table 2, namely mandatory dividend, shows that mandatory dividends are used *only* in French-civil-law countries. This result is broadly consistent with the rest of our evidence and suggests that mandatory dividends are indeed a remedial legal protection for shareholders who have relatively few other legal rights.

The results in panel B of table 2 suggest that the differences in the various measures of shareholder rights between different legal families are often significant and almost always significant when common- and civil-law families are compared. One further question is whether the difference in scores by legal origin just reflects differences in per capita income levels. To address this question, table 3 divides all countries into the bottom 25 percent, middle 50 percent, and top 25 percent by gross national product per capita. The results show, in particular, that antidirector rights scores are independent of per capita income, rejecting the notion that legal rules that are more protective of investors are a reflection of higher per capita income.

In sum, common-law countries have the relatively strongest, and

TABLE 3

DEVELOPMENT AND INVESTOR RIGHTS

Countries Sorted by GNP per Capita	GNP per Capita	One Share–One Vote	Antidirector Rights	Mandatory Dividend	Creditor Rights	Legal Reserve as a Percentage of Capital
			A. Means			
Bottom 25%	705	.17	2.92	.08	3.18	.15
Mid 50%	9,465	.32	3.16	.05	2.13	.16
Highest 25%	25,130	.08	2.75	.00	1.83	.15
Total average	11,156	.22	3.00	.05	2.30	.15
			B. Tests of Means (t-Statistics)			
Bottom 25% vs. mid 50%	−4.59*	−.97	−.56	.54	2.08**	−.20
Bottom 25% vs. top 25%	−18.63*	.60	.30	1.48	2.49**	−.05
Mid 50% vs. top 25%	−7.44*	1.58	.85	2.02***	.69	.16

* Significant at the 1 percent level.
** Significant at the 5 percent level.
*** Significant at the 10 percent level.

the French-civil-law countries the weakest, protections of shareholders, independent of per capita income. Minority shareholders in Australia can vote by mail, can trade their shares during a shareholders' meeting, are protected from certain expropriations by directors, and need to organize only 5 percent of the votes to call an extraordinary meeting. Minority shareholders in Belgium, in contrast, cannot vote by mail, have their shares blocked during the shareholder meeting, are not protected from expropriation by directors, and need 20 percent of share capital to call for an extraordinary meeting. The differences between legal families come out clearly from this analysis of shareholder rights.

IV. Creditor Rights

Conceptually, creditor rights are more complex than shareholder rights, for two reasons. First, there may be different kinds of creditors, with different interests, so protecting rights of some creditors has the effect of reducing the rights of others. For example, in the case of a default, senior secured creditors may have a simple interest in getting possession of collateral no matter what happens to the firm, whereas junior unsecured creditors may wish to preserve the firm as a going concern so that they can hope to get some of their money back if the firm turns a profit. In assessing creditor rights, we take the perspective of senior secured creditors, in part for concreteness and in part because much of the debt in the world has that character.

Second, there are two general creditor strategies of dealing with a defaulting firm: liquidation and reorganization, which require different rights to be effective. The most basic right of a senior collateralized creditor is the right to repossess—and then liquidate or keep—collateral when a loan is in default (see Hart 1995). In some countries, law makes it difficult for such creditors to repossess collateral, in part because such repossession leads to liquidation of firms, which is viewed as socially undesirable. In these countries, creditors may still have powers against borrowers, namely their votes in the decisions for how to reorganize the company. The debate between the wisdom of reorganization and liquidation from the social viewpoint has been extensive (Aghion, Hart, and Moore 1992; White 1993; Baird 1995) and has raised the question of whether both procedures or just one is needed to protect creditors. Thus a country with a perfect liquidation procedure but totally ineffective reorganization might be extremely protective of creditors simply because reorganization never needs to be used. We score creditor rights in both reorganization and liquidation and add up the scores to create a creditor rights index, in part because almost all countries rely to some extent on both procedures.

We use five creditor rights variables in this analysis. First, in some countries, the reorganization procedure imposes an automatic stay on the assets, thereby preventing secured creditors from getting possession of loan collateral. This rule obviously protects managers and unsecured creditors against secured creditors and prevents automatic liquidation. In Greece, for example, secured creditors have the right to foreclose on their property when their claim matures and not when the borrower defaults (Houghton and Atkinson 1993, p. 112). In other countries, in contrast, secured creditors can pull collateral from firms being reorganized without waiting for completion of reorganization, a right that is obviously of value to them.

Second, some countries do not assure the secured creditors the right to collateral in reorganization. In these, admittedly rare, countries, secured creditors are in line behind the government and workers, who have absolute priority over them. In Mexico, for example, various social constituencies need to be repaid before the secured creditors, often leaving the latter with no assets to back up their claims.

Third, management in some countries can seek protection from creditors unilaterally by filing for reorganization, without creditor consent. Such protection is called Chapter 11 in the United States and gives management a great deal of power, since at best creditors can get their money or collateral only with a delay. In other countries, in contrast, creditor consent is needed to file for reorganization, and hence managers cannot so easily escape creditor demands.

Finally, in some countries, management stays pending the resolution of the reorganization procedure, whereas in other countries, such as Malaysia, management is replaced by a party appointed by the court or the creditors. This threat of dismissal may enhance creditors' power.

As with shareholder rights, we use one remedial creditor rights measure, namely the existence of a legal reserve requirement. This requirement forces firms to maintain a certain level of capital to avoid automatic liquidation. It protects creditors who have few other powers by forcing an automatic liquidation before all the capital is stolen or wasted by the insiders.

The results on creditor rights are presented in table 4. In general, the protections of creditor rights analyzed here occur more frequently than the protections of shareholder rights. Nearly half of the countries do not have an automatic stay on assets, 81 percent

TABLE 4

CREDITOR RIGHTS AROUND THE WORLD

Country	No Automatic Stay on Assets	Secured Creditors First Paid	Restrictions for Going into Reorganization	Management Does Not Stay in Reorganization	Creditor Rights	Legal Reserve Required as a Percentage of Capital
	A. Creditor Rights (1 = Creditor Protection Is the Law)					
Australia	0	1	0	0	1	.00
Canada	0	1	0	0	1	.00
Hong Kong	1	1	1	1	4	.00
India	1	1	1	1	4	.00
Ireland	0	1	0	0	1	.00
Israel	1	1	1	1	4	.00
Kenya	1	1	1	1	4	.00
Malaysia	1	0	1	1	4	.00
New Zealand	1	1	1	1	3	.00
Nigeria	1	1	1	1	4	.00
Pakistan	1	1	1	1	4	.00
Singapore	1	1	1	1	4	.00
South Africa	0	0	1	1	3	.00
Sri Lanka	1	1	1	1	3	.10
Thailand	1	1	0	1	3	.00
United Kingdom	1	1	1	1	4	.00
United States	0	1	0	0	1	.00
Zimbabwe	1	1	1	1	4	.01
English-origin average	**.72**	**.89**	**.72**	**.78**	**3.11**	**.01**
Argentina	0	1	0	0	1	.20
Belgium	1	1	0	0	2	.10
Brazil	0	0	1	0	1	.20
Chile	0	1	1	0	2	.20
Colombia	0	0	0	0	0	.50
Ecuador	1	1	1	1	4	.50
Egypt	1	1	1	1	4	.50
France	0	0	0	1	0	.10
Greece	0	0	0	1	1	.33
Indonesia	1	1	1	1	4	.00

Italy	0	1	1	0	2	.20
Jordan	na	na	na	na	na	.25
Mexico	0	0	0	0	0	.20
Netherlands	0	1	1	0	2	.00
Peru	0	0	0	0	0	.20
Philippines	0	1	0	0	0	.00
Portugal	1	1	0	0	1	.20
Spain	0	1	1	0	2	.20
Turkey	0	1	1	0	2	.20
Uruguay	0	1	0	1	2	.20
Venezuela	na	na	na	na	na	.10
French-origin average	**.26**	**.65**	**.42**	**.26**	**1.58**	**.21**
Austria	1	1	1	0	3	.10
Germany	1	1	1	0	3	.10
Japan	0	1	0	1	2	.25
South Korea	1	1	0	1	3	.50
Switzerland	0	1	0	0	1	.50
Taiwan	1	1	0	0	2	1.00
German-origin average	**.67**	**1.00**	**.33**	**.33**	**2.33**	**.41**
Denmark	1	1	1	0	3	.25
Finland	0	1	0	0	1	.00
Norway	0	1	1	0	2	.20
Sweden	0	1	1	0	2	.20
Scandinavian-origin average	**.25**	**1.00**	**.75**	**.00**	**2.00**	**.16**
Sample average	**.49**	**.81**	**.55**	**.45**	**2.30**	**.15**

B. Tests of Means (*t*-Statistics)

Common vs. civil law	2.65*	1.04	1.86***	4.13*	3.61*	−4.82*
English vs. French origin	3.06*	1.75**	1.89***	3.55*	3.61*	−5.75*
English vs. German origin	.25	−1.46	1.74***	2.10**	1.43	−5.21*
English vs. Scandinavian origin	1.83***	−1.46	−.11	7.71*	1.71***	−5.90*
French vs. German origin	−1.85***	−3.20*	.37	−.32	−1.29	−2.14**
French vs. Scandinavian origin	.05	−3.20*	−1.18	2.54**	−.60	.59
German vs. Scandinavian origin	1.27	.00	−1.26	1.58	.63	1.37

* Significant at the 1 percent level.
** Significant at the 5 percent level.
*** Significant at the 10 percent level.

pay secured creditors first, over half restrict the managers' right to seek protection from creditors unilaterally, and 45 percent remove management in reorganization proceedings.

As in table 2, we see that, for many creditor rights, the legal origin matters. Common-law countries offer creditors stronger legal protections against managers. They have the highest (72 percent) incidence of no automatic stay on assets; with two exceptions, they guarantee that secured creditors are paid first (the German-civil-law and Scandinavian families have no exceptions); they frequently (72 percent, behind only Scandinavia) preclude managers from unilaterally seeking court protection from creditors; and they have far and away the highest (78 percent) incidence of removing managers in reorganization proceedings. The United States is actually one of the most anticreditor common-law countries: it permits automatic stay on assets, allows unimpeded petition for reorganization, and lets managers keep their jobs in reorganization. The average aggregate creditor rights score for common-law countries is 3.11—by far the highest among the four families—but this score is only 1 for the United States.

The French-civil-law countries offer creditors the weakest protections. Few of them (26 percent, tied with Scandinavia) have no automatic stay on assets; relatively few (65 percent) assure that secured creditors are paid first; few (42 percent—still more than German-civil-law countries) place restrictions on managers seeking court protection from creditors; and relatively few (26 percent) remove managers in reorganization proceedings. The average aggregate creditor rights score for the French-civil-law countries is 1.58, or roughly half of that for the common-law family.

On some measures, countries in the German-civil-law family are strongly pro-creditor. For instance, 67 percent of them have no automatic stay, and secured creditors in all of them are paid first. On the other hand, relatively few of these countries (33 percent) prevent managers from getting protection from creditors unilaterally, and most (67 percent) allow managers to stay in reorganization. One view of this evidence is that the German-civil-law countries are very responsive to secured creditors by not allowing automatic stay and by letting them pull collateral. As a consequence of making liquidation easy, these countries rely less on reorganization of defaulting firms, and hence being soft on such firms by letting managers stay may not be a big problem. The overall average creditor rights score of 2.33 for the German family may therefore understate the extent to which secured creditors are protected.

Finally, Scandinavia has an overall average score of 2.00, which is a bit lower than that of the German family but higher than that of the French.

The evidence on the one remedial pro-creditor legal rule in the sample, the legal reserve requirement, shows that it is almost never used in common-law countries, where other investor protections presumably suffice, but is more common in all civil-law families. Since this requirement is likely to protect unsecured creditors in particular, it is not surprising that it is relatively common in the German-civil-law countries, which tend to be as unprotective as the French-civil-law countries of unsecured creditors. The evidence suggests that, for creditors as well, remedial rights are used as a substitute for the weakness of other investor protections.

From table 4, we see that the ranking of legal families is roughly the same for creditor and shareholder protections. It is not the case that some legal families protect shareholders and others protect creditors. This result can be confirmed formally by looking at the (unreported) correlations of creditor and shareholder rights scores across countries, which are generally positive. The one possible exception is that German-civil-law countries are protective of secured creditors, though generally not of shareholders. A final interesting result, presented in table 3, is that creditor rights are, if anything, stronger in poorer than in richer countries, perhaps because poor countries adapt their laws to facilitate secured lending for lack of other financing opportunities.

In summary so far, laws differ a great deal across countries, and in particular they differ because they come from different legal families. Relatively speaking, common-law countries protect investors the most, and French-civil-law countries protect them the least. German-civil-law countries are in the middle, though closer to the civil-law group. The one exception is the strong protections that German-civil-law countries afford secured creditors. Scandinavian countries are in the middle as well. The evidence also indicates that these results are not a consequence of richer countries' having stronger investor rights; if anything, the results for creditors are the reverse.[7]

If poor investor protections are actually costly to companies in terms of their ability to raise funds, then do countries compensate for these shortcomings in other ways? We have already shown that French-civil-law countries have a higher incidence of remedial legal protections, such as mandatory dividends and legal reserves. But

---

[7] We have also examined whether investor rights are a consequence of geography by dividing the world into Australia, Europe, Africa, Asia, and America. They do not appear to be.

there may be other strategies to compensate, at least in part, for investor-unfriendly laws. One of them—examined in Section V—is strict and effective enforcement of the laws that do exist. The other—examined in Section VI—is concentrated ownership.

V. Enforcement

In principle, a strong system of legal enforcement could substitute for weak rules since active and well-functioning courts can step in and rescue investors abused by the management. To address these issues, we examine proxies for the quality of enforcement of these rights, namely estimates of "law and order" in different countries compiled by private credit risk agencies for the use of foreign investors interested in doing business in the respective countries. We use five of these measures: efficiency of the judicial system, rule of law, corruption, risk of expropriation—meaning outright confiscation or forced nationalization—by the government, and likelihood of contract repudiation by the government. The first two of these measures obviously pertain to law enforcement proper; the last three deal more generally with the government's stance toward business. Some of these measures have been previously shown to affect national growth rates (Knack and Keefer 1995).

In addition, we use an estimate of the quality of a country's accounting standards. Accounting plays a potentially crucial role in corporate governance. For investors to know anything about the companies they invest in, basic accounting standards are needed to render company disclosures interpretable. Even more important, contracts between managers and investors typically rely on the verifiability in court of some measures of firms' income or assets. If a bond covenant stipulates immediate repayment when income falls below a certain level, this level of income must be verifiable for the bond contract to be enforceable in court even in principle. Accounting standards might then be necessary for financial contracting, especially if investor rights are weak (Hay et al. 1996). The measure of accounting standards we use, like the rule of law measures, is a privately constructed index based on examination of company reports from different countries. Unfortunately, it is available for only 44 countries, 41 of which are in our sample.[8]

---

[8] The measure of accounting standards we use was published in 1991. At around the same time, European countries began to harmonize their accounting standards under pressure from the European Community. Over time, accounting standards may converge in Europe. However, for the purposes of our analysis of country differences and of determinants of ownership, historical differences in the quality of standards are obviously more important than the future convergence.

Table 5 presents country scores for the various rule of law measures, as well as for their accounting standards. It arranges countries by legal origin and presents tests of equality of means between families. The table suggests that quality of law enforcement differs across legal families. In law enforcement, Scandinavian countries are clearly on top, with German-civil-law countries close behind. These families have the highest scores of any group on the efficiency of the judicial system, the rule of law, corruption, risk of expropriation, and risk of contract repudiation by the government. On all the measures of rule of law, common-law countries are behind the leaders but ahead of the French-civil-law countries. The statistical significance of these results varies from variable to variable.

With quality of accounting, Scandinavia still comes out on top, though common-law countries are second, statistically significantly ahead of the German-civil-law countries. The French family has the weakest quality of accounting.

These results do not support the conclusion that the quality of law enforcement substitutes or compensates for the quality of laws. An investor in a French-civil-law country is poorly protected by both the laws and the system that enforces them. The converse is true for an investor in a common-law country, on average.

An inspection of table 5 suggests that, for the enforcement measures, the level of per capita income may have a more important confounding effect than it did for the laws themselves. In table 6, we investigate whether quality of enforcement is different in different legal families through regression analysis across countries, controlling for each country's level of per capita income. The omitted dummy in the regressions is the one for common-law countries.[9]

By every single measure, richer countries have higher quality of law enforcement. Nonetheless, even when one controls for per capita income, the legal family matters for the quality of enforcement and the accounting standards. A great deal of the cross-sectional variance in these rule of law scores is explained by per capita income and the legal origin. In some cases, these variables together explain around 80 percent of the cross-sectional variation in rule of law scores, with the lion's share of the explanatory power coming from per capita income.

Once income is controlled for, French-civil-law countries still score lower on every single measure, and statistically significantly

[9] We have also estimated these equations using Tobits, with very similar results. One difference is that the Tobit procedure does not produce a standard error on the Scandinavian dummy because all Scandinavian countries have the same values for some of the variables.

TABLE 5
RULE OF LAW

COUNTRY	Efficiency of Judicial System	Rule of Law	ENFORCEMENT VARIABLES			ACCOUNTING: Rating on Accounting Standards	GNP PER CAPITA (U.S. $)
			Corruption	Risk of Expropriation	Risk of Contract Repudiation		
			A. Country Scores				
Australia	10.00	10.00	8.52	9.27	8.71	75	17,500
Canada	9.25	10.00	10.00	9.67	8.96	74	19,970
Hong Kong	10.00	8.22	8.52	8.29	8.82	69	18,060
India	8.00	4.17	4.58	7.75	6.11	57	300
Ireland	8.75	7.80	8.52	9.67	8.96	na	13,000
Israel	10.00	4.82	8.33	8.25	7.54	64	13,920
Kenya	5.75	5.42	4.82	5.98	5.66	na	270
Malaysia	9.00	6.78	7.38	7.95	7.43	76	3,140
New Zealand	10.00	10.00	10.00	9.69	9.29	70	12,600
Nigeria	7.25	2.73	3.03	5.33	4.36	59	300
Pakistan	5.00	3.03	2.98	5.62	4.87	na	430
Singapore	10.00	8.57	8.22	9.30	8.86	78	19,850
South Africa	6.00	4.42	8.92	6.88	7.27	70	2,980
Sri Lanka	7.00	1.90	5.00	6.05	5.25	na	600
Thailand	3.25	6.25	5.18	7.42	7.57	64	2,110
United Kingdom	10.00	8.57	9.10	9.71	9.63	78	18,060
United States	10.00	10.00	8.63	9.98	9.00	71	24,740
Zimbabwe	7.50	3.68	5.42	5.61	5.04	na	520
English-origin average	**8.15**	**6.46**	**7.06**	**7.91**	**7.41**	**69.62**	**9,353**
Argentina	6.00	5.35	6.02	5.91	4.91	45	7,220
Belgium	9.50	10.00	8.82	9.63	9.48	61	21,650
Brazil	5.75	6.32	6.32	7.62	6.30	54	2,930
Chile	7.25	7.02	5.30	7.50	6.80	52	3,170
Colombia	7.25	2.08	5.00	6.95	7.02	50	1,400
Ecuador	6.25	6.67	5.18	6.57	5.18	na	1,200
Egypt	6.50	4.17	3.87	6.30	6.05	24	660
France	8.00	8.98	9.05	9.65	9.19	69	22,490
Greece	7.00	6.18	7.27	7.12	6.62	55	7,390

Indonesia	2.50	3.98	2.15	7.16	6.09	na	740
Italy	6.75	8.33	6.13	9.35	9.17	62	19,840
Jordan	8.66	4.35	5.48	6.07	4.86	na	1,190
Mexico	6.00	5.35	4.77	7.29	6.55	60	3,610
Netherlands	10.00	10.00	10.00	9.98	9.35	64	20,950
Peru	6.75	2.50	4.70	5.54	4.68	38	1,490
Philippines	4.75	2.73	2.92	5.22	4.80	65	850
Portugal	5.50	8.68	7.38	8.90	8.57	36	9,130
Spain	6.25	7.80	7.38	9.52	8.40	64	13,590
Turkey	4.00	5.18	5.18	7.00	5.95	51	2,970
Uruguay	6.50	5.00	5.00	6.58	7.29	31	3,830
Venezuela	6.50	6.37	4.70	6.89	6.30	40	2,840
French-origin average	**6.56**	**6.05**	**5.84**	**7.46**	**6.84**	**51.17**	**7,102**
Austria	9.50	10.00	8.57	9.69	9.60	54	23,510
Germany	9.00	9.23	8.93	9.90	9.77	62	23,560
Japan	10.00	8.98	8.52	9.67	9.69	65	31,490
South Korea	6.00	5.35	5.30	8.31	8.59	62	7,660
Switzerland	10.00	10.00	10.00	9.98	9.98	68	35,760
Taiwan	6.75	8.52	6.85	9.12	9.16	65	10,425
German-origin average	**8.54**	**8.68**	**8.03**	**9.45**	**9.47**	**62.67**	**22,067**
Denmark	10.00	10.00	10.00	9.67	9.31	62	26,730
Finland	10.00	10.00	10.00	9.67	9.15	77	19,300
Norway	10.00	10.00	10.00	9.88	9.71	74	25,970
Sweden	10.00	10.00	10.00	9.40	9.58	83	24,740
Scandinavian-origin average	**10.00**	**10.00**	**10.00**	**9.66**	**9.44**	**74.00**	**24,185**
Sample average	**7.67**	**6.85**	**6.90**	**8.05**	**7.58**	**60.93**	**11,156**
B. Tests of Means between Origins (t-Statistics)							
Common vs. civil law	1.27	-.77	.39	-.46	-.51	3.12*	
English vs. French origin	2.65*	.51	1.79***	.90	1.06	4.66*	
English vs. German origin	-.41	-1.82***	-.93	-2.19**	-2.79**	2.22**	
English vs. Scandinavian origin	-3.78*	-15.57*	-5.38***	-2.06**	-2.26**	-1.05	
French vs. German origin	-2.53*	-2.55*	-2.49*	-3.20*	-3.90*	-2.10**	
French vs. Scandinavian origin	-9.34*	-20.80*	-9.77*	-2.94*	-3.17*	-3.32*	
German vs. Scandinavian origin	-2.06***	-11.29*	-2.88*	-.63	.10	-2.66**	

* Significant at the 1 percent level.
** Significant at the 5 percent level.
*** Significant at the 10 percent level.

TABLE 6

ORDINARY LEAST SQUARES REGRESSIONS: CROSS SECTION OF 49 COUNTRIES

DEPENDENT VARIABLE

INDEPENDENT VARIABLE	Efficiency of Judiciary System (N = 49)		Rule of Law (N = 49)		Corruption (N = 49)		Risk of Expropriation (N = 49)		Repudiation of Contracts by Government (N = 49)		Accounting Standards (N = 41)	
	(1)	(2)	(1)	(2)	(1)	(2)	(1)	(2)	(1)	(2)	(1)	(2)
Log of GNP per capita	.8421* (.1450)	.9763* (.1355)	1.4761* (.1584)	1.5541* (.1379)	1.3088* (.1138)	1.4020* (.0993)	.9099* (.0932)	.9679* (.0772)	.9951* (.0832)	1.0976* (.0734)	4.3348* (1.2453)	5.7747* (1.2908)
Civil-law dummy[a]	...	-1.3774* (.4235)	...	-.3642 (.4290)	...	-1.1388* (.3024)	...	-.3855*** (.2132)	...	-.4111*** (.2228)	...	-14.331* (2.7407)
French origin	-1.6609* (.4796)	...	-.5250 (.4563)	...	-1.3236* (.3190)	...	-.5164** (.2518)	...	-.6459** (.2520)	...	-17.366* (2.9445)	...
German origin	-1.0305*** (.6033)	...	-.2715 (.6312)	...	-1.2422* (.4749)	...	-.0009 (.2097)	...	.3803*** (.1946)	...	-11.890* (2.9104)	...
Scandinavian origin	.2392 (.3550)	...	.7174 (.4681)	...	.4369 (.3152)	...	.0054 (.2242)	...	.1300 (.2095)	...	-1.5272 (4.7556)	...
Intercept	1.2677 (1.3598)	.1702 (1.2862)	-5.6050* (1.3600)	-6.2421* (1.2087)	-3.6367* (.9881)	-4.3986* (.8711)	.4732 (.8431)	-.0018 (.7181)	-.7290 (.7250)	-1.5671* (.6493)	31.807* (10.844)	19.249 (11.442)
Adjusted R^2	.5719	.5185	.7744	.7605	.8442	.8056	.8120	.7998	.8465	.8146	.6125	.5131

NOTE.—Robust standard errors are in parentheses.

[a] The dummy variable civil law takes a value equal to one when the country belongs to the civil-law tradition (i.e., all French, German, and Scandinavian codes) and zero when the country belongs to the common-law tradition (i.e., English common law).

* Significant at the 1 percent level.
** Significant at the 5 percent level.
*** Significant at the 10 percent level.

lower for almost all measures, than the common-law countries do. However, German-civil-law countries now tend to score lower than the common-law countries on all measures other than repudiation of contracts by government, although the effect is significant only for the efficiency of the judiciary and the accounting standards. Scandinavian countries are similar to common-law countries in rule of law measures. The regression results continue to show that legal families with investor-friendlier laws are also the ones with stronger enforcement of laws. Poor enforcement and accounting standards aggravate, rather than cure, the difficulties faced by investors in the French-civil-law countries.

VI. Ownership

In this section, we explore the hypothesis that companies in countries with poor investor protection have more concentrated ownership of their shares. There are at least two reasons why ownership in such countries would be more concentrated. First, large, or even dominant, shareholders who monitor the managers might need to own more capital, ceteris paribus, to exercise their control rights and thus to avoid being expropriated by the managers. This would be especially true when there are some legal or economic reasons for large shareholders to own significant cash flow rights as well as votes. Second, when they are poorly protected, small investors might be willing to buy corporate shares only at such low prices that make it unattractive for corporations to issue new shares to the public. Such low demand for corporate shares by minority investors would indirectly stimulate ownership concentration. Of course, it is often efficient to have some ownership concentration in companies since large shareholders might monitor managers and thus increase the value of the firm (Shleifer and Vishny 1986). But with poor investor protection, ownership concentration becomes a substitute for legal protection, because only large shareholders can hope to receive a return on their investment.

To evaluate this hypothesis, we have assembled a database of up to the 10 largest (by market capitalization) nonfinancial (i.e., no banks or insurance companies), domestic (i.e., no foreign multinationals), totally private (i.e., no government ownership), publicly traded (i.e., not 100 percent privately held) companies in each country in our sample. For some countries, including Egypt, India, Nigeria, Philippines, and Zimbabwe, we could not find 10 such companies and settled for at least five.

For each company, we collected data on its three largest shareholders and computed the combined (cash flow) ownership stake

of these three shareholders. We did not correct for the possibility
that some of the large shareholders are affiliated with each other or
that the company itself owns the shares of its shareholders. Both of
these corrections would raise effective concentration of cash flow
ownership. On the other hand, we also did not examine the complete ownership structure of firms, taking account of pyramidal
structures and the fact that corporate shareholders themselves have
owners. Doing this is likely to reduce our measure of ownership concentration. Finally, we could not distinguish empirically between
large shareholders who are the management, are affiliated with the
management, or are separate from the management. It is not clear
that a conceptual line between management and, say, a 40 percent
shareholder can be drawn.

Subject to these caveats, it is possible to construct measures of
ownership concentration for 45 of our 49 countries. For each country, we took the average and the median ownership stake of the three
largest shareholders among its 10 largest publicly traded companies.
This measure resembles measures of ownership concentration used
for American companies by Demsetz and Lehn (1985) and Mørck,
Shleifer, and Vishny (1988).

Table 7 presents, by legal origin, this concentration variable for
each country. In the world as a whole, the average ownership of the
three largest shareholders is 46 percent, and the median is 45 percent. Dispersed ownership in large public companies is simply a
myth. Even in the United States, the average for the 10 most valuable
companies is 20 percent (which is partly explained by the fact that
Microsoft, Walmart, Coca-Cola, and Intel are on the list and all have
significant ownership concentration), and the median is 12 percent.
The average concentration measure we use is under 30 percent only
for the United States, Australia, United Kingdom, Taiwan, Japan,
Korea, and Sweden. Presumably, if we looked at smaller companies,
the numbers we would get for ownership concentration would be
even larger. The finance textbook model of management faced by
multitudes of dispersed shareholders is an exception and not the
rule.

Table 7 also shows that ownership concentration varies by legal
origin. By far the highest concentration of ownership is found in the
French-civil-law countries, with the average ownership by the three
largest shareholders a whopping 54 percent for the 10 largest non-
government firms. The lowest concentration, in the German-civil-
law countries, is 34 percent. This puzzlingly low concentration comes
from East Asia, where as we already mentioned company law has
been significantly influenced by the United States, rather than from
Germany, Austria, or Switzerland. Scandinavian countries are also

TABLE 7

OWNERSHIP OF 10 LARGEST NONFINANCIAL DOMESTIC FIRMS BY LARGE
SHAREHOLDERS: CROSS SECTION OF 49 COUNTRIES

	OWNERSHIP BY THREE LARGEST SHAREHOLDERS		AVERAGE MARKET CAPITALIZATION OF FIRMS (Millions
COUNTRY	Mean	Median	of U.S. $)
	A. Ownership		
Australia	.28	.28	5,943
Canada	.40	.24	3,015
Hong Kong	.54	.54	4,282
India	.40	.43	1,721
Ireland	.39	.36	944
Israel	.51	.55	428
Kenya	na	na	27
Malaysia	.54	.52	2,013
New Zealand	.48	.51	1,019
Nigeria	.40	.45	39
Pakistan	.37	.41	49
Singapore	.49	.53	1,637
South Africa	.52	.52	6,238
Sri Lanka	.60	.61	4
Thailand	.47	.48	996
United Kingdom	.19	.15	18,511
United States	.20	.12	71,650
Zimbabwe	.55	.51	28
English-origin average	**.43**	**.42**	**6,586**
Argentina	.53	.55	2,185
Belgium	.54	.62	3,467
Brazil	.57	.63	1,237
Chile	.45	.38	2,330
Colombia	.63	.68	457
Ecuador	na	na	na
Egypt	.62	.62	104
France	.34	.24	8,914
Greece	.67	.68	163
Indonesia	.58	.62	882
Italy	.58	.60	3,140
Jordan	na	na	63
Mexico	.64	.67	2,984
Netherlands	.39	.31	6,400
Peru	.56	.57	154
Philippines	.57	.51	156
Portugal	.52	.59	259
Spain	.51	.50	1,256
Turkey	.59	.58	477
Uruguay	na	na	na
Venezuela	.51	.49	423
French-origin average	**.54**	**.55**	**1,844**
Austria	.58	.51	325
Germany	.48	.50	8,540
Japan	.18	.13	26,677
South Korea	.23	.20	1,034

TABLE 7 (*Continued*)

COUNTRY	OWNERSHIP BY THREE LARGEST SHAREHOLDERS		AVERAGE MARKET CAPITALIZATION OF FIRMS (Millions of U.S. $)
	Mean	Median	
A. Ownership			
Switzerland	.41	.48	9,578
Taiwan	.18	.14	2,186
German-origin average	**.34**	**.33**	**8,057**
Denmark	.45	.40	1,273
Finland	.37	.34	1,980
Norway	.36	.31	1,106
Sweden	.28	.28	6,216
Scandinavian-origin average	**.37**	**.33**	**2,644**
Sample average	**.46**	**.45**	**4,521**
B. Tests of Means (*t*-Statistics)			
Common vs. civil law	−1.10	−.91	1.00
English vs. French origin	−3.24*	−2.68*	1.22
English vs. German origin	1.38	1.31	−.20
English vs. Scandinavian origin	1.05	1.22	.46
French vs. German origin	3.87*	3.29*	−2.61**
French vs. Scandinavian origin	3.93*	3.32*	−.61
German vs. Scandinavian origin	−.24	−.06	1.05

NOTE.—A firm is considered privately owned if the state is not a known shareholder in it.
* Significant at the 1 percent level.
** Significant at the 5 percent level.
*** Significant at the 10 percent level.

relatively low, with a 37 percent concentration. Finally, common-law countries are in the middle, with a 43 percent average ownership concentration. The differences between the French and other legal families are statistically significant, although other differences are not. In sum, these data indicate that the French-civil-law countries have unusually high ownership concentration. These results are at least suggestive that concentration of ownership is an adaptation to poor legal protection.

In table 8, we examine empirically the determinants of ownership concentration, in two steps. First, we regress ownership concentration on legal origin dummies and several control variables to see whether origin matters. The controls we use are (the logarithm of) GNP per capita on the theory that richer countries may have different ownership patterns; (the logarithm of) total GNP on the theory that larger economies have larger firms, which might therefore have a lower ownership concentration; and the Gini coefficient for a country's income on the theory that more unequal societies have a

TABLE 8

ORDINARY LEAST SQUARES REGRESSIONS: CROSS SECTION OF 49 COUNTRIES

Dependent Variable: Mean Ownership

Independent Variable	Basic Regression	Shareholder and Creditor Rights
Log of GNP per capita	.0077	.0397
	(.0097)	(.0242)
Log of GNP	−.0442*	−.0428*
	(.0119)	(.0118)
Gini coefficient	.0024***	.0027
	(.0014)	(.0023)
Rule of law		−.0143
		(.0115)
Accounting		−.0029***
		(.0016)
French origin	.1296*	.0733
	(.0261)	(.0802)
German origin	−.0113	−.0025
	(.0666)	(.0728)
Scandinavian origin	−.0496	−.0430
	(.0371)	(.0473)
Antidirector rights		−.0315**
		(.0150)
One share–one vote		−.0497
		(.0406)
Mandatory dividend		.2197***
		(.1113)
Creditor rights		−.0128
		(.0171)
Legal reserve required		−.2237**
		(.0766)
Intercept	.7785*	.8686*
	(.1505)	(.2952)
Number of observations	45	39
Adjusted R^2	.5582	.7348

NOTE.—Variables are defined in table 1. Robust standard errors are in parentheses.
* Significant at the 1 percent level.
** Significant at the 5 percent level.
*** Significant at the 10 percent level.

higher ownership concentration. Second, we add to the first regression several measures of legal protections, including accounting standards, enforcement quality, shareholder rights, creditor rights, and remedial rights. Given the large number of variables collected for this paper, we cannot estimate all the possible regressions, and we need to make some choices. We pick "rule of law" as our measure of quality of enforcement and use aggregate antidirector and creditor rights scores from tables 2 and 4. The results we present are representative of other specifications.

The first regression in table 8, with all 45 observations, has an adjusted R^2 of 56 percent. It shows that larger economies have a lower ownership concentration and more unequal countries have a higher ownership concentration, consistent with the conjectured effects of these controls. In addition, this regression confirms the sharply higher concentration of ownership in the French-civil-law countries. The second regression in table 8 adds investor rights, rule of law, and accounting standards. It has only 39 observations because the data on accounting standards are incomplete. Still, the adjusted R^2 rises to 73 percent. The coefficient on the logarithm of GNP remains significant, but not that on the Gini coefficient. The coefficient on the French-origin dummy turns insignificant, which suggests that our measures of investor protections actually capture the limitations of the French-civil-law system. Indeed, countries with better accounting standards have a (marginally) statistically significantly lower concentration of ownership, though rule of law is insignificant. A 20-point increase in the accounting score (roughly the distance between the common-law and French-civil-law averages) reduces average ownership concentration by six percentage points. Countries with better antidirector rights, as measured by our aggregate variable, also have a statistically significantly lower concentration of ownership. A 1.6-point increase in the antidirector rights score (roughly the distance between common-law and French-civil-law averages) reduces ownership concentration by five percentage points. In contrast, one share–one vote is not significant.

The creditor rights score is insignificant. One could argue that when creditor rights are good, bank borrowing becomes more common, and small shareholders can free-ride on the monitoring by banks, making dispersed ownership possible. One could alternatively argue that easier bank borrowing enables firms to finance their investment through debt rather than equity, leading to a higher ownership concentration in equilibrium.

Finally, the regression shows a large positive effect of the mandatory dividend rule and a large negative effect of the legal reserve requirement on ownership concentration. The former variable is correlated with the French origin and the latter with the German origin.

Some of our independent variables, but particularly accounting standards, might be endogenous. Countries that for some reason have heavily concentrated ownership and small stock markets might have little use for good accounting standards, and so fail to develop them. The causality in this case would go from ownership concentration to accounting standards rather than the other way around. Since we have no instruments that we believe determine accounting but not ownership concentration, we cannot reject this hypothesis.

More generally, the only truly exogenous variable in these regressions is the legal origin, and hence the result that is most plausibly interpreted as causal is the positive effect of French origin on ownership concentration.

In sum, the message of this section is that the quality of legal protection of shareholders helps determine ownership concentration, accounting for the higher concentration of ownership in the French-civil-law countries. The results support the idea that heavily concentrated ownership results from, and perhaps substitutes for, weak protection of investors in a corporate governance system. The evidence indicates that weak laws actually make a difference and may have costs. One of these costs of heavily concentrated ownership in large firms is that their core investors are not diversified. The other cost is that these firms probably face difficulty raising equity finance, since minority investors fear expropriation by managers and concentrated owners.

VII. Conclusion

In this paper, we have examined laws governing investor protection, the quality of enforcement of these laws, and ownership concentration in 49 countries around the world. The analysis suggests three broad conclusions.

First, laws differ markedly around the world, though in most places they tend to give investors a rather limited bundle of rights. In particular, countries whose legal rules originate in the common-law tradition tend to protect investors considerably more than the countries whose laws originate in the civil-law, and especially the French-civil-law, tradition. The German-civil-law and the Scandinavian countries take an intermediate stance toward investor protections. There is no clear evidence that different countries favor different types of investors; the evidence rather points to a relatively stronger stance favoring all investors in common-law countries. This evidence confirms our basic hypothesis that being a shareholder, or a creditor, in different legal jurisdictions entitles an investor to very different bundles of rights. These rights are determined by laws; they are not inherent in securities themselves.

Second, law enforcement differs a great deal around the world. German-civil-law and Scandinavian countries have the best quality of law enforcement. Law enforcement is strong in common-law countries as well, whereas it is the weakest in the French-civil-law countries. These rankings also hold for one critical input into law enforcement in the area of investor protections: the accounting standards. The quality of law enforcement, unlike the legal rights themselves, improves sharply with the level of income.

Third, the data support the hypothesis that countries develop substitute mechanisms for poor investor protection. Some of these mechanisms are statutory, as in the case of remedial rules such as mandatory dividends or legal reserve requirements. We document the higher incidence of such adaptive legal mechanisms in civil-law countries. Another adaptive response to poor investor protection is ownership concentration. We find that ownership concentration is extremely high around the world, consistent with our evidence that laws, on average, are only weakly protective of shareholders. In an average country, close to half the equity in a publicly traded company is owned by the three largest shareholders. Furthermore, good accounting standards and shareholder protection measures are associated with a lower concentration of ownership, indicating that concentration is indeed a response to poor investor protection.

The ultimate question, of course, is whether countries with poor investor protections—either laws or their enforcement—actually do suffer. Recent research has begun to provide partial answers to this question. King and Levine (1993) and Levine and Zervos (1998) find that developed debt and equity markets contribute to economic growth. In a similar vein, Rajan and Zingales (1998) find that countries with better developed financial systems show superior growth in capital-intensive sectors that rely particularly heavily on external finance. Levine (1998) confirms the King-Levine findings that financial development promotes economic growth using our legal origin variable as an instrument for his measures of financial development. And finally, La Porta et al. (1997) show that countries with poor investor protections indeed have significantly smaller debt and equity markets.[10] Taken together, this evidence describes a link from the legal system to economic development. It is important to remember, however, that while the shortcomings of investor protection described in this paper appear to have adverse consequences for financial development and growth, they are unlikely to be an insurmountable bottleneck. France and Belgium, after all, are both very rich countries.

References

Aghion, Philippe; Hart, Oliver; and Moore, John. "The Economics of Bankruptcy Reform." *J. Law, Econ., and Organization* 8 (October 1992): 523–46.

[10] La Porta et al. (1997) use the original La Porta et al. (1996) data. We have reconfirmed their results using the refined measures presented in this paper.

LAW AND FINANCE   1153

American Bar Association. *Multinational Commercial Insolvency*. Chicago: American Bar Assoc., 1989, 1993.

Andenas, Mads, and Kenyon-Slade, Stephen, eds. *E.C. Financial Market Regulation and Company Law*. London: Sweet and Maxwell, 1993.

Baird, Douglas. "The Hidden Values of Chapter 11: An Overview of the Law and Economics of Financially Distressed Firms." Manuscript. Chicago: Univ. Chicago, Law School, 1995.

Bebchuk, Lucian A. "Efficient and Inefficient Sales of Corporate Control." *Q.J.E.* 109 (November 1994): 957–93.

Berglof, Erik, and Perotti, Enrico. "The Governance Structure of the Japanese Financial Keiretsu." *J. Financial Econ.* 36 (October 1994): 259–84.

Berle, Adolf A., and Means, Gardiner C. *The Modern Corporation and Private Property*. New York: Harcourt, Brace and World, 1932.

Boycko, Maxim; Shleifer, Andrei; and Vishny, Robert W. "Privatizing Russia." *Brookings Papers Econ. Activity*, no. 2 (1993), pp. 139–81.

Deininger, Klaus, and Squire, Lyn. "Measuring Income Inequality: A New Data-Base." Manuscript. Washington: World Bank, 1996.

Demsetz, Harold, and Lehn, Kenneth. "The Structure of Corporate Ownership: Causes and Consequences." *J.P.E.* 93 (December 1985): 1155–77.

Easterbrook, Frank H., and Fischel, Daniel R. *The Economic Structure of Corporate Law*. Cambridge, Mass.: Harvard Univ. Press, 1991.

Edwards, Jeremy, and Fischer, Klaus. *Banks, Finance and Investment in West Germany since 1970*. Cambridge: Cambridge Univ. Press, 1994.

Glendon, Mary Ann; Gordon, Michael W.; and Osakwe, Christopher. *Comparative Legal Traditions: Text, Materials and Cases on the Civil and Common Law Traditions, with Special References to French, German and English*. St. Paul, Minn.: West, 1994.

Gorton, Gary, and Schmidt, Frank. "Universal Banking and the Performance of German Firms." Working Paper no. 5453. Cambridge, Mass.: NBER, February 1996.

Gromb, Denis. "Is One-Share–One-Vote Optimal?" Manuscript. London: London School Econ., 1993.

Grossman, Sanford J., and Hart, Oliver. "One Share–One Vote and the Market for Corporate Control." *J. Financial Econ.* 20 (January/March 1988): 175–202.

Harris, Milton, and Raviv, Artur. "Corporate Governance: Voting Rights and Majority Rules." *J. Financial Econ.* 20 (January/March 1988): 203–35.

Hart, Oliver. *Firms, Contracts, and Financial Structure*. London: Oxford Univ. Press, 1995.

Hay, Jonathan R.; Shleifer, Andrei; and Vishny, Robert W. "Toward a Theory of Legal Reform." *European Econ. Rev.* 40 (April 1996): 559–67.

Houghton, Anthony R., and Atkinson, Nigel G. *Guide to Insolvency in Europe*. Chicago: Commerce Clearing House (for Deloitte Touche Tohmatsu Internat.), 1993.

Institutional Shareholder Services. *Proxy Voting Guidelines*. Washington: ISS Global Proxy Services, 1994.

Investor Responsibility Research Center. *Proxy Voting Guide*. Washington: Investor Responsibility Res. Center, 1994, 1995.

Jensen, Michael C., and Meckling, William H. "Theory of the Firm: Managerial Behavior, Agency Costs and Ownership Structure." *J. Financial Econ.* 3 (October 1976): 305–60.

Kaplan, Steven N., and Minton, Bernadette A. "Appointments of Outsiders to Japanese Boards: Determinants and Implications for Managers." *J. Financial Econ.* 36 (October 1994): 225–57.

King, Robert G., and Levine, Ross. "Finance and Growth: Schumpeter Might Be Right." *Q.J.E.* 108 (August 1993): 717–37.

Knack, Stephen, and Keefer, Philip. "Institutions and Economic Performance: Cross-Country Tests Using Alternative Institutional Measures." *Econ. and Politics* 7 (November 1995): 207–27.

La Porta, Rafael; Lopez-de-Silanes, Florencio; Shleifer, Andrei; and Vishny, Robert W. "Law and Finance." Working Paper no. 5661. Cambridge, Mass.: NBER, July 1996.

———. "Legal Determinants of External Finance." *J. Finance* 52 (July 1997): 1131–50.

Levine, Ross. "The Legal Environment, Banks, and Long-Run Economic Growth." *J. Money, Credit and Banking* 30, no. 3, pt. 2 (August 1998).

Levine, Ross, and Zervos, Sara. "Stock Markets, Banks, and Economic Growth." *A.E.R.* 88 (June 1998): 537–58.

Levy, Haim. "Economic Evaluation of Voting Power of Common Stock." *J. Finance* 38 (March 1983): 79–93.

Merryman, John H. *The Civil Law Tradition: An Introduction to the Legal Systems of Western Europe and Latin America.* Stanford, Calif.: Stanford Univ. Press, 1969.

Modigliani, Franco, and Miller, Merton H. "The Cost of Capital, Corporation Finance and the Theory of Investment." *A.E.R.* 48 (June 1958): 261–97.

Mørck, Randall; Shleifer, Andrei; and Vishny, Robert W. "Management Ownership and Market Valuation: An Empirical Analysis." *J. Financial Econ.* 20 (January/March 1988): 293–315.

Pagano, Marco; Panetta, F.; and Zingales, Luigi. "Why Do Companies Go Public: An Empirical Analysis." *J. Finance* 53 (February 1998): 27–64.

Rajan, Raghuram G., and Zingales, Luigi. "What Do We Know about Capital Structure? Some Evidence from International Data." *J. Finance* 50 (December 1995): 1421–60.

———. "Financial Dependence and Growth." *A.E.R.* 88 (June 1998): 559–86.

Reynolds, Thomas H., and Flores, Arturo A. *Foreign Law: Current Sources of Codes and Basic Legislation in Jurisdictions of the World.* Littleton, Colo.: Rothman, 1989.

Roe, Mark J. *Strong Managers, Weak Owners: The Political Roots of American Corporate Finance.* Princeton, N.J.: Princeton Univ. Press, 1994.

Rydquist, Kristian. "Empirical Investigation of the Voting Premium." Working Paper no. 35. Evanston, Ill.: Northwestern Univ., 1987.

Shleifer, Andrei, and Vishny, Robert W. "Large Shareholders and Corporate Control." *J.P.E.* 94, no. 3, pt. 1 (June 1986): 461–88.

———. "A Survey of Corporate Governance." *J. Finance* 52 (June 1997): 737–83.

Vishny, Paul. *Guide to International Commerce Law.* New York: McGraw-Hill, 1994.

Watson, Alan. *Legal Transplants: An Approach to Comparative Law.* Charlottesville: Univ. Virginia Press, 1974.

Werlauff, Erik. *EC Company Law: The Common Denominator for Business Undertakings in 12 States.* Copenhagen: Jurist- og Okonomforbundets Forlag, 1993.

White, Michelle. "The Costs of Corporate Bankruptcy: The U.S.-European Comparison." Manuscript. Ann Arbor: Univ. Michigan, Dept. Econ., 1993.

World Bank. *Social Indicators of Development, 1991–1992.* Baltimore: Johns Hopkins Univ. Press, 1993. (*a*)

———. *World Development Report.* Washington: Oxford Univ. Press, 1993. (*b*)

Zingales, Luigi. "The Value of the Voting Right: A Study of the Milan Stock Exchange Experience." *Rev. Financial Studies* 7 (Spring 1994): 125–48.

———. "What Determines the Value of Corporate Votes?" *Q.J.E.* 110 (November 1995): 1047–73.

Zweigert, Konrad, and Kotz, Hein. *An Introduction to Comparative Law.* 2d rev. ed. Oxford: Clarendon, 1987.

[3]

Available online at www.sciencedirect.com

SCIENCE @ DIRECT®

Journal of Financial Economics 69 (2003) 5–50

JOURNAL OF
Financial
ECONOMICS

www.elsevier.com/locate/econbase

ELSEVIER

The great reversals: the politics of financial development in the twentieth century ☆

Raghuram G. Rajan*, Luigi Zingales

The University of Chicago Graduate School of Business, 1101 E. 58th St., Chicago, IL 60637, USA

Abstract

The state of development of the financial sector does not change monotonically over time. In particular, by most measures, countries were more financially developed in 1913 than in 1980 and only recently have they surpassed their 1913 levels. To explain these changes, we propose an interest group theory of financial development where incumbents oppose financial development because it breeds competition. The theory predicts that incumbents' opposition will be weaker when an economy allows both cross-border trade and capital flows. This theory can go some way in accounting for the cross-country differences in, and the time-series variation of, financial development.
© 2003 Elsevier Science B.V. All rights reserved.

JEL classification: G100; G180; G200; G380; O160; P000

Keywords: Financial markets; Growth; Politics; Financial development; Reversals; Trade; Capital flows

☆This paper is a development of some ideas in a previous working paper entitled "The Politics of Financial Development." We thank the Bradley Foundation, the George J. Stigler Center for the Study of the Economy and the State, the Center for Research in Securities Prices, the Kauffman Foundation, and the World Bank for funding support. Rajan also thanks the National Science Foundation and M.I.T. for research support. Claudio Callegari, Henrik Cronqvist, Shola Fafunso, Isidro Ferrer, Jorg Kukies, Roger Laeven, Jamers Mello, Galina Ovtcharova, Nahid Rahman, Sofia Ramos, Ruy Ribeiro, Amir Sasson, and Elfani Wen provided excellent research assistantship and Arnoud Boot, Pratip Kar, Claus Parum, Kristian Rydqvist, and Elu Von Thadden provided invaluable help. We benefited from comments by Lucian Bebchuk, Stijn Claessens, Peter Hogfeldt, Louis Kaplow, Colin Mayer, Mark Ramseyer, Eric Rasmussen, Mark Roe, Andrei Shleifer, Richard Sylla, and an anonymous referee.
    *Corresponding author. Tel.: +1-773-702-4437; fax: +1-773-834-8172.
    E-mail address: raghuram.rajan@gsb.uchicago.edu (R.G. Rajan).

6   R.G. Rajan, L. Zingales / Journal of Financial Economics 69 (2003) 5–50

1. Introduction

There is a growing body of evidence indicating that the development of a country's financial sector greatly facilitates its economic growth (e.g., Demirguc-Kunt and Maksimovic, 1998; King and Levine, 1993; Jayaratne and Strahan, 1996; Rajan and Zingales, 1998a). Why then do so many countries still have underdeveloped financial sectors?

The simple answer, and one favored by many economists, is the absence of demand. Certainly demand is a prime driver of financial development, but it cannot be the only explanation. Demand (as proxied for by level of industrialization or economic development) cannot explain why countries at similar levels of economic development differ so much in the level of their financial development. For instance, why was France's stock market much bigger as a fraction of its gross domestic product (GDP) than markets in the United States in 1913, even though the per capita GDP in the United States was not any lower than France's? It is hard to imagine that the demand for financing in the United States at that time was inadequate. At the time, the demand for more, and cheaper, credit was a recurrent theme in political debates in the United States, and it was among the most industrialized countries in the world even then.

An alternative explanation is that there are structural impediments to supply rising to meet demand. Perhaps a country does not have the necessary levels of social capital (Guiso et al., 2000) or "savoir faire" to create a viable financial sector (e.g., Bencivenga and Smith, 1991; Greenwood and Jovanovic, 1990). Or perhaps it has not inherited the right legal, cultural, or political system. In particular, the seminal work of La Porta et al. (1997, 1998) shows that countries with a Common Law origin seem to have better minority investor protection, and furthermore, these countries have more highly developed equity markets. There has been some debate as to the precise channel through which a country's institutional inheritance affects its financial development (e.g., Berglof and Von Thadden, 1999; Coffee, 2000; Holmen and Hogfeldt, 2000; La Porta, et al., 1999a, 1999b; Rajan and Zingales, 1999; Stulz and Williamson, 2001). Some question whether the influence of certain forms of Civil Law heritage can be distinguished from the influence of a Common Law heritage (e.g., Beck et al., 1999). Yet, there is a burgeoning literature suggesting that a country's "structure" matters.

There are other implications, however, of structural theories of financial development. For instance, once a country has overcome the structural impediments, the supply of finance should rise to meet demand. In other words, we should not see measures of financial development waxing and waning independent of demand. Similarly, conditional on demand, the relative position of different countries should not change dramatically over time. If some countries have a system that is pre-disposed towards finance, that pre-disposition should continue to be relatively strong since structural factors are relatively time-invariant.

To test these implications, we collect various indicators of financial development for developed countries over the twentieth century. By most measures, countries were more financially developed in 1913 than in 1980 and only recently have they

R.G. Rajan, L. Zingales / Journal of Financial Economics 69 (2003) 5–50   7

surpassed their 1913 levels. Furthermore, even after controlling for the different levels of industrialization, the pattern across countries is quite different from the 1990s. In 1913, France's stock market capitalization (as a fraction of GDP) was almost twice that of the United States (0.78 vs. 0.39) even though the French Civil Code has never been friendly to investors (La Porta et al., 1998). By 1980, roles had reversed dramatically. France's capitalization was now barely one-fourth the capitalization in the United States (0.09 vs. 0.46). And in 1999, the two countries seem to be converging (1.17 vs. 1.52). More generally, in 1913, the main countries of continental Europe were more developed financially than the United States. What is especially interesting is that indicators of financial development fell in all countries after 1929, reaching their nadir around 1980. Since then, there has been a revival of financial markets.

In fact, in contrast to the findings of La Porta et al. (1997) for the 1990s, we find that countries with Common Law systems were not more financially developed in 1913. There is some indication that these differences had to do with differences in financial infrastructure. Tilly (1992) indicates that corporate share issues in Germany in the beginning of the Twentieth Century were greater than in England. He suggests this is because of the "paucity of information and relatively weak financial controls on the operations of company founders and insiders" (p. 103) in England. The common wisdom today is the reverse, that German corporations are much less transparent than corporations in the United Kingdom, as reflected by their lower scores on accounting standards.

The disruption in demand caused by the Great Depression and World War II are not sufficient to explain the reversal in financial markets. The economies of the hardest-hit countries recovered within a decade or two. Why did it take financial markets until the late 1980s to stage a recovery? Moreover, such a delay was not seen after the World War I.

All this is not to suggest that structural theories are incorrect, but that they are incomplete. A theory with a more variable factor is needed to explain both the time-series variation in financial development as well as the cross-sectional differences. In our view, the strength of political forces in favor of financial development is a major variable factor. The challenge for such a theory is to identify who is opposed to something as economically beneficial as financial development. We believe that incumbents, in the financial sector and in industry, can be hostile to arm's length markets. This is because arm's length financial markets do not respect the value of incumbency and instead can give birth to competition. There are occasions, however, when the incentives, or the ability, of incumbents to oppose development is muted. In particular, we argue that when a country's borders are open to both trade and capital flows, we see the opposition to financial development will be most muted and development will flourish.

Of course, the decision to open to trade and capital flows is also partly political. This raises two questions. First, why do some countries become more open than others, or open up at some times rather than at others—do the incumbents not oppose opening up? And second, how can we provide evidence of a causal link rather than simply a correlation: How can we argue that the link between openness and financial development should be interpreted as one causing the other rather than simply as evidence that incumbents who favor openness also favor financial development?

Let us answer the first question first. Some countries have no choice. Because they are small, or because they are close to other countries, they are likely to have more trade. Therefore, these countries are likely open for reasons that are not political. Also, even if the decision is political, countries' decisions whether to open up are likely strategic complements. If important parts of the world are open, then natural leakages across borders (the gray trade, smuggling, under-invoicing, over-invoicing, etc.) are likely to be high and make it hard for a country to remain closed. Moreover, groups that are in favor of openness (for example, exporters) are likely to gain in prospective profitability and strength relative to those who rely on controls, and they are likely to have more success in pressing for openness (e.g., Becker, 1983). The economic importance of other countries that are open can be thought of as largely exogenous to a country's domestic politics.

These observations suggest ways to test whether openness has a causal effect. First, in examining the link between trade openness and financial development, we instrument trade openness with a measure of natural openness (largely based on a country's distance from its trading partners) developed by Frankel and Romer (1999). We thus focus on the exogenous component of a country's trade. Because distance matters less for capital, we do not have a similar instrument for cross-border capital flows. But precisely because capital is more mobile, the strategic complementarities in cross-border capital flows are likely to be stronger. So we can use world-wide cross-border capital flows over time as an exogenous measure of whether countries are more open to capital flows. International capital mobility is high both in the beginning and towards the end of the twentieth century for most countries. Thus, we test in the cross-section of countries if financial development is positively correlated with the exogenous component of a country's openness to trade (correcting for the demand for finance), both in the beginning of the century and towards the end of the century, and it is.

By contrast, in the intermediate periods (from the 1930s to the 1970s) when cross-border capital flows had dwindled to a trickle for a variety of reasons, we find that trade openness did not have as strong a positive correlation (if at all) with financial development. These findings suggest that it takes the combination of openness in product and financial markets to mute incumbent incentives to oppose financial development. They also suggest a rationale for why indicators of financial development fell between the 1930s and the 1970s. Cross-border flows, especially of capital, were relatively small, so incumbents could oppose financial development without constraints.

We are, of course, not the first to point to the influence of private interests on financial development, though our focus is quite different from previous work. Jensen (1991) argues that legislation motivated by potential targets crimped the market for corporate control even while it was having salutary effects on US industry. Kroszner and Strahan (1999) explain the timing of financial liberalization across states in the United States in the 1970s and 1980s with variables that relate to

R.G. Rajan, L. Zingales / Journal of Financial Economics 69 (2003) 5–50   9

the power of private interest groups. Morck et al. (2000) find that the share prices of heir-controlled Canadian firms fell on news that the Canada–US free-trade agreement would be ratified. One reason they suggest is that the treaty had a provision for greater capital market openness, which would reduce the advantage heir-controlled firms had from access to capital. Bebchuk and Roe (1999) argue that corporate governance regimes will be strongly influenced by the initial positions of owners. Our paper is related to all these in that we also emphasize the role of private interests in retarding financial development, but we differ in that we attempt to find general patterns across countries.

We will postpone a discussion of the other related literature until we present the theoretical reasoning and tests. The rest of the paper is as follows. Section 2 describes how we collect the data and presents measures of financial-sector development in different countries at various points in the twentieth century. Section 3 presents our interest group theory of why some countries develop their financial systems (and others not) and argues why this could explain the reversals in the data. Section 4 tests both the time-series and cross-sectional implications of this theory. Section 5 concludes.

2. Evolution of financial development over the twentieth century

We are faced with two problems in analyzing the historical evolution of financial development over the twentieth century. First, it is difficult to obtain reliable sources for historical information about financial markets. In Appendix A, we describe how we deal with this problem. The second problem is how to measure financial development.

2.1. What do we mean by financial development?

The right measure would capture the ease with which any entrepreneur or company with a sound project can obtain finance, and the confidence with which investors anticipate an adequate return. Presumably, also, a developed financial sector can gauge, subdivide, and spread difficult risks, letting them rest where they can best be borne. Finally, it should do all this at low cost.

In our view, the most important word in the above definition is "any." In a perfect financial system, it will be the quality of the underlying assets or ideas that will determine whether finance is forthcoming, and the identity of the owner (to the extent it is orthogonal to the owner's capability of carrying out the project) will be irrelevant. Because our focus is on how easy it is to raise finance without prior connections or wealth, our measures of financial development will emphasize the availability of arm's length market finance (and if the data were available, the availability of non-relationship-based bank finance).

This choice is not innocuous. In some financial systems, capital is easily available for anyone within a circle of firms and financiers, but it does not percolate outside (e.g., Hellwig, 2000; Rajan and Zingales, 1998b). Most investment opportunities originate within this closed group, and this group can undertake more daring investment than would be possible in an economy with more widespread access. We would not deem this economy to be financially developed. In a sense, we adopt the Schumpeterian view that a critical role of finance is creative destruction, and this is possible only if there is a constant flow of capital into new firms and out of old firms.

Our definition of development then suggests different ratios of the size of arm's length markets to the size of the economy as our measures of financial development. For example, measures include ratios such as equity market capitalization to GDP, volume of equity issues to gross fixed-capital formation, or number of listed firms to population in millions. While they are no doubt crude proxies, these ratios broadly capture a country's level of financial sophistication and they are standard in the literature. For the sake of comparison, we will also report a measure of the development of the banking sector.

2.2. Various measures of financial development

Let us now describe the various indicators of financial development we use.

2.2.1. Banking sector

We use the ratio of deposits (commercial banks plus savings banks) to GDP as a measure of the development of the banking sector. One shortcoming is that this measure captures only the liability side of banks, ignoring differences in the composition of the banks' assets. Another shortcoming is that this measure cannot indicate if banks operate as a cartel, forming a closed shop to new industrial entrants. Despite this shortcoming, the measure has the virtue that it is available for a long time-series and for a large cross-section of countries. In more recent periods, we have domestic credit from the private sector to GDP, which will be our measure of banking-sector development.

2.2.2. Equity issues

One measure of the importance of equity markets is the fraction of investments that are funded through equity issues. The proxy we use is the ratio of equity issues by domestic corporations to gross fixed capital formation (GFCF) during the year. Ideally, we would have liked to normalize corporate equity issues by the amount of corporate investments, but this datum is not consistently available. In interpreting the results, therefore, it is important to realize that our measure will tend to underestimate the level of financial development of countries where agriculture (which does not enter in corporate investments but does enter in total investments) is more significant. It will also tend to underestimate the level of financial development in the earlier part of the century, when corporate investments were a smaller fraction of total investments.

Another drawback of this measure stems from the well-known cyclicality of equity issues. A disproportionate amount of equity issues are concentrated during boom years (Choe et al., 1993). This can bias cross-country comparisons to the extent stock market booms are not contemporaneous across economies. It also biases the

R.G. Rajan, L. Zingales / Journal of Financial Economics 69 (2003) 5–50   11

time-series comparisons if one of the reference years is a boom year. To minimize the problem, we average issues over a number of years when we have easy access to annual data.

2.2.3. Capitalization

A more stable measure of the importance of the equity market is the total stock market capitalization. A drawback is this measure captures the amount of equity listed, not the amount of equity raised. Thus, the presence of few companies that have greatly appreciated in value can give the impression of an important equity market even when the amount of funds raised in the market is tiny. On the positive side, however, this measure is less cyclical than the previous one and thus is better for making comparisons across countries and across time periods.

In measuring both equity issues and stock market capitalization we restrict ourselves whenever possible to domestic companies. At the beginning of the twentieth century, London and Paris attracted foreign listings. More recently, New York attracts many foreign listings. We are especially interested, however, in how a country's financial and legal institutions help domestic industries raise funds, and as some have argued (e.g., Kennedy, 1989), the financial sector's ability to fund foreigners may not imply an ability to fund domestic firms. Moreover, our focus reduces the possibility of mechanical correlations in our tests. This is why we limit ourselves to domestic companies.

2.2.4. Number of companies listed

A final indicator of the importance of equity markets is the number of publicly traded domestic companies per million of population. This is a measure that is not tainted by fluctuations in stock market valuations and possible mismeasurement of the level of GDP. This also suggests a drawback. It could be too slow-moving a measure to fully capture high frequency changes in the environment. Also, the measure will be affected by the process of consolidation as well as by the fragmentation of the industrial structure. Countries with a more concentrated industrial structure will have fewer, but larger, companies and thus might score low according to this measure. Since concentration will reflect, only in part, limited access to finance, this measure will be a noisy proxy for what we want to capture.

One indicator that is missing from our list is the volume of securities traded. Unfortunately, the way volume is recorded (even today) is quite controversial. The Federation Internationale Bourses Valeurs (FIBV) classifies data on volume traded into two groups: trading system view (TSV) and regulated environment view (REV). The TSV system counts as volume only those transactions which pass through the exchange's trading floor, or which take place on the exchange's trading floor. The REV system includes in volume all the transactions subject to supervision by the market authority, with no distinction between on- and off-market transactions. As the FIBV warns, comparisons are not valid between stock exchanges belonging to different groups, because the numbers differ substantially depending on method used. For example, in Paris, according to the TSV method the volume of equity traded in 1999 was $770,076 million, while the REV method suggests a volume four

12   R.G. Rajan, L. Zingales / Journal of Financial Economics 69 (2003) 5–50

times greater ($2,892,301 million). Given the magnitude of the difference and the impossibility of obtaining consistent data both across countries and over time, we chose to disregard this indicator.

In sum, any indicator has its own drawbacks. This is the reason why they should be looked at together to get a better sense of the development of a country's financial structure.

2.3. Stylized facts

In Table 1, we report the average value of our four indicators of financial development for the period 1913–1999. The countries in our sample are those for which we could get pre-World War II financial market data. Since the availability of data on financial development has exploded recently, we include all the countries whose data we can get in our tests for the most recent years. For every indicator we report both the average across all available observations and the average for the countries with observations throughout the sample period. In Tables 2–5 we report the value of each indicator for each country. An examination of these tables suggests the following facts.

2.3.1. Financial systems were highly developed in 1913
Regardless of the way we measure, the average level of financial development in 1913 is quite high, comparable to that in 1980 or 1990. The average ratio of deposits to GDP in 1913 is very similar to that in 1980 (see Table 1). The absence of an upward trend reflects the fact that countries depend less on banks and more on financial markets as they develop economically. But the data on the capitalization of the stock market (Tables 1 and 3) suggest that in most countries equity markets were bigger relative to GDP in 1913 than in 1980. Only by the end of the 1990s do they seem to exceed their 1913 level.

Equity issues also an important source of funds for corporate investments than 1980 (and even 1990) for most countries whose data we have (see Tables 1 and 4). This is particularly noteworthy when we recognize that the 1913 figures are biased downwards relative to the 1990 ones, because we normalize by Gross Fixed Capital Formation, and corporate investments represent a much smaller proportion of GFCF in 1913 than in 1990.

Most countries have the same number of listed companies per million people in 1913 as in 1980 (see Tables 1 and 5). In some countries, even with the explosion of financial markets during the late 1990s, the 1913 level has not been surpassed.

While, in general, the richest countries had highly developed financial sectors in 1913, the degree of development does vary widely. The level of economic development explains only 14% of the cross-country variation in the deposit-to-GDP ratio and it is not even statistically significant in explaining the level of equity market capitalization. For example, in 1913 Argentina shows about the same per capita GDP as Germany and France, but its level of deposits is only about two-thirds that of France and Germany. Similarly, our data show that in 1913

R.G. Rajan, L. Zingales / Journal of Financial Economics 69 (2003) 5–50   13

Table 1
Evolution of the different indicators of financial development

Whole sample indicates an average across all the countries we have data for. Constant sample indicates an average across countries for which we have data every year. Deposits to GDP is the ratio of commercial and savings bank deposits to GDP. Stock market cap to GDP is the ratio of the aggregate market value of equity of domestic companies divided by GDP. Number of companies to population is the ratio of number of domestic companies whose equity is publicly traded in a domestic stock exchange to the country's population in millions. Equity issues to GFCF is the ratio of funds raised through public equity offerings (both initial public offerings and seasoned equity issues) by domestic companies to gross fixed capital formation. N is the number of observations. Sources are in the Data Appendix, which is available on request from the authors.

Year	Deposits to GDP			Stock market cap to GDP			No. of companies to population			Equity issues to GFCF		
	Whole	N	Constant sample (N=20)	Whole	N	Constant sample	Whole	N	Constant sample	Whole	N	Constant sample (N=7)
1913	0.38	22	0.40	0.57	22	0.40	28.68	22	24.00	0.12	12	0.13
1929	0.49	21	0.51	0.60	11	0.53	33.80	14	27.75	0.35	15	0.34
1938	0.45	21	0.46	0.58	13	0.57	30.12	13	27.69	0.13	12	0.10
1950	0.33	22	0.34	0.30	14	0.27	38.63	16	23.80	0.06	11	0.03
1960	0.31	22	0.33	0.47	18	0.44	31.85	19	22.38	0.07	16	0.05
1970	0.31	22	0.33	0.49	19	0.42	23.66	21	21.22	0.06	16	0.02
1980	0.34	22	0.35	0.26	22	0.25	26.70	22	23.71	0.03	18	0.03
1990	0.41	21	0.40	0.57	21	0.51	22.18	22	23.21	0.05	20	0.05
1999	0.46	21	0.45	1.02	23	1.08	26.30		24.46	0.13	20	0.18

Table 2
Evolution of the ratio of deposits to GDP
Deposits to GDP is the ratio of commercial and savings deposits divided by GDP. Until 1990 the source is
Mitchell (1995). We extrapolate the 1999 data from the 1994 data in Mitchell using the rate of growth of
deposits as reported in *International Financial Statistics* published by the International Monetary Fund.

Country	Year								
	1913	1929	1938	1950	1960	1970	1980	1990	1999
Argentina	0.29	0.36	0.36	0.30	0.22	0.19	0.28	0.07	0.24
Australia	0.37	0.45	0.45	0.69	0.43	0.38	0.29	0.42	0.49
Austria	1.12	0.37	0.33	0.21	0.28	0.31	0.62	0.73	0.70
Belgium	0.68	0.48	0.69	0.44	0.35	0.40	0.39	0.38	0.85
Brazil	0.12	0.16	0.21	0.20	0.15	0.12	0.17		
Canada	0.22	0.13	0.16	0.17	0.13	0.37	0.47	0.49	0.61
Chile	0.16	0.15	0.09	0.10	0.06	0.07	0.07	0.12	0.19
Cuba									
Denmark	0.76	0.46	0.39	0.32	0.27	0.25	0.28	0.55	0.54
Egypt				0.17	0.17	0.14	0.31	0.67	0.51
France	0.42	0.44	0.36	0.24	0.30	0.33	0.45	0.42	0.47
Germany	0.53	0.27	0.25	0.15	0.23	0.29	0.30	0.32	0.35
India	0.04	0.09	0.12	0.08	0.08	0.09	0.08	0.09	0.09
Italy	0.23	0.21	0.31	0.23	0.81	0.54	0.59	0.40	0.28
Japan	0.13	0.22	0.52	0.14	0.21	0.33	0.48	0.51	0.53
Netherlands	0.22	0.32	0.52	0.28	0.28	0.26	0.25	0.73	0.69
Norway	0.65	0.89	0.56	0.52	0.43	0.49	0.30	0.50	0.49
Russia	0.21								
South Africa	0.09	0.09	0.16	0.18	0.18	0.16	0.12	0.16	0.21
Spain	0.07	0.24	0.24	0.33	0.37	0.53	0.44	0.66	0.71
Sweden	0.69	0.69	0.73	0.59	0.54	0.50	0.48	0.40	0.39
Switzerland	0.93	1.08	1.13	0.79	0.78	0.69	0.69	0.54	0.66
UK	0.10	2.88	1.34	0.67	0.32	0.22	0.14	0.33	0.39
US	0.33	0.33	0.44	0.40	0.30	0.25	0.18	0.19	0.17

Argentina's per capita GDP was three times as big as Japan's, but the relative size of
its equity market was only one-third of Japan's.

2.3.2. Countries most advanced in 1913 do not necessarily stay advanced

By our measures, countries that were financially developed in 1913 do not
necessarily continue to be so. In 1913, equity issues appear more important in
France, Belgium, and Russia than in the United States. Thus, by this measure, some
continental European markets seem at least as developed as the US market at that
time. The data on market capitalization in Table 3 confirm this impression. While
the UK had a high capitalization in 1913, Belgium, France, Germany, and Sweden
were all ahead of the United States. Recent studies highlight the distinction between
Civil Law continental European economies and Common Law Anglo-American
economies, but the early data do not confirm this. In fact, this distinction seems to be
a post-World War II phenomenon implying financial markets in Civil Law countries

R.G. Rajan, L. Zingales / Journal of Financial Economics 69 (2003) 5–50   15

Table 3

Evolution of stock market capitalization over GDP

Stock market capitalization to GDP is the ratio of the aggregate market value of equity of domestic companies to GDP. Sources are in the Data Appendix, which is available on request from the authors.

Country	Year								
	1913	1929	1938	1950	1960	1970	1980	1990	1999
Argentina	0.17				0.05	0.03	0.11		0.15
Australia	0.39	0.50	0.91	0.75	0.94	0.76	0.38	0.37	1.13
Austria	0.76					0.09	0.03	0.17	0.17
Belgium	0.99	1.31			0.32	0.23	0.09	0.31	0.82
Brazil	0.25						0.05	0.08	0.45
Canada	0.74		1.00	0.57	1.59	1.75	0.46	1.22	1.22
Chile	0.17				0.12	0.00	0.34	0.50	1.05
Cuba	2.19								
Denmark	0.36	0.17	0.25	0.10	0.14	0.17	0.09	0.67	0.67
Egypt	1.09				0.16		0.01	0.06	0.29
France	0.78		0.19	0.08	0.28	0.16	0.09	0.24	1.17
Germany	0.44	0.35	0.18	0.15	0.35	0.16	0.09	0.20	0.67
India	0.02	0.07	0.07	0.07	0.07	0.06	0.05	0.16	0.46
Italy	0.17	0.23	0.26	0.07	0.42	0.14	0.07	0.13	0.68
Japan	0.49	1.20	1.81	0.05	0.36	0.23	0.33	1.64	0.95
Netherlands	0.56		0.74	0.25	0.67	0.42	0.19	0.50	2.03
Norway	0.16	0.22	0.18	0.21	0.26	0.23	0.54	0.23	0.70
Russia	0.18								0.11
South Africa				0.68	0.91	1.97	1.23	1.33	1.20
Spain							0.17	0.41	0.69
Sweden	0.47	0.41	0.30	0.18	0.24	0.14	0.11	0.39	1.77
Switzerland	0.58					0.50	0.44	1.93	3.23
UK	1.09	1.38	1.14	0.77	1.06	1.63	0.38	0.81	2.25
US	0.39	0.75	0.56	0.33	0.61	0.66	0.46	0.54	1.52

appear to have declined more between 1913 and the early 1990s (though the gap has narrowed since).

Another way of seeing the change in patterns is to compute the correlation between indicators of financial development at different points in time. Using the Spearman rank correlation test, we find a correlation of 0.4 between capitalization to GDP in 1913 and capitalization to GDP in 1999. We reject the hypothesis that the two distributions across countries are independent at the 10% level (21 observations). The cross-country pattern of financial development in 1999 is positively correlated with that in 1913. However, this is not true a decade earlier. The correlation of the 1913 data with 1990 and 1980 data is lower (0.21 in 1990, −0.07 in 1980), and we cannot reject the hypothesis that the distributions are independent.

By way of comparison, consider the cross-country correlation of per-capita GDP measured at two different points in time. Using the Spearman rank correlation test, we find a correlation of 0.55 between per-capita GDP in 1913 and per-capita GDP in 1999 (independence rejected at the 1% level with 22 observations). The correlation of the 1913 data with 1990 and 1980 data is equally high (0.62 for 1990, 0.73 for 1980).

16   *R.G. Rajan, L. Zingales / Journal of Financial Economics 69 (2003) 5–50*

Table 4
Evolution of fraction of gross fixed-capital formation raised via equity
Amount of funds raised through public equity offerings (both initial public offerings and seasoned equity issues) by domestic companies divided by gross fixed capital formation. Sources are in the Data Appendix, which is available on request from the authors.

Country	Year								
	1913	1929	1938	1950	1960	1970	1980	1990	1999
Argentina					0.01		0.01	0.10	0.02
Australia		0.13		0.19	0.09	0.05	0.05	0.09	0.24
Austria		0.07			0.04	0.07	0.00	0.07	0.03
Belgium	0.23	0.85	0.03		0.09	0.08	0.03	0.01	0.06
Brazil				0.20	0.19	0.19	0.06	0.01	0.07
Canada		1.34	0.02	0.03	0.03	0.01	0.04	0.01	0.07
Chile									
Cuba									
Denmark		0.03	0.01				0.01	0.08	0.09
Egypt									0.31
France	0.14	0.26	0.03	0.02	0.04	0.04	0.06	0.02	0.09
Germany	0.07	0.17	0.06	0.00	0.04	0.02	0.01	0.04	0.06
India						0.00	0.00	0.00	0.08
Italy	0.07	0.26	0.03	0.02	0.08	0.02	0.04	0.04	0.12
Japan	0.08	0.13	0.75		0.15	0.03	0.01	0.02	0.08
Netherlands	0.38	0.61	0.45	0.02	0.02	0.00	0.01	0.10	0.67
Norway		0.05	0.01					0.04	0.06
Russia	0.17								
South Africa						0.33	0.08	0.10	0.14
Spain	0.01	0.33		0.08	0.11	0.07	0.03	0.06	0.10
Sweden	0.08	0.34	0.06	0.01	0.03	0.00	0.00	0.03	0.10
Switzerland	0.03				0.02			0.02	
UK	0.14	0.35	0.09	0.08	0.09	0.01	0.04	0.06	0.09
US	0.04	0.38	0.01	0.04	0.02	0.07	0.04	0.04	0.12

Thus over long periods, the relative ranking of countries according to financial development seems more volatile than ranking according to economic development.

2.3.3. Indicators of financial development fall then rise between 1913 and 1999

The most striking fact that emerges from Table 1 is that indicators of financial development fall considerably and then rise again. It is not easy to define precisely where the indicators start falling, but the data suggest that the turning point is somewhere in the 1930s or 1940s.

It is worth noting that the decline in indicators is not limited to the countries that lost the war, although it is more pronounced for such countries. It is not even seen only in countries involved in the war, since we see it in Sweden, Argentina, and Brazil. Finally, it cannot be attributed to a decline in the standard of living, since during the period (from 1938 to 1950) the average per-capita GDP in 1990 dollars increased from $4,036 to $4,644.

Table 5

Evolution of number of listed companies per million people

The number of listed companies per million people is the number of domestic companies whose equity is publicly traded in a domestic stock exchange divided by the population in millions. Sources are in the Data Appendix, which is available on request from the authors.

Country	Year								
	1913	1929	1938	1950	1960	1970	1980	1990	1999
Argentina	15.29				26.78	15.58	9.85	5.54	3.63
Australia	61.74	76.92	84.88	122.05	93.72		68.53	63.89	64.91
Austria	38.72	42.62	30.06	16.29	13.34	12.05	8.74	12.57	12.02
Belgium	108.7			55.09	42.60	38.39	22.85	18.50	14.33
Brazil	12.43	9.85	5.17	41.02		4.32	4.06	3.86	3.18
Canada	14.65			66.61	62.43	55.20	50.52	42.99	130.13
Chile	20.62				44.52	38.72	23.78	16.32	19.03
Cuba	12.69								
Denmark	38.22	54.86	85.25	81.28	75.75	52.14	42.54	50.18	44.80
Egypt	16.58	13.44			10.58	1.76		11.01	13.71
France	13.29		24.64	26.20	18.34	15.98	13.99	15.05	
Germany	27.96	19.73	10.91	13.22	11.33	9.07	7.46	6.53	12.74
India	0.82	1.81	2.59	3.13	0.00	0.00	3.11	7.31	6.48
Italy	6.32	6.40	3.11	2.70	2.79	2.46	2.36	3.82	4.54
Japan	7.53	16.65	19.48	9.15	8.35	15.19	14.80	16.76	20.00
Netherlands	65.87	95.48			21.42	15.95	15.12	17.39	15.14
Norway	33.51	41.50	45.98	37.98	37.10	37.90	44.53	44.80	49.62
Russia	2.02								0.81
South Africa				69.05	60.93	51.39	42.48	20.75	15.86
Spain							25.20	10.96	22.25
Sweden	20.64	16.36	14.93	12.83	14.04	13.18	12.39	14.14	31.46
Switzerland	61.53	67.80	55.46	52.47	51.74	58.72	78.03	49.61	34.01
UK	47.06						47.22	29.63	31.11
US	4.75	9.72	9.16	8.94	9.33	11.48	23.11	26.41	28.88

While we cannot also date the recovery in indicators precisely, the turning point lies somewhere in the 1970s or 1980s. Over the 1980s and 1990s, for the countries reporting throughout, the average ratio of deposits to GDP increased by 35%, the average ratio of stock market capitalization to GDP increased four times, as did the fraction of GFCF raised via equity. The number of listed domestic companies shows a more modest increase (30%).

3. An interest group theory of financial development

We now describe a parsimonious theory to explain broad patterns in the data. In essence, our theory suggests why financial development can differ so much between countries at similar levels of economic and industrial development. It also suggests a reason for reversals. No doubt, the specifics of each country will differ and the theory, on occasion, can seem a caricature, but this is the price we have to pay for parsimony.

18   *R.G. Rajan, L. Zingales / Journal of Financial Economics 69 (2003) 5–50*

3.1. The necessity for government intervention

The essential ingredients of a developed financial system include the following: (1) respect for property rights, (2) an accounting and disclosure system that promotes transparency, (3) a legal system that enforces arm's length contracts cheaply, and (4) a regulatory infrastructure that protects consumers, promotes competition, and controls egregious risk-taking.

No doubt, private arrangements could go some way in achieving all this. But the government has the ability to coordinate standards and enforce non-monetary punishments such as jail terms. Such power gives it some advantage in laying out and policing the ducts in which financial plumbing will go. For instance, a number of studies suggest that the mandatory disclosures required by the Securities Act of 1933 did improve the accuracy of pricing of securities (e.g., Simon, 1989). Given that government action is needed for financial development, the focus of our inquiry then shifts to when there is a political will to undertake these actions.

3.2. The political economy of financial development

Financial development is so beneficial that it seems strange that anyone would oppose it. However, financial development is not always win-win. It could pose a threat to some.

Consider, for instance, established large industrial firms in an economy, a group we will call industrial incumbents. In normal times, these incumbents do not require a developed financial system. They can finance new projects out of earnings (as most established firms do) without accessing external capital markets. Even when their business does not generate sufficient cash to fund desired investments, they can use the collateral from existing projects and their prior reputation to borrow. Such borrowing does not require much sophistication from the financial system. Even a primitive system will provide funds willingly against collateral. Because of their privileged access to finance in underdeveloped financial systems, incumbents enjoy a positional rent. Anybody else who starts a promising business has to sell it to the incumbents or get them to fund it. Thus, not only do incumbents enjoy some rents in the markets they operate in, but they also end up appropriating most of the returns from new ventures.

These rents will be impaired by financial development. Better disclosure rules and enforcement in a developed financial market will reduce the relative importance of incumbents' collateral and reputation, while permitting newcomers to enter and compete away profits.

Similar arguments apply to incumbent financiers. While financial development provides them with an opportunity to expand their activities, it also strikes at their very source of comparative advantage. In the absence of good disclosure and proper enforcement, financing is typically relationship-based. The financier uses connections to obtain information to monitor loans, and uses various informal levers of power to cajole repayment. The key, therefore, to the ability to lend is relationships with those who have influence over the firm (managers, other lenders, suppliers, politicians, etc.)

R.G. Rajan, L. Zingales / Journal of Financial Economics 69 (2003) 5–50   19

and the ability to monopolize the provision of finance to a client (either through a monopoly over firm-specific information, or through a friendly cartel amongst financiers). Disclosure and impartial enforcement tend to level the playing field and reduce barriers to an entrance into the financial sector. The incumbent financier's old skills become redundant, while new ones of credit evaluation and risk management become necessary. Financial development not only introduces competition, which destroys the financial institution's rents and relationships (e.g., Petersen and Rajan, 1995), it also destroys the financier's human capital.[1]

In sum, a more efficient financial system facilitates entry, and thus leads to lower profits for incumbent firms and financial institutions. From the perspective of incumbents, the competition-enhancing effects of financial development can offset the other undoubted benefits that financial development brings. Moreover, markets tend to be democratic, and they particularly jeopardize ways of doing business that rely on unequal access. Thus, not only are incumbents likely to benefit less from financial development, they can actually lose. This would imply that as a collective, incumbents have a vested interest in preventing financial development. They may also be small enough (e.g., Olson, 1965; Stigler, 1971) to organize successfully against financial development. In doing so, they will rely on other incumbent groups (such as organized labor). Previous studies show such groups benefit from an economy with limited competition. For example, Salinger (1984) and Rose (1987) provide evidence that unions share in rents from industrial concentration.

Critical to the above arguments is that financial development aids the entrance of new firms, thus enhancing competition. There is some evidence for this. In a comparative study of the textile industry in Mexico and Brazil around the beginning of the twentieth century, Haber (1997) shows that Brazil, following its political revolution, liberalized finance, and saw the textile industry grow faster and become less concentrated than the Mexican textile industry. Porfirio Diaz, the Mexican dictator during this period, was much more a prisoner of incumbent interests. Mexico's financial markets remained underdeveloped during his regime, with the consequence that Mexico's textile industry, while starting out larger and relatively more competitive, had less opportunities for entry, and ended up smaller and more concentrated than Brazil's.

Studies of larger samples of countries support the idea that financial development facilitates the entry of newcomers. Rajan and Zingales (1998a) find that the growth in the number of new establishments is significantly higher in industries dependent on external finance when the economy is financially developed. In a study of trade credit in transitional economies, Johnson et al. (2000) find that an important consequence of an effective legal system is that a firm offers more trade credit to new trading partners. Firms that believe in the effectiveness of the legal system are also more likely to seek out new trading partners.

---

[1] One could also argue for the existence of political incumbents. The relationship between financial development and political incumbency is less clear-cut.

20   *R.G. Rajan, L. Zingales / Journal of Financial Economics 69 (2003) 5–50*

3.3. Financial repression is not the only way to protect incumbent rents

Financial underdevelopment is not the only barrier to newcomers. Incumbents with political influence could restrict or prevent entry into their industry directly through some kind of licensing scheme. There are, however, reasons why some prefer financial underdevelopment to more direct barriers.

First, direct-entry restrictions often require very costly enforcement. Enforcement becomes particularly difficult, if not impossible, when innovation can create substitutes for the product whose market is restricted. Each new threatening innovation has to be identified, categorized, and then banned. Second, the active enforcement of restrictions on entry is very public and, therefore, politically transparent. Citizens are unlikely to remain rationally ignorant when confronted with such blatant opportunism, especially when they face the poor service and extortionate prices of the local monopoly. By contrast, the malign neglect that leads to financial underdevelopment is less noticeable (it goes with the grain to have comatose bureaucrats who do not act rather than have overly active ones) and can be disguised under more noble motives such as protecting citizens from charlatans. Leaving finance underdeveloped is an act of omission with few of the costs entailed by an act of commission such as the use of the apparatus of the state to stamp out entry.

In general, however, we would expect direct entry restrictions and financial underdevelopment to be used as complementary tools. In Fig. 1, we graph the Djankov et al. (2002) measure of the number of procedures in different countries to start a business (a measure of the direct barriers to entry) against the size of equity

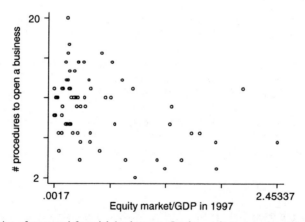

Fig. 1. Regulation of entry and financial development. On the *x*-axis we report a measure of financial development: the ratio of equity market capitalization to GDP in 1997 (average 1996–1998, from the World Bank's World Development Indicators). On the *y*-axis we report a measure of direct regulation of entry. As a measure of direct regulation we use the number of procedures necessary to open a business, as computed by Djankov et al. (2002). As the graph shows there is a clear negative correlation between the two. Countries that regulate entry more tend also to be less financially developed.

markets relative to GDP in that country. The correlation is significantly negative, and regression estimates (not reported) show that it persists after correcting for the level of GDP. Financial underdevelopment does seem present along with other bureaucratic barriers, and this suggests a common purpose.

3.4. What determines outcomes?

In an industrialized economy, incumbent industrialists and financiers ordinarily would have enough political power, because of their large economic weight and small numbers, to collectively decide the development of the economy's financial sector. In earlier times, the landed gentry could have been more powerful in many developed countries than the "commercial" interests. How their power waned is a matter beyond the scope of this paper (though see Rajan and Zingales (2003) for one account). So financial development will take place only when the country's political structure changes dramatically, or when the incumbents want development to take place.

By creating a fresh power structure, political change can foster anti-incumbent institutions, one of which is financial infrastructure. For example, a number of new mortgage banks and institutions like the Credit Mobilier were supported by the government of Louis Napoleon after its coming to power in 1848. They were meant as a counter to the Bank of France and the Rothschilds who were thought to be sympathetic to the deposed monarchy (e.g., Cameron, 1961). More recently, Weber and Davis (2000) find that a country's transition to a multi-party democracy increases its estimated rate of creation of a stock exchange by 134% during the subsequent 3 years.

If, however, we examine a period of relatively little structural political change, we should see finance develop faster when both financial and industrial incumbents will it to do so and slower when both are against it. When one of these powerful groups is for development and the other is against, predictions are more ambiguous.

Incumbent incentives are powerfully affected by competition, especially that emanating from outside their political borders, which they cannot control. The degree to which a country's borders are open to both the flow of trade and capital is thus likely to matter. Of course, an important question is what causes a country to be open. We will address this shortly. But first let us examine how incumbent incentives can altered by cross-border competition.

3.5. Financial development and openness

Consider a country that is open to trade. While foreign markets bring opportunity, openness also brings foreign competitors to domestic markets. Foreign entry drives down domestic rents. Lower profits means established firms have lower internal cash flow, making them more dependent on external finance. At the same time, outside opportunities (or the need to defend domestic markets against superior foreign technologies) increase the need for incumbents to invest more.

Unfortunately, the need for external finance need not translate into reforms that improve transparency and access in the financial system. In fact, given their greater need for finance, industrial incumbents can press for greater financial repression so that the available finance flows their way. Financial incumbents can also be unwilling to accept the increased competition in the financial sector (from greater transparency and access) in exchange for the additional industrial clientele that reforms generate. It may be far more profitable to support the existing relationships with industrial incumbents and ply them with greater amounts of capital they now need.

Industrial incumbents can also petition the government for loan subsidies in the face of foreign competition, instead of improving the quality of the domestic financial system. Selective government intervention can further reduce the transparency of, and the access to, the financial system. Thus openness to trade flows (i.e., industrial sector openness) alone may not be enough to convince either, or both, dominant interest groups to support financial development.

Consider next the possibility of cross-border capital flows (or financial openness) alone. Free access to international capital markets will allow the largest and best-known domestic firms to tap foreign markets for funds. But in the absence of domestic or foreign competition in product markets, these firms will have little need to access external funds. And given the state of information asymmetries across markets, it is unlikely that small domestic firms are financed directly by foreign investors. If potential domestic entrants are not financed by foreigners, industrial incumbents will still retain an incentive to keep entrants at bay by opposing financial development. The domestic financial sector will see its sizeable profits from providing finance and services to the largest industrial firms diminish as these firms threaten to tap foreign financial markets and institutions. It will face the opposition of domestic industrial incumbents if it tries to liberalize access and improve transparency. So cross-border capital flows alone are unlikely to convince both our interest groups to push for financial development.

It is when both cross-border trade flows and capital flows are unimpeded that industrial and financial incumbents will have convergent incentives to push for financial development. Industrial incumbents, with depleted profits and the need for new investment, will need funds to meet foreign challenges. But with free cross-border capital flows, the government's role in directing credit to incumbents will become more circumscribed. As product markets become more competitive, the risks in, and information requirements for, lending will increase. The potential for large errors from the centralized direction of credit will increase. Moreover, the ability of the government to provide large subsidized loans to favored firms will decrease as mobile capital forces governments to maintain macro-economic prudence. For example, Loriaux (1997), provides a description of the constraints on French intervention in domestic credit in the 1980s. The government's role in the financial sector will diminish.

The healthiest industrial incumbents will tap the now open foreign markets for finance. These firms, able to compete in international markets, may not be much worried, or affected, by domestic entry, and thus may not oppose domestic financial development. While the not-so-healthy industrial incumbents can be the hardest hit

R.G. Rajan, L. Zingales / Journal of Financial Economics 69 (2003) 5–50   23

by foreign product market competition, there are reasons why they, too, will not oppose financial development and in fact support it. They will need finance. And their existing financiers will be reluctant to lend to them on the old cozy terms. Because of product market competition, these firms will now be much less profitable, while needing much more investment. Moreover, competition in financial markets will make long-term relationships, through which the traditional financier could have hoped to recover investments, more difficult. Both factors would combine to make finance more difficult. Difficulty in financing will lead these firms to push for greater transparency and access so that their own access to finance improves. Unlike the case when the country is only open to capital flows, industrial incumbents now will also push for financial development. The accompanying threat of domestic industrial entry will now seem relatively minor, given the competitive state of product markets.

Moreover, as the domestic financial sector loses some of its best clients, domestic financial institutions will want to seek new clients among the unborn or younger industrial firms that hitherto did not have the relationships to obtain finance. Since these clients will be riskier, and less well known, financial institutions will have no alternative but to press for improved disclosure and better contract enforcement. In turn, this leveling of the playing field will create the conditions for more entry and competition in the financial sector.

An example of such a virtuous circle is provided by Rosenbluth (1989). As the most reputable Japanese exporters escaped their financial system in the 1980s to raise arm's length finance from the Euromarkets, Japanese banks were forced to change their practices. One beneficial outcome is that access to the Japanese corporate bond markets, that hitherto had been tightly controlled by the banks, is now liberalized.

Other influences will kick in over time. As the domestic financial incumbents improve their skills, they will seek to compete abroad. As they look for new clients outside, they will be forced as a quid pro quo to increase access for foreigners and dismantle domestic regulations that give them their privileged competitive positions. For example, the German government banned lead underwriting of Deutschmark bonds by Japanese financial institutions until Japan agreed in 1985 to allow foreign securities firms to act as lead underwriters for Euroyen bonds (e.g., Rosenbluth, 1989). Foreign financial firms that enter the domestic market are another powerful constituency for financial development. Since they are not part of the domestic social and political networks, they would prefer transparent arm's length contracts and enforcement procedures to opaque negotiated arrangements. It is not a coincidence that these are the very requirements of would-be domestic entrepreneurs who are also outsiders to the domestic clubs.

4. A test of the private interest theory of financial development

Direct measures of the political power of interest groups and their ability to influence outcomes are controversial at best. The following example should illustrate the problems. French financial liberalization was kicked off in 1983 by a Socialist government. Socialists do not seem to be an interest group that would push for liberalization. A more detailed examination of the facts (e.g., Helleiner, 1994) suggests that there was a liberalizing faction in the French Socialist party, led by Prime Minister Pierre Mauroy and Finance Minister Jacques Delors, whose hand was strengthened by France's increased trade integration into the European Community. This faction argued that liberalization was necessary to preserve trade and won the day. How could one ever hope to capture the strength of such factions in a large sample cross-country study without a subjective country-by-country exercise?

Our theory, however, does lead to some indirect, but more objective, tests. According to it, incumbent interests are least able to coordinate to obstruct or reverse financial development when a country is open to both trade and capital flows. When a country is open to neither, they coordinate to keep finance under heel. Matters are unlikely to be much better when a country is open only to capital flows or only to trade. In the former case, incumbent industrial interests can hold back financial development, fearful of the domestic competition that might be financed. In the latter case, both industrial and financial incumbents want to strengthen existing financial relationships to combat the foreign threat. Free access and transparency are likely to get short shrift at such times.

4.1. A test

To test the theory, we need a measure of financial development. The amount of funds raised from arm's length financial markets or the amount of credit offered by competitive banking systems could be measures (albeit crude) of financial development. Unfortunately, we do not know how competitive the banking system is. Instead, we only have measures of the quantity of deposits. The banking system could be concentrated and captive to incumbent interests, dominated by state owned banks, or just plain inefficient. Therefore, we prefer to use the size of the arm's length financial markets as our measure of development. This also accords well with the view that arm's length markets will emerge only when financial infrastructure such as disclosure requirements (e.g., Sylla and Smith, 1995) and investor protection are reasonably developed (e.g., La Porta et al., 1998). Meanwhile banks can exist even when infrastructure is primitive (e.g., Rajan and Zingales, 1998b).

The obvious test would be to regress measures of financial development against measures of openness. But we are immediately faced with another issue. A country's openness to trade and capital flows is also a matter of government policy, liable to influence by different interest groups. A large literature (e.g., Gourevitch, 1986; Rogowski, 1989; O'Rourke and Williamson, 1999) suggests that the decision to open up or close down an economy to trade is a political one, based on the relative strengths of the sectors that stand to gain or lose from openness. This creates a potential problem. A country may open to trade when it sees opportunity, yet is also likely to be a time that financial markets expand. A correlation between trade openness and the size of financial markets can simply reflect a common driving force (opportunity) rather than a causal relationship. In independent work Svaleryd and Vlachos (2002) explore the Granger causality between openness and financial

R.G. Rajan, L. Zingales / Journal of Financial Economics 69 (2003) 5–50   25

development. While they find evidence that openness can cause financial development, they do not find evidence in the opposite direction.

We have a way to deal with this problem when we consider openness to trade as
the explanatory variable. For we can instrument trade openness with measures of a
country's natural propensity to trade—because of its small size or its proximity to
trading partners. If the exogenous component of trade correlates with financial
development, we can be more confident that openness indeed causes financial
development.

Openness to capital flows is more problematic. First, the extent to which capital
flows into a particular country may directly reflect the sophistication of its financial
system. Moreover, unlike with trade, no obvious instruments present themselves.
The mobility of capital, however, suggests a way out.

The decision to open up to capital flows is likely to be a strategic complement.
When the rest of the world is open, it is both more difficult for a country to prevent
cross-border capital movement and less attractive for it to do so. It is more difficult
to prevent capital movements because the openness of the rest of the world makes it
easier for domestic agents to expatriate funds to a safe haven or borrow funds from
it, despite domestic controls. These leakages are especially likely for countries that
are more open to trade. In open countries, funds can be transferred through
underinvoicing or overinvoicing of trade, transfer pricing between units of a
multinational, etc. A country can also find controlling capital flows unattractive
when others are open. Its domestic financial institutions can find themselves at a
comparative disadvantage. For example, a domestic exchange may not be able to
provide as much liquidity as exchanges in other countries that are open to capital
movements. In fact, competition between New York, London, and Tokyo to become
global financial centers was responsible for the rapid demise of capital controls in
these countries after the collapse of Bretton Woods (e.g., Helleiner, 1994).

Given all this, for each individual country the decision to allow capital to flow
across its borders is strongly influenced by overall global conditions, which can be
regarded as exogenous to specific domestic political considerations. And there is
considerable variation in the flow of capital across borders during the twentieth
century. Consider the mean absolute value of current account over GDP over five-
year intervals for a sample of fourteen developed countries as calculated by Taylor
(1998) and extended by us until 1999. This indicator suggests international capital
mobility remained high only up to 1930s (3.8% before World War I and 3.2% in the
1920s, dropping to 1.6% in the 1930s). Following the Depression and the Bretton
Woods agreement, capital movement remained severely curtailed till the 1980s
(oscillating around 1.4%). The United States opened up in the mid 1970s, United
Kingdom and Japan in 1980, while the countries of Continental Europe only in the
late 1980s. As a result, the indicator rose to 2.1% in the 1980s and 2.6% in the 1990s.

In what follows, we will instrument openness to trade to get an exogenous
measure, while we will use the variation in global capital flows over time as an
exogenous measure of a country's variation in openness to capital flows. Let us now
frame the hypothesis. In periods of high capital mobility, countries that conduct a lot
of foreign trade are also likely to have well-developed capital markets. Countries that

26   *R.G. Rajan, L. Zingales / Journal of Financial Economics 69 (2003) 5–50*

conduct little trade are unlikely to have developed capital markets (they are open on only one dimension). So

(1) *For any given level of demand for financing, a country's domestic financial development should be positively correlated with trade openness at a time when the world is open to cross-border capital flows.*

Changes in capital mobility over time give us the data to test the other dimension of our theory:

(2) *The positive correlation between a country's trade openness and financial development should be weaker when worldwide cross-border capital flows are low.*

We will need a proxy for the demand for financing. Bairoch (1982) computes an index of industrialization across a group of countries for a number of years. The index number in a year reflects a country's absolute level of industrialization in that year, with England in 1900 set at one hundred. The index is calculated on the basis of data on per-capita consumption of manufactured goods and from the sectoral distribution of labor. The index is computed in two stages, with the data for the UK calculated in the first stage and the relative importance, sector by sector, of other countries calculated in the second stage. There are measurement issues with any index, but this one seems well accepted among economic historians. Bairoch's index is our preferred control for the demand for financing whenever it is available. This is because GDP is a poorer proxy for the demand for financing in earlier years, when much of GDP was generated by agriculture. We will use per-capita GDP when Bairoch's numbers are not available, though sectoral differences between countries at very different levels of development will add noise.

To test the first hypothesis, we examine the correlation between openness and financial development in 1913, the earliest date for which we have data for a sizeable number of countries, and 1996–1998, the last period for which we have data. Capital flows are relatively free in both periods.

4.2. Financial development in 1913

Consider first financial development in 1913, a period of relatively free capital flows and varying degrees of openness to trade. We present summary statistics and pairwise correlations in Table 6 Panels A and B. Equity market capitalization to GDP is positively correlated with Bairoch's index of industrialization (0.58, $p = 0.01$), with openness (0.33, $p = 0.19$), and negatively correlated with tariffs on manufacturing (-0.37, $p = 0.15$). Its correlation with the interaction (between the index of industrialization and openness) is both high and very significant (0.67, $p = 0.002$).

In Table 7, Panel A, the ratio of stock market capitalization to GDP is our measure of financial development. As the estimates in Column (i) show, more industrialized countries have more developed financial markets. More relevant to our hypothesis, more open countries have more developed financial markets, but due to the small number of observations, this effect is not statistically significant at

R.G. Rajan, L. Zingales / Journal of Financial Economics 69 (2003) 5–50   27

Table 6

Summary statistics

Equity market cap./GDP is the equity market capitalization of domestic companies to GDP in 1913. Issues to GDP is the sum of equity and bond issues by domestic firms in 1912 to GDP in 1913. Per Capita Industrialization is the index of industrialization for that country in 1913 as computed by Bairoch (1982). Openness is the sum of exports and imports of goods in 1913 (obtained from the League of Nations Yearbook) divided by GDP in 1913. Tariffs are import duties as a percentage of special total imports (1909–1913) obtained from Bairoch (1989).

	Mean	Standard deviation	Minimum	Maximum	Observations
Panel A. Summary statistics					
Equity market capital/GDP	0.490	0.294	0.02	1.09	18
Issues to GDP in 1912	0.022	0.015	0.002	0.055	17
Per capita industrialization	49.5	37.08	2	126	18
Openness (trade volume/GDP)	0.59	0.51	0.11	2.32	18
Tariffs	13.0	9.5	0.4	37.4	17
Interaction of per capita industrialization and openness	29.1	31.1	0.36	118.67	18

Panel B. Pairwise correlations between variables (significance in parentheses)

	Equity market cap to GDP	Per capita industrialization	Openness (trade volume/GDP)	Tariffs
Per capita industrialization	0.58 (0.01)			
Openness (trade volume/GDP)	0.33 (0.19)	0.01 (0.98)		
Tariffs	−0.37 (0.15)	−0.24 (0.35)	−0.37 (0.15)	
Interaction of per capita industrialization and openness	0.67 (0.00)	0.55 (0.02)	0.69 (0.00)	−0.37 (0.15)

conventional level. Our hypothesis, however, is that for any given level, more openness should lead to more financial development. Therefore, in column (ii) we include the interaction between openness and the index of industrialization, which is our proxy for the demand for finance. The coefficient estimate for the interaction term is highly statistically significant ($p = 0.034$). The magnitude of the effect is also large. A one standard deviation increase in the interaction term increases the ratio of stock market capitalization to GDP by 50% of its standard deviation. Since we have so few observations, we plot the data in Fig. 2 to show the result is not driven by outliers.

We can try to tell the effect of openness (apart from the effect of openness working through demand) by including both the level of openness and the interaction term in Column (iii). It turns out that only the interaction has a positive coefficient estimate, and the explanatory power of the specification in Column (ii) is not enhanced by including openness. The magnitude of the interaction coefficient is higher than in Column (ii) but its standard error also goes up. The problem is that openness and the interaction are highly correlated ($=0.69$), so it is hard to tell their effects apart with

Table 7

Financial development and openness in 1913

In Panel A the dependent variable is equity market capitalization of domestic companies to GDP in 1913, in Panel B it is the number of listed companies per million of population in 1913, and in Panel C it is the total amount of securities issued to GDP, which is the sum of equity and bond issues by domestic firms in 1912 to GDP. Per Capita Industrialization is the index of industrialization for that country in 1913 as computed by Bairoch (1982). Openness is the sum of exports and imports of goods in 1913 (obtained from the League of Nations Yearbook) divided by GDP in 1913. Tariffs are import duties as a percentage of special total imports (1909–1913) obtained from Bairoch (1989). Coefficient estimates for per capita industrialization, its interaction with openness, and the corresponding standard errors are multiplied by one thousand. Columns (iv)–(v) report instrumental variable estimates, where the instrument for openness is population size. All the regressions include a constant, whose coefficient is not reported. Standard errors are in parentheses. (*) indicates significance at the 10% level, (**) at the 5% level, (***) at the 1% level.

Dependent variable	Equity market capitalization/GDP				
	(i)	(ii)	(iii)	(iv)	(v)
Panel A. Equity market capitalization/GDP					
Per capita industrialization	4.61***	2.42	2.11	1.55	8.77**
	(1.52)	(1.71)	(2.25)	(2.05)	(3.18)
Openness	0.18		-0.04		
	(0.11)		(0.19)		
Interaction of per-capita industrialization and openness		4.76** (2.03)	5.44 (3.69)	6.62** (3.08)	
Interaction of per-capita industrialization and tariffs					-0.38* (0.22)
Adjusted R^2	0.37	0.45	0.42		
Observations	18	18	18	18	17

Panel B. Number of domestic companies listed/million population

Dependent variable	No. of companies/million population				
	(i)	(ii)	(iii)	(iv)	(v)
Per-capita industrialization	215.8	-210.6	-199.5	-252.0*	927.7**
	(133.6)	(116.0)	(152.8)	(137.0)	(442.3)
Openness	38.8***		-1.5		
	(9.6)		(12.7)		
Interaction of per-capita industrialization and openness		924.1*** (138.1)	899.8*** (250.8)	1012.8*** (206.0)	
Interaction of per-capita industrialization and tariffs					-60.9** (29.9)
Adjusted R^2	0.50	0.74	0.72		
Observations	18	18	18	18	17

Panel C. Total securities issued/GDP

Dependent variable	Securities issued/GDP				
	(i)	(ii)	(iii)	(iv)	(v)
Per-capita industrialization	0.17	0.02	-0.09	-0.02	0.52**
	(0.10)	(0.10)	(0.12)	(0.11)	(0.22)
Openness	0.01		-0.01		
	(0.01)		(0.01)		
Interaction of per-capita industrialization and openness		0.33** (0.11)	0.56** (0.19)	0.41** (0.17)	
Interaction of per-capita industrialization and tariffs					-0.03* (0.01)
Adjusted R^2	0.14	0.39	0.44		
Observations	17	17	17	17	17

R.G. Rajan, L. Zingales / Journal of Financial Economics 69 (2003) 5–50   29

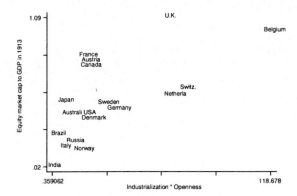

Fig. 2. Market capitalization versus interaction between industrialization and openness. On the *x*-axis we report the product between the level of per capita industrialization of a country and its level of openness. Per capita industrialization is the index of industrialization for that country in 1913 as computed by Bairoch (1982). Openness is the sum of exports and imports of goods in 1913 (obtained from the League of Nations Yearbook) divided by GDP in 1913. On the *y*-axis we report a measure of financial development: the equity market capitalization to GDP ratio in 1923. As the graph shows there is a clear positive correlation between the two, which is not driven by any particular outlier.

so few observations. Since the correct specification could be debated, in what follows we present estimates for both the effect of openness and the effect of the interaction. Our claim is that openness matters, not that we can separate a direct effect of openness from an interaction between openness and our proxy for the demand for finance. Between the two we expect the interaction to be more important, because it is more directly linked to what the theory predicts.

The results thus far indicate that in more open countries, a given demand for finance is correlated with more financial development. Because openness and financial development could be simultaneously determined by some omitted variable, we instrument openness with the size of a country's population in Column (iv). Small countries typically have to be more open since it is difficult to manufacture everything internally (e.g., Katzenstein, 1985). The point estimate of the effect of openness interacted with industrialization increases by 50% and, in spite of an inevitable increase of the standard error, remains statistically significant at the 5% level.

Another concern is that we proxy for openness with the volume of goods traded, and there can be a disguised link between the volume of trade and the volume of financing. One measure of openness that is not directly a measure of volume is the tariff on manufactured goods. We use this as a proxy for the extent of openness in Column (v), and the two-stage least-squares estimate (using the same instrument as in the previous column) is negative and significant.

As discussed before, the ratio of equity market capitalization to GDP is a very imperfect measure of financial development. It is sensitive to fluctuations in relative valuations and to mistakes in the computation of the GDP (national accounts statistics were widely calculated only after WWII, all previous numbers are estimates computed in recent years). An alternative measure, which is immune to both these criticisms, is the ratio of the number of publicly listed companies to population. In Panel B of Table 7, we re-estimate the specifications in Table 7's Panel with this alternative dependent variable. The correlations are even stronger. Openness has a positive and significant correlation with development even when included alone. When both openness and openness interacted are included, the latter remains statistically significant at the 5% level.

Finally, our measure of financial development captures only the size of the equity market, even though the bond market plays an important role in some of these countries. Unfortunately, we were unable to obtain data for the size of the corporate bond market for the same set of countries. We did obtain data, however, from the 1915 Bulletin of the International Institute of Statistics (IIS) in Vienna on the total issues of public corporate securities (both equity and corporate bonds) by domestic firms in a set of countries in 1912. The IIS sample is slightly different from our 1913 sample (which we have put together from different sources for each country). We have checked that the data in the IIS sample seem accurate by comparing with independent sources, and they do seem to represent net rather than gross issues.

In Panel C of Table 7, we re-estimate the same specifications using total issues to GDP in 1912 as dependent variable. As a denominator we use GDP rather than GFCF to maximize the number of observations available. Here again, the interaction between industrialization and openness has a positive and statistically significant coefficient. A one-standard deviation increase in the interaction term increases the ratio of total issues to GDP by 68% of its standard deviation.

4.3. Financial development in the late 1990s

Regardless of the measure used, openness seems to have facilitated financial development in 1913. The paucity of observations, however, is worrisome. But our hypothesis suggests the results should also be present in recent times, when cross-border capital flows have regained the levels they had reached in the early part of the twentieth century.

In Table 8, we re-estimate the specifications in Table 7 using the largest cross-section of data available today. We obtain data for market capitalization from the World Bank's World Development Indicators, data on the number of domestic listed companies from the Emerging Market Factbook, and data on security issues from Beck et al. (1999). Since Bairoch's index of industrialization is not available, we use instead the log of per-capital GDP in PPP dollar, also from the World Bank's World Development Indicators.

To smooth the effects of the East Asian financial crisis we averaged the dependent variable across three years (1996–1998). As Table 8's Panel A (with dependent variable equity market capitalization to GDP) shows, the results are very similar to those in 1913. Openness has a positive and statistically significant effect on financial development. This is true both if we use openness directly (see Column (i)) and if we

R.G. Rajan, L. Zingales / Journal of Financial Economics 69 (2003) 5–50   31

Table 8

Financial development and openness in the late 1990s

In Panel A the dependent variable is the ratio of equity market capitalization to gross domestic product averaged over 1996 to 1998 from the World Development Indicators (World Bank). In Panel B the dependent variable is the number of domestic companies listed over million inhabitants in 1997 from the Emerging Market Factbook. In Panel C the dependent variable is the sum of equity and long-term private debt issues to GDP averaged over the 1990s from Beck et al. (1999). Log per-capita gross domestic product is the logarithm of the per-capita GDP in PPP dollars as reported in the World Development Indicators. Openness is the average of the sum of exports and imports of goods divided by GDP across 1996–1998 (source: World Bank). In Column (iii) the interaction between logarithm of the per-capita GDP and openness is instrumented by the interaction between logarithm of the per-capita GDP and constructed trade share in Frankel and Romer (1999). All the regressions include a constant, whose coefficient is not reported. The standard errors are in parentheses. (*) indicates significance at the 10% level, (**) at the 5% level, (***) at the 1% level.

	(i)	(ii)	(iii)
Panel A. Equity market capitalization/GDP			
Log per-capita GDP	0.264***	0.243***	0.198***
	(0.044)	(0.046)	(0.063)
Openness	0.214***		
	(0.082)		
Interaction of log per-capita GDP and openness		0.025***	0.048***
		(0.009)	(0.024)
Adjusted R^2	0.34	0.34	
Observations	96	96	82
Panel B. Number of domestic companies listed/million population			
	(i)	(ii)	(iii)
Log per-capita GDP	10.96***	8.86**	4.26
	(3.83)	(3.98)	(4.71)
Openness	25.10***		
	(7.11)		
Interaction of log per-capita GDP and openness		2.69***	5.35***
		(0.76)	(1.78)
Adjusted R^2	0.20	0.20	
Observations	91	91	81
Panel C. Security issues/GDP			
	(i)	(ii)	(iii)
Log per-capita GDP	0.026***	0.025***	0.018*
	(0.007)	(0.007)	(0.009)
Openness	0.022**		
	(0.011)		
Interaction of log per-capita GDP and openness		0.002*	0.006**
		(0.001)	(0.003)
Adjusted R^2	0.39	0.38	
Observations	34	34	34

interact it with our proxy for the demand for finance, the log of per capital GDP (see Column (ii)). A one-standard deviation increase in the interaction term corresponds to an increase in the ratio of stock market capitalization to GDP by 25% of its standard deviation. In spite of the very high correlation between openness and the interaction between openness and log per-capita income, the larger cross-section allows us to distinguish the two, and it is the interaction that is positively significantly correlated (estimates not reported).

Frankel and Romer (1999) predict bilateral trade between two countries using an expanded version of the gravity model of trade (where trade is a function of the distance between the countries, their size, and whether they have a common border). Their constructed trade share, then, is simply the sum of these fitted values across all possible trading partners and is a good instrument for trade (perhaps better than population) which is all that we have in 1913. When we use this instrument, the estimated coefficient almost doubles (see Column (iii)) and remains statistically significant at the 1% level.

We show these results hold for other measures of financial development. In Panel B the dependent variable is the number of domestic companies listed per million inhabitants in 1997, while in Panel C it is the sum of equity and long-term private debt issues to GDP. To deal with the cyclicality of equity and debt issues, we use an average across all the years during the 1990s that are available in Beck et al. (1999). These panels confirm the finding that financial development is higher for any level of demand when a country is more open.

4.3.1. Robustness

The greater availability of data at the end of 1990s allows us to explore the robustness of our results. La Porta et al. (1997) suggest that a better measure of financial development than market capitalization is the amount of equity held by outsiders. Using this measure of development, openness or openness interacted with GDP per-capita have a positive and statistically significant correlation with equity held by outsiders (estimates not reported). Similarly, a good indicator of the ability to raise external funds, and thus a measure of the development of a financial market, is the quality of the accounting standards, as measured by the Center for International Financial Analysis and Research. This measure is available only for 39 countries, nevertheless openness alone and openness interacted with GDP per-capita are positively and statistically significantly correlated with it (estimates not reported).

One might worry that there is a mechanical link between openness and financial market development. We know that financial liberalization leads to an increase in stock prices (e.g., Henry, 2000) and, thus, at least temporarily to an increase in the ratio of stock market capitalization to GDP, which is one of our measures of financial development. For example, a large trade deficit has to be financed through capital inflows. If domestic government assets are insufficient, and if foreign direct investment is small, the inflows will be reflected in a larger private market for financial assets. Is the link we have found merely the flip side of a trade deficit? We re-estimate the basic specification using the ratio of trade surplus to GDP as a

R.G. Rajan, L. Zingales / Journal of Financial Economics 69 (2003) 5–50   33

substitute for openness (estimates not reported). Trade surplus does not seem to be correlated with domestic financial development. When we include the interaction of openness with log per-capita GDP, trade surplus loses statistical significance, while the interaction term remains positive and statistically significant.

Another way of getting at this is to look at a form of financing that may not be arm's length (domestic bank credit) and is therefore less likely to be influenced by openness. Openness does not seem to be statistically significantly correlated with the ratio of domestic credit to the private sector to GDP (obtained from Beck et al., 1999). Thus there does not seem to be a mechanical link between openness and financing. Instead the link is to arm's length financing (or we conjecture, if we could measure it, competitive private credit).

4.4. Financial development over time

Our results thus far indicate that both before World War I and in the late 1990s, measures of financial development were higher in countries more open to trade. Of course, many good institutions are associated with more trade. For example, Wei (2000) finds lower corruption in countries that trade more. But our second hypothesis suggests that trade openness is particularly effective when it is accompanied by capital mobility and offers a way of distinguishing our theory from the more general observation that trade is good for institutions. We hypothesize the correlation between trade openness and financial development to be stronger in periods of high international capital mobility than in periods of low mobility.

To begin with, we estimate our basic regression (specification (ii) in Table 7, Panel A) year by year. Unfortunately, we do not have Bairoch's measure of per-capita industrialization over the entire period. Thus, the first seven cross-sections (for the years 1913, 1929, 1938, 1950, 1960, 1970, and 1980) use Bairoch's index as a proxy for demand, while the last two use the logarithm of per capita GDP adjusted for difference in the purchasing power parity (as computed by the World Bank). Consequently, the magnitude of the coefficient before 1980 and after 1981 are not directly comparable.

As Table 9 shows, the interaction between openness and demand for finance has a reliable and statistically significant positive correlation with financial development both at the beginning and at the end of the sample (1913, 1929, and 1997), which correspond to the periods of high international capital mobility. During the period of low capital mobility, the effect is statistically insignificant or even negative when we measure financial development by the ratio of equity market capitalization to GDP.

To formally test whether the effect of openness is smaller during periods of low capital mobility, we pool the different cross-sections. We first report the results for the panel 1913–1980 in Table 10, Column (i), where Bairoch's index is our measure of demand. The specification is the same as Column (iv) of Table 7, with the inclusion of an additional slope term for the years of low capital mobility and year indicators. As an instrument for openness, we use the constructed trade shares

Table 9
Financial development and openness over time

The dependent variable in each regression is a measure of financial development (equity market capital to GDP and number of companies per million inhabitants). The explanatory variables are a constant (coefficient not reported), a measure of industrialization (coefficients not reported), and the interaction between this measure of industrialization and openness (the only coefficient reported). For the period 1913–1980 the measure of industrialization is Bairoch (1982)'s index of industrialization, for the period 1981–1997 it is the logarithm of the per capita GDP in PPP dollars as reported in the World Development Indicators. Coefficient estimates for the interaction of the per capita industrialization index with openness and the corresponding standard errors are multiplied by 1000. Standard errors are in parentheses. Coefficients in bold are statistically different from zero at the 10% level.

Dependent variable	Year								
	1913	1929	1938	1950	1960	1970	1980	1981	1997
	Coefficient of Interaction Term (Demand = Index of Industrialization)						Coefficient of Interaction Term (Demand = Log Per Capita GDP)		
Equity market capitalization to GDP	**4.76**	7.02	5.53	1.76	−1.90	−1.39	−0.65	0.036	**0.046**
	(2.03)	(4.94)	(14.25)	(3.19)	(2.85)	(2.28)	(0.89)	(0.05)	**(0.01)**
Adjusted R^2	0.45	0.13	−0.14	−0.07	−0.14	−0.13	−0.09	0.56	0.46
N	18	10	12	13	13	16	18	45	45
Number of Companies per Million	**924.1**	**1741.7**	**1627.5**	**552.3**	190.6	**128.5**	35.7	**1.78**	**2.71**
	(138.1)	**(531.6)**	**(675.8)**	**(388.5)**	(181.9)	**(63.8)**	(68.3)	**(0.72)**	**(0.53)**
Adjusted R^2	0.74	0.45	0.26	0.00	−0.07	0.17	−0.06	0.21	0.53
N	18	12	12	15	14	15	18	49	49

Table 10

Financial development and variation in capital flows

The dependent variable is the ratio of equity market capitalization to gross domestic product measure in a year. In Column (i), we pool the cross-sections from the following years: 1913, 1929, 1938, 1950, 1960, 1970, and 1980. In Column (ii), we pool the data averaged over 1980–1982 with the data averaged over 1996–1998. In Columns (iii) and (iv) we pool data for 1990 and 1999 with the data used for the estimates in Column (i). All estimates are obtained by instrumental variables, where openness is instrumented by constructed trade share in Frankel and Romer (1999). In the first column the proxy for demand for finance is the index of industrialization for that country in that year as computed by Bairoch (1982) divided by one thousand. In the other columns it is the logarithm of the per-capita GDP. Openness is the ratio of the sum of exports and imports of goods to GDP that year. The indicator for low international capital mobility equals one in the years from 1938–1980 and zero otherwise. The level of capital mobility is the mean absolute level of current account to GDP in 14 countries as computed by Taylor (1998) and extended by us to 1999. All regressions include a calendar year dummy. The standard errors, which are corrected for possible clustering of the residual at a country level, are in parentheses. (*) indicates significance at the 10% level, (**) at the 5% level, (***) at the 1% level.

Sample period:	1913–1980 (i)	1981–1997 (ii)	1913–1999 (iii)	1913–1999 (iv)
Demand for finance	1.201	0.127**	0.143	0.145
	(1.220)	(0.054)	(0.106)	(0.108)
Interaction of demand for finance and openness	6.549***	0.062**	0.037	−0.162
	(0.976)	(0.024)	(0.036)	(0.097)
Interaction of demand for finance and openness *dummy = 1 if period of low international capital mobility	−10.420***	−0.034**	−0.077*	
	(0.222)	(0.015)	(0.040)	
Interaction of demand for finance and openness * level of international capital mobility				6.695**
				(3.038)
Observations	100	90	151	151

computed by Frankel and Romer (1999). While this instrument will be weaker as we go back in time because it is constructed based on country borders in the 1990s, all we care about is that it be correlated with trade and not with financial development. We use population in Table 7 as an instrument because it is available contemporaneously in 1913, but we check that the results hold even when we use the Frankel and Romer instrument. The interaction term is significantly positive, and the additional effect in periods of low capital mobility is significantly negative as predicted.

In Table 10, Column (ii), we report the results for the panel 1981–1997, where the log of per-capita GDP is our measure of demand. The specification is the same as Column (iii) of Table 8, with the inclusion of an additional slope term for the years of low capital mobility. Again, the interaction term is significantly positive, and the additional effect in periods of low capital mobility is significantly negative as predicted.

As discussed earlier, Bairoch's index is probably a better measure of demand for finance in the early years than per-capita industrialization. Since we do not have it

36   *R.G. Rajan, L. Zingales / Journal of Financial Economics 69 (2003) 5–50*

for later years, the only panel we can estimate for all the years is one with log of per-capita GDP as a measure of demand. This is what we report in Column (iii). The interaction effect is positive (though not statistically significant) and it is significantly lower in years of low capital mobility.

Finally, perhaps we should let the data define periods of low and high capital mobility. In Column (iv), instead of multiplying by a dummy indicating periods of low capital mobility, we multiply the interaction by the ratio of cross border flows to GDP in that year (obtained from Taylor, 1998). The coefficient estimates indicate, as predicted, that the interaction is significantly higher in periods of high capital mobility.

We obtain qualitatively similar results to those in Table 10 (not reported) when we use the ratio of number of domestic firms listed to million inhabitants as a measure of financial development or when we use openness rather than openness interacted with demand.

Overall, these results suggest that the positive correlation between openness and financial development re-emerged, and became stronger, in the last two decades of the Twentieth Century, in concert with the increased cross-border capital mobility.

4.5. Summary of results

Overall, the results suggest that financial development is positively correlated with trade openness in periods when cross-border capital flows are high, but less so, or not at all, when cross-border capital flows are low. This is consistent with our theory that incumbents are most able to coordinate opposition to financial development when cross-border capital and trade flows ebb but not when they are vibrant. Of course, other theories could be consistent with our evidence. Nevertheless, when viewed in conjunction with the descriptive histories of financial development in the twentieth century (see below for examples), our theory seems to be an important part of the explanation.

The reversal in financial development in the data is then explained by the diminution of cross-border capital flows that started during the Depression and continued post-World War II until the breakdown of the Bretton Woods agreement. Of course, this raises the question of why most countries collectively shut their borders in the 1930s and 1940s and fully opened up again only recently. While a complete explanation is beyond the scope of this paper, in what follows we try to sketch our main arguments.

4.6. Shutting and re-opening borders

In the 1930s openness fell victim to the Great Depression. The extremely high level of unemployment created by the Great Depression increased the demand for government intervention, which could not take place within the narrow margins of discretion allowed by the Gold Standard. The Gold Standard simply did not allow governments to dislocate their budgets to provide social security and welfare support

R.G. Rajan, L. Zingales / Journal of Financial Economics 69 (2003) 5–50   37

to the needy (e.g., Eichengreen, 1996) even if they wanted to. When the political demand for some form of support became irresistible, country after country abandoned the Gold Standard and devalued its currency. This reaction triggered a round of competitive devaluations between trade partners. To minimize the economic consequences of these competitive devaluations most governments introduced tariffs. Hence, the Great Depression ignited a chain reaction beyond the control of any single country, which almost inevitably led to protectionism. To better understand why this took place in the 1930s, however, we have to analyze the changed political and social conditions after WWI.

4.6.1. The rising political demand for insurance

In the open developed economies in the beginning of the twentieth century, the role of the government was relatively small. Government expenditure as a fraction of GDP was only 12.7% in 1913 for a sample of 17 developed countries, compared to 45.6% in 1996 (e.g., Tanzi and Schuknecht, 2000). Part of the reason for the relatively small role played by the government was that it did not provide insurance to the people to the extent it now does. Only 20% of the labor force in western Europe had some form of pension insurance in 1910, and only 22% had health insurance (vs. 93% and 90% respectively in 1975).

Before World War I, there were a number of reasons why the government played such a small role in social insurance. The prevailing liberal belief in the relentless logic of the market suggested it was unwise for governments to interfere. Intervention, it was thought, would only prolong the pain. The rigidity of the Gold Standard system prevented governments from running large deficits. Last but not least, the poorer sections of society (the workers, the small farmers, and the unemployed) were not organized and had little political voice (e.g., Maier, 1987; Eichengreen, 1996).

World War I and the Great Depression, which followed a decade after, were huge consecutive political and economic shocks, which combined to create an organized demand for insurance and triggered a coordinated response by governments.

Labor was organized by the war. The senseless carnage of a war that left all its main protagonists worse off led many to doubt the caliber and motives of their political leaders and discredited the pre-war free-market consensus. The trenches during the war served as classrooms where the working class absorbed radical ideas. Labor, with its newly found ideas and organization, gave notice even in the 1920s that it would no longer continue unquestioningly to absorb the costs of adjustment to the rigors of the Gold Standard.

The onset of the Depression immensely increased the size of economic adjustments countries would have to undergo to stay on the Gold Standard. Classical liberal economics indicated the cure to falling output was a steep fall in wages. This was simply not acceptable to labor. Faced with increasing resistance from labor, politicians saw little reward in paying a political price to adhere to the Gold Standard. With little thought for the collective consequences, they also started erecting barriers to imports in an attempt to trade their way out of depression. As everyone attempted to beggar their neighbors, trade and capital flows ceased.

Clearly, incumbents were not idle in the policy debates in the 1930s. Equally clearly, many of them welcomed the descent into autarky, for it strengthened their positions. But it would be incorrect to claim that broad policy was shaped primarily, or even largely, by these interests. The Depression had affected too many people for business as usual to prevail. For example, in Sweden, labor and agrarian interests came together in 1932 in what has been termed the "cow trade." Labor accepted higher food prices and price supports in return for stable wages, policies for full employment, and social services. The business interests opposed this coalition at first, but became more accommodating when the party representing labor, the Social Democrats, became stronger in the election of 1936.

Economic policy in the developed democracies was thus broadly a response to the large, across-the-board, adverse shock affecting the uninsured masses. Autarky allowed the governments to implement various insurance schemes that may have been more difficult had the economies been open and the Gold Standard in place. The increase in insurance coverage was significant. Over 56% of the workforce in western Europe was covered by pension insurance by 1935 and 47% had health insurance coverage. Unemployment insurance was introduced for the first time in a number of countries, including the United States, during the Depression.

Incumbents used the protection afforded by autarky to mould policies in their own favor. Thus, Japan, for example, moved from an economy with a flourishing financial market, and a competitive banking system, to an economy with small financial markets and a concentrated banking system. These moves had the support of the government, which felt it could better control resource allocation if funds were channeled largely through the banks. The reversal in openness provided the conditions under which financial markets could be, and indeed were, repressed (see Rajan and Zingales (2003) for a more detailed account).

4.6.2. Why did financial markets take so long to recover?

The disruption to international trade caused by the two wars and the Great Depression was significant. While the average degree of export openness (merchandise exports as a percentage of GDP) was 8.2 in 1913, it was just 5.2 in 1950 (e.g., O'Rourke and Williamson, 1999, p. 30). In contrast to much of the developed world, the United States emerged from World War II with its industries largely intact and highly competitive. Clearly, it had a strong incentive to press for open trade since its markets were likely to expand. Meanwhile, its wartime role as the "Arsenal of Democracy" gave it the political clout to press its agenda. But in return for agreeing to free trade, other developed countries wanted some restrictions on cross-border capital flows.

The rationale was clear. If capital were allowed to flow freely, it would hamper the ability of governments to provide the various kinds of insurance that was increasingly being expected of them by their citizens, especially given the terrible state of post-war government finances. Thus the argument for controlling capital flows and the second-class status accorded to finance in the post-war economic order. As Keynes was one of the architects of the Bretton Woods agreement, which set the stage for the post-war international order. He said (cited in Helleiner, 1994,

p. 164): "Not merely as a feature of the transition but as a permanent arrangement, the plan accords every member government the explicit right to control all capital movements. What used to be heresy is now endorsed as orthodoxy."

This should be contrasted with the general desire of countries after World War I to return to the Gold Standard and thus reduce barriers to capital flow. If openness to trade is, by itself, insufficient to force financial development, then the restrictions on capital movements after WWII can explain why financial markets did not take off even though trade expanded. After all, they recovered rapidly after WWI. Even though the toll taken by the wars was admittedly very different, an important part of the explanation must be that there was no Bretton Woods after World War I endorsing capital controls.

4.6.3. The end of capital controls

The breakdown of the Bretton Woods system (e.g., Eichengreen, 1996, for a lucid exposition of the causes), led to the dismantling of capital controls, and could have been the precipitating factor for financial development across the world. Starting with the Euromarkets, spreading to the United States, and then moving to Europe and Japan, cross-border capital flows went from a trickle to a torrent. Accounts of the process by which this happened suggest that the cross-border flows increased despite, rather than because of, the efforts of domestic interest groups (e.g., Helleiner, 1994). Given the growing volume of trade, it was simply too difficult to control the potential leakage of capital, especially when there were countries abroad where the money could be deposited.

By the end of the 1980s, controls had effectively been removed throughout western Europe, Scandinavia, and Japan. The competition generated by trade and free international capital movements forced a modernization of the financial system and a progressive withdrawal of the State from the economy, through privatization in the industrial and banking sectors. This then would explain the other leg of the reversal. Before we go further, let us take a look at two case studies.

4.7. The case of Japan

Japan, as our data suggest, was making rapid strides to developing a strong financial sector before World War I. Until 1918, there were no restrictions on entry into banking, provided minimum capital requirements were met. There were over 2,000 banks in 1920. The five large Zaibatsu (translated as financial cliques) banks accounted for only 20.5% of the deposits before the war, and there were many small banks. (Aoki et al., 1994; Hoshi and Kashyap, 2001).

As a result of increased competition in the post-World War I years and the Great Tokyo Earthquake in 1923, which caused damage estimated at an incredible 38% of GDP, more and more banks became troubled. This gave the government the excuse to enact regulations promoting mergers in the name of stability. By 1945, there were only 65 banks, and the share of Zaibatsu banks in total deposits had increased to 45.7%. (Aoki et al., 1994).

40   *R.G. Rajan, L. Zingales / Journal of Financial Economics 69 (2003) 5-50*

At the same time as the banking system was becoming more concentrated, the government's control over it was increasing. This became especially pronounced as the government sought to direct funds towards supplying the war against China in 1937. With the Temporary Fund Adjustment Act in 1937 and the Corporate Profits Distribution and Fund Raising Act in 1939, the government, through the Industrial Bank of Japan, assumed control of financing. All security issuances and lending decisions above a certain amount had to be approved by the government, and those that were not related to the war effort were typically not approved. Further Acts simply strengthened the government's control and this culminated in the designated lending system by which each munitions company was designated a major bank which would take care of all its credit needs. By the end of the war, the banking system was not only concentrated, but well and truly under the control of the government.

The accompanying demise of the arm's length financial markets was aided and abetted by the banks. In 1929, 26% of the liability side of large Japanese firm balance sheets consisted of bonds while only 17% was bank debt (see Teranishi, 1994). As bond defaults increased as a result of the earlier crisis and depression, a group of banks together with trust and insurance companies seized on the poor economic conditions to agree in 1931 to make all subsequent bond issues secured in principle. This immediately made it harder for their clients to issue public debt. With the acquiescence of the Ministry of Finance, the agreement was formalized in 1933 through the formation of a Bond Committee. The Committee determined which firms could issue bonds, on what terms, and when. All bonds were required to be collateralized, and banks were to serve as trustees for the collateral in exchange for a substantial fee. Giving banks the responsibility for determining firms' right to access the public bond markets was like giving a fox who resided in a chicken coop the right to determine which chickens could leave. Hoshi and Kashyap (2001) add further support to the claim that this was a cartel by the observation that security houses that were not part of the 1931 agreement started competing fiercely for underwriting business and continued to underwrite unsecured bonds. Thus the market itself did not appear to develop a distaste for unsecured bonds. The obvious outcome was that a flourishing bond market was killed off. By 1936, bonds were down to 14% while bank debt was up to 24% of the liability side. By 1943, 47 percent of liabilities were bank debt while only 6% were bonds.

Japan illustrates yet another point. Entrenched hierarchies have the power to defend themselves. For example, despite their best efforts to break up bank-firm established during the period of militarization, the post-war American occupying forces could not prevent them re-emerging as the Keiretsu or main bank system (e.g., Hoshi and Kashyap (2001), though see Miwa and Ramseyer (2002) who suggest a contrary view that Keiretsus are fiction). Similarly, the Bond Committee, set up ostensibly to improve the quality of bond issuance during the Depression, survived until the 1980s. Even as Japanese industrial firms invaded the rest of the world in the 1970s, their bond markets remained miniscule, and Hitachi, an AA credit, was denied the ability to issue unsecured bonds. It was only in the early 1980s, as Japanese firms decided to borrow abroad in the Euromarkets rather than depend on

R.G. Rajan, L. Zingales / Journal of Financial Economics 69 (2003) 5–50   41

their antiquated financial system that Japanese banks had to loosen their stranglehold. The powers of the bond committee were eventually curtailed, not by a far-seeing government, but by the forces of outside competition.

4.8. Why not the United States?

As with any large sample study, there are exceptions. The United States undertook a variety of market-friendly actions including passing legislation requiring greater disclosure in financial markets, setting up the Securities and Exchange Commission, and passing the Glass Steagall Act, which brought more competition among financial institutions by breaking up the universal banks. Was the United States an exception to the trend at this time?

First, it is possible to overstate the extent to which the legislation was market friendly. The National Recovery Administration, which was set up under the New Deal, sought to fix prices in industry in order to eliminate "ruinous" competition, while Regulation Q attempted to do the same thing in the banking sector. The US government defaulted on the Gold Clause to the detriment of creditors, and the sanctity of contracts (e.g., Kroszner, 1999). Markets and competition were not seriously affected in the long run. This was not for the want of effort by the New Deal politicians. But legislative zeal in the United States was also tempered by checks imposed by the judiciary, a characteristic of Common Law countries (though it was the independent judiciary rather than Common Law that was the source of the check). Roosevelt's primary method of intervention, the National Recovery Administration, was declared unconstitutional by the Supreme Court (Kennedy, 1999, p. 328). When the Supreme Court eventually became more pliant after threats to pack its bench with government supporters, Congress became more nervous about growing executive powers, and growing threats to property, and became the main obstacle to proposed New Deal legislation (Kennedy, 1999, p. 341).

Checks and balances are not sufficient to explain the pro-market legislation. Of course, the legislation was not as pro-market as it is often made out to be. Mahoney (2001) argues that the ostensibly pro-market and pro-competitive Securities Act of 1933 and the Glass Steagall Act, were really protection in disguise for established investment bankers. Various aspects of the Securities Act reduced price competition among investment bankers, while the Glass Steagall Act forced commercial banks out of the underwriting business. Mahoney provides evidence that the Securities Act increased concentration in the underwriting business.

Nevertheless, even if private interests were at work, the United States did not go the way of Japan. In part, the private interests were more fragmented. Investment banks did not see eye to eye with commercial banks, nor did large banks form common cause with small banks. The variety of conflicting private interests and the variety of political support they could count on at both the state and national level, more than any other factor, could have been the reason why outcomes in the United States were not more anti-competitive. There was no way markets could be closed down without hurting some powerful faction in the financial sector.

42 *R.G. Rajan, L. Zingales / Journal of Financial Economics 69 (2003) 5–50*

So this then leaves us with the final question. Why were there so many different groups within the financial sector? Roe (1994) suggests an answer. He claims that there has always been an undercurrent of opposition in the United States to anyone getting overly powerful in the financial sector. Whether it be the setting up of the Federal Reserve to undercut the power of JP Morgan, the Glass Steagall Act to curtail the power of large universal banks, or the refusal of the Federal Reserve to act to save Drexel Burnham, the United States has managed to cut powerful financiers down to size. Perhaps it was its ability to ensure even in normal times that no small group of incumbents ever became really powerful that enabled the United States to pass through crisis relatively unscathed.

4.9. How does structure matter?

Since the work of La Porta et al. (1997, 1998), there has been some debate over why the legal origin of a country appears to matter so much for financial markets. Some suggest it reflects the inherent superiority of Common Law over Civil Law for financial transactions and investor protection. Others argue it matters because it reflects something about a country's culture, religion, or politics (e.g., Acemoglu et al., 2001; Beck et al., 1999; Berglof and Von Thadden, 1999; La Porta et al., 1999; Rajan and Zingales, 1999; Stulz and Williamson, 2001).

Our finding that financial markets in countries with a Civil Law system were not less developed than those in countries with Common Law in 1913 and in 1929 but only after World War II suggests a deeper look at the underlying mechanism for why legal origin seems to matter.

Rajan and Zingales (1999) argue that many complex legal constructs that first emerged in Common Law, such as limited liability, were readily imitated by Civil Law countries. In fact, they argue, when the government has a will, Civil Law countries have a greater ability to translate governmental policy into law because laws emanate from the center rather than evolving through judicial decisions. Private interests therefore have a greater chance of seeing their agenda enacted in a Civil Law country.

One reason is simply that if the governance system is more centralized, it is easier for small private interests to capture it. If, in addition, the legal system is important for validating and enforcing new policy, the Civil Law system is again easier to capture. The focus of influence activity in a Civil Law country only has to be the legislator. By contrast, the judiciary in a Common Law country can restrain a new political climate, and because it is dispersed and subject to local influences, is less easy to capture.

A second reason is that Common Law evolves at the periphery, and innovates around legislative or administrative roadblocks set up by the center. In England, for instance, after the Bubble Act placed constraints on the incorporation of limited liability companies in 1720 (primarily to bolster the position of companies that were already incorporated), Common Law courts continuously evolved their own interpretation of which companies did not contravene the spirit of that law. It was precisely to overcome this ability of the judiciary to defy the will of the center that

Napoleon introduced the Civil Code as a way to prevail over judges still loyal to the *Ancien Regime*.

In summary, in a Civil Law country, it is easier for a small group representing private interests, such as large incumbent industrialists and financiers to influence the implementation of friendly policies. This need not be all bad. When these private interests are aligned with the national interests, good policy can also be implemented quickly. But when interests are misaligned, matters can become much worse. Empirically, this would suggest that Civil Law countries went further in repressing financial markets when borders closed down (explaining the La Porta et al. findings in the mid-1990s), but have also begun developing them again as borders have opened up again in recent years (explaining the convergence seen in the most recent data). In summary, structure might matter, not so much in directly favoring or disfavoring financial development, but in filtering the impact of interest groups and the forces that affect their incentives.

The data seem to support this view. In Table 11 Columns (i) and (ii) regress the change in the stock market capitalization for a country between 1913 and the breakdown of Bretton Woods (1970) against the changes in its per-capita income in constant dollars and an indicator for Civil Law. Both when we compute change as a change in level and as a change in percentage, the coefficient estimate for the Civil Law indicator is strongly negative, suggesting that stock markets in Civil Law countries did indeed fall by more over the period of the reversal. In Columns (iii) and (iv), the dependent variable is the change in stock market capitalization for a country between the beginning of Bretton Woods's breakdown (1970) and the end of our sample period (1999). In this case, the coefficient estimate for the Civil Law indicator is strongly positive, suggesting that stock markets in Civil Law countries did indeed recover by more in recent times.

While certainly not a test, this evidence suggests that structure may have been found to matter for financial development in recent papers because Civil Law systems can have more exaggerated reactions to changes in private interests. A related finding is that a country's cultural heritage plays the strongest role when the country is shielded from foreign competition and private interests can reign unhindered. Stulz and Williamson (2001) find that the correlation between creditor rights and religion weakens when a country is more open to trade. If we compare systems at a time of transition, we come away with the impression that structure has a strong influence on levels of development even though it has more of an influence on rates of change.

4.10. Related literature

Our view that institutional differences between countries serve to modify the impact of private interests offers a different view of convergence across countries than Coffee (2000). In his view, financial development will take place through changes in practices when a constituency emerges that demands it. Much later, the formal legal system will adapt to reflect these demands. Thus he attributes the convergence to Anglo-Saxon norms of corporate governance practices in continental

Table 11
Openness and legal system over time
In the first two columns the dependent variable is the change in the ratio of equity market capitalization to
gross domestic product between 1913 and 1970 (in the first column, it is the absolute change, in the second,
the % change). In the next two columns the dependent variable is the change in the ratio of equity market
capitalization to gross domestic product between 1970 and 1999 (in the third column, it is the absolute
change, in the fourth the % change). In the first two columns the proxy for the change in the demand for
finance is the change in the index of industrialization for that country in that year as computed by Bairoch
(1982) divided by 1000. In the next two columns the proxy for the change in demand for finance is the
change in the logarithm of the per-capita GDP in PPP dollars as reported in the World Development
Indicators. The indicator for Civil Law is one in countries with Civil Law and is zero otherwise. All
regressions include calendar year indicators. The standard errors, which are corrected for possible
clustering of the residual at a country level, are in parentheses. (*) indicates significance at the 10% level,
(**) at the 5% level, (***) at the 1% level.

	Change in stock market capitalization/GDP over the 1913–1970 period		Change in stock market capitalization/GDP over the 1970–1999 period	
	Changes in level	Percent change	Changes in level	Percent change
Change in demand for finance	0.655	−2.270**	−0.398	−3.650
	(0.792)	(1.063)	(1.014)	(3.687)
Civil law indicator	−0.745***	−1.551***	0.762*	3.207**
	(0.165)	(0.221)	(0.393)	(1.428)
R^2	0.57	0.77	0.10	0.16
Observations	16	16	18	18

Europe to the privatization in the 1980s, which created a constituency of minority shareholders. We differ primarily in that we attribute a strong role to private interests (not just for, but also against, development) and potentially, a role for structure in modifying the influence of private interests.

Before concluding this section, we must note two other explanations for the reversals. Roe (1999) suggests that corporations in continental Europe became more closely held because of the potential for higher agency costs there as a result of pro-labor legislation passed in the 1920s and 1930s. This diminished the size of public markets. While we do believe that the shrinkage of public equity markets and the passage of pro-labor legislation were coincident in some countries, his theory does not account for the greater government intervention and cartelization witnessed in many countries, or for the demise of corporate bond markets in some.

Pagano and Volpin (2000) develop a model in which entrepreneurs, who have already raised finance, want low investor protection (so as to indulge in private benefits) and get the support of workers by promising them high employment protection. This model of incumbent interests (entrepreneurs who already have finance) is similar to ours. It suggests a different explanation for the correlation Roe finds by saying that incumbent industrialists bribed workers with pro-worker legislation to go along with anti-finance legislation. Our emphasis on openness as a modifying influence is different, and it helps us explain both pro-market and anti-market legislation.

R.G. Rajan, L. Zingales / Journal of Financial Economics 69 (2003) 5–50   45

5. Conclusion

We see four contributions of this work. The first is to show the reversal in financial markets, a finding inconsistent with pure structural theories of financial market development. The second is to add a new fact, which is that trade openness is correlated with financial market development, especially when cross-border capital flows are free. The third is to argue that these findings are consistent with interest group politics being an important factor in financial development across countries. The last is to suggest that a county's institutions might slow or speed-up interest group activities. This might indicate that institutions matter, though the way they matter might primarily be in tempering interest group activities.

If our understanding of the impediments to financial development is correct, then it suggests that the exhortations by international development institutions to countries to develop institutions to aid economic growth are not be enough. It is not that the cognoscenti in developing countries are not aware that the country needs good institutions, it is simply that too many interests will lose out if the institutions are developed (e.g., Olson, 1982). More emphasis needs to be placed on establishing political pre-conditions for institutions.

More thought has to be given then to how interest groups can be reined in. Openness clearly will help. Policies that tend to promote efficient, competitive industries rather than inefficient, rent-seeking ones will also tend to pave the way for institutional development, as will public awareness of the hidden costs of policies that ostensibly promote economic stability. Finally, insurance schemes that will soften the impact of economic adversity on individuals will help ward off an anti-market reaction. How such policies fit together clearly requires more thought and suggests ample scope for further research. In further work, Rajan and Zingales (2003) provide a preliminary effort.

Appendix A. Important notes on data collection

A.1. Historical differences in reporting data

A formidable challenge, specific to the historical nature of our analysis, is the difficulty in obtaining reliable sources for historical information about financial markets. Primary sources are often lost or inaccessible, while secondary sources are contradictory or repeat uncritically the same primary sources. To further complicate our task, the type of information statisticians and governing bodies of stock exchanges were interested in at the beginning of the twentieth century seems quite different from the ones we are interested in today (this seems a topic worthy of a separate study). We discuss some of these differences because they help shed some light on the different perceptions of the nature and role of financial instruments at that time.

A number that is often reported is the total nominal value of securities outstanding in a country. This joins together not only stocks and corporate bonds, but also Government bonds, making the number difficult to interpret. The clubbing of information on corporate bonds and stocks, which is pervasive even in the United Kingdom, probably the most sophisticated financial market at that time, reflects the similarity of these two instruments at that time. The use of preferred stock paying a fixed dividend was widespread. Also, common stock paid very high dividends, making them more similar to bonds. One consequence of the high dividend payout ratio was that most stocks traded fairly closely to their nominal value. In fact, stock prices in many countries were quoted as a percentage of their nominal value. Thus, even from an investor's point of view, bonds and stocks were perceived as very close substitutes.

A second problem is that the official statistics at the beginning of the twentieth century report the total universe of corporations existing at that time, rather then the subset of those that are publicly traded. To make the numbers more comparable across time, we classify companies as publicly traded only if the firm is quoted during the year. Even with this requirement, we may still have very infrequently traded stock.

A final problem comes from the existence of regional exchanges. At the beginning of the century, not only was trading more fragmented across exchanges, but so was listing. For example, the Banco do Brazil is listed in the Rio Stock Exchange but not in San Paulo. Companies listed only in Osaka represent a considerable portion of the total companies listed in Japan. Most extreme is Germany, probably as a consequence of the delayed political reunification. In 1913 Germany had nine major stock exchanges and Berlin represented only about 50% of the total capitalization.

Data for regional (or secondary) stock exchanges are especially challenging. Since many have disappeared or have been absorbed by the main exchange, they tend not to be well documented. We try, as best as possible, to reconstruct a measure that includes all the major stock exchanges, eliminating double listing. When this is not possible for the date of interest, we compute the ratio of the capitalization of the secondary exchanges to main exchange at the earliest date available and then use this ratio to extrapolate backwards the value of these exchanges. Since the importance of regional exchanges has gone down over time, this procedure clearly biases downwards the estimate of the total stock market capitalization in countries with fragmented stock markets. This should be kept in mind in the analysis.

A.2. Stock market capitalization and number of companies listed

Our starting point was the official publication of the stock exchanges as well as those of the Federation Internationale des Bourses Valeurs (FIBV). These provide extensive information only starting in 1980. Official publications of individual stock exchanges often go back only to WWII. When these are not available, we use information contained in private guides to stock exchanges. Only for Japan and the United States did we find official publications before WWII.

To assess the importance of the equity market in 1913 we rely on two approaches. Whenever possible we secure a copy of a stock exchange handbook in 1913 (or the

R.G. Rajan, L. Zingales / Journal of Financial Economics 69 (2003) 5–50   47

closest year before 1913). Using the handbook we identify the number of domestic companies listed, the number of shares of each company, and the price per share. We then compute the total stock market capitalization as the sum of the product of price times the number of shares. We were able to do this for Australia, Brazil, Canada, Cuba, Denmark, Germany, Italy, Netherlands, Russia, Sweden, Switzerland, the United Kingdom, and the United States.

A second source was various issues of the Bulletin of the International Institute of Statistics (IIS). Starting in the late nineteenth century, statisticians from all over the world met every year for a conference. This association formed a special group to compute the importance of security markets in different countries. Unfortunately, many of the reports club together stocks and bonds but we do obtain some disaggregate information for some countries.

A.3. Data on equity issues

Data on equity issues are relatively easier to get for the pre-WWII period than for the period immediately after the war. For example, the *League of Nations* statistics include this information, even though it is not contained in more modern publications like the *United Nations Statistics* or the *Financial Statistics of the International Monetary Fund*. This could reflect the greater importance attributed to this information before World War II. When not available from official statistics, we gather this information from financial newspapers of that time such as the *Economist, Commercial and Financial Chronicle, Deutsche Oekonomiste*, etc.

A.4. Data on deposits and national accounts data

Data on deposits, national income, and gross fixed-capital formation come from Mitchell (various issues). Mitchell's data are available until the mid-1990s. We extrapolate this to 1999 for deposits by using the growth rate of deposits from the IMF's International Financial Statistics. For national accounts, we use the data from the NBER website whenever available. Post WWII national accounts data come from the IMF's International Financial Statistics. We indicate whenever data come from a different source. A comprehensive data appendix is available on request.

References

Acemoglu, D., Johnson, S., Robinson, J., 2001. The colonial origins of comparative development: an empirical study. American Economic Review 91, 1369–1401.

Aoki, M., Patrick, H., Sheard, P., 1994. The Japanese main bank system: introductory overview. In: Aoki, M., Patrick, H. (Eds.), The Japanese Main Bank System: Its Relevance for Developing and Transferring Economies. Oxford University Press, New York, pp. 3–50.

Bairoch, P., 1982. International industrialization levels from 1750 to 1980. Journal of European Economic History 11, 269–334.

Bairoch, P., 1989. European trade policy, 1815–1914. In: Mathias, P., Pollard, S. (Eds.), The Cambridge Economic History of Europe, Vol. VIII. Cambridge University Press, Cambridge, England.

Bebchuk, L., Roe, M., 1999. A theory of path dependence in corporate ownership and governance. Stanford Law Review 52, 127–170.

Beck, T., Demirguc-Kunt, A., Levine, R., 1999. A new database on financial development and structure. Unpublished Working Paper 2784. The World Bank, Washington.

Becker, G., 1983. A theory of the competition among pressure groups for political influence. The Quarterly Journal of Economics 98, 371–400.

Bencivenga, V., Smith, B., 1991. Financial intermediation and endogenous growth. Review of Economic Studies 58, 195–209.

Berglof, E., Von Thadden, E.L., 1999. The changing corporate governance paradigm: implications for transition and developing countries. Unpublished working paper. Stockholm School of Economics, Stockholm, Sweden.

Cameron, R., 1961. France and the Economic Development of Europe, 1800–1914. Princeton University Press, Princeton, NJ.

Choe, H., Masulis, R., Nanda, V., 1993. Common stock offerings across the business cycle: theory and evidence. Journal of Empirical Finance 1, 3–31.

Coffee, J., 2000. Convergence and its critics: what are the preconditions to the separation of ownership and control? Unpublished working paper, Columbia University, New York.

Demirguc-Kunt, A., Maksimovic, V., 1998. Law, finance, and firm growth. Journal of Finance 53, 2107–2138.

Djankov, S., La Porta, R., Lopez-de-Silanes, F., Shleifer, A., 2002. The regulation of entry. Quarterly Journal of Economics 117, 1–37.

Eichengreen, B., 1996. Globalizing Capital: A history of the international monetary system. Princeton University Press, Princeton, NJ.

Frankel, J.A., Romer, D., 1999. Does trade cause growth? American Economic Review 89, 379–399.

Gourevitch, P., 1986. Politics in Hard Times: Comparative Responses to International Economic Crises. Cornell University Press, Ithaca, NY.

Greenwood, J., Jovanovic, B., 1990. Financial development, growth, and the distribution of income. Journal of Political Economy 98, 1076–1107.

Guiso, L., Sapienza, P., Zingales, L., 2000. The role of social capital in financial development. Unpublished working paper 7563, NBER, Cambridge, MA.

Haber, S., 1997. Financial markets and industrial development. A comparative study of government regulation, financial innovation, and industrial structure in Brazil and Mexico, 1840–1930. In: Haber, S. (Ed.), How Latin America Fell Behind: Essays on the Economic Histories of Brazil and Mexico. Stanford University Press, Stanford, CA, pp. 1800–1914.

Helleiner, E., 1994. From Bretton Woods to global finance: a world turned upside down. In: Stubbs, R., Underhill, G. (Eds.), Political Economy and the Changing Global Order. Oxford University Press, Toronto, pp. 244.

Hellwig, M., 2000. On the economics and politics of corporate finance and corporate control. In: Vives, X. (Ed.), Corporate Governance: Theoretical and Empirical Perspectives. Cambridge University Press, Cambridge, England, pp. 95–136.

Henry, P.B., 2000. Stock market liberalization, economic reform, and emerging market equity prices. Journal of Finance 55, 529–564.

Holmen, M., Hogfeldt, P., 2000. A law and finance analysis of initial public offerings. Unpublished working paper, University of Chicago.

Hoshi, T., Kashyap, A., 2001. Corporate Finance and Government in Japan. M.I.T. Press, Cambridge, MA.

Jayaratne, J., Strahan, P.E., 1996. The finance-growth nexus: evidence from bank branch deregulation. Quarterly Journal of Economics 111, 639–670.

Jensen, M., 1991. Corporate control and the politics of finance. Continental Bank Journal of Applied Corporate Finance 4, 13–33.

Johnson, S., McMillan, J., Woodruff, C., 2000. Courts and relational contracts. Unpublished working paper, M.I.T, Cambridge, MA.

Katzenstein, P., 1985. Small States in World Markets: Industrial Policy in Europe. Cornell University Press, Ithaca, NY.

Kennedy, D., 1999. Freedom from fear: The American people in depression and war, 1929–1945. In: Oxford History of the United States. Oxford University Press, New York.

Kennedy, W., 1989. Industrial Structure, Capital Markets, and the Origins of British Economic Decline. Cambridge University Press, Cambridge, England.

King, R., Levine, R., 1993. Finance and growth: schumpeter might be right. The Quarterly Journal of Economics 108, 681–737.

Kroszner, R., 1999. Is it better to forgive than to receive? Evidence from the abrogation of gold indexation clauses in long-term debt during the Great Depression, Unpublished working paper. The University of Chicago, Chicago.

Kroszner, R., Strahan, P., 1999. What drives deregulation? Economics and politics of the relaxation of bank branching restrictions. Quarterly Journal of Economics 114, 1437–1467.

La Porta, R., Lopez-de-Silanes, F., Shleifer, A., Vishny, R., 1997. The legal determinants of external finance. Journal of Finance 52, 1131–1150.

La Porta, R., Lopez-de-Silanes, F., Shleifer, A., Vishny, R., 1998. Law and finance. Journal of Political Economy 106, 1113–1155.

La Porta, R., Lopez-de-Silanes, F., Shleifer, A., Vishny, R., 1999a. The quality of government. Journal of Law, Economics, and Organization 15, 222–279.

La Porta, R., Lopez-de-Silanes, F., Shleifer, A., Vishny, R., 1999b. Investor protection: origins, consequences, and reform. Unpublished Working Paper 7428, NBER, Cambridge, MA.

Loriaux, M., 1997. Capital Ungoverned. Cornell University Press, Ithaca, NY.

Mahoney, P. G., 2001. The political economy of the Securities Act of 1933. Journal of Legal Studies 30.

Maier, C., 1987. In Search of Stability. Cambridge University Press, Cambridge, England.

Mitchell, B., 1995. International Historical Statistics. Stockton Press, London.

Miwa, Y., Ramseyer, J.M., 2002. The myth of the main bank: Japan and comparative corporate governance. Law and Social Inquiry 27, 401–424.

Morck, R., Strangeland, D., Yeung, B., 2000. Inherited wealth, corporate control, and economic growth: the canadian disease? In: Morck, R.K. (Ed.), Concentrated Capital Ownership. University of Chicago Press, Chicago.

Olson, M., 1965. The Logic of Collective Action. Harvard University Press, Cambridge, MA.

Olson, M., 1982. The Rise and Decline of Nations: Economic growth, Stagflation, and Social Rigidities. Yale University Press, New Haven.

O'Rourke, K., Williamson, J., 1999. Globalization and History: The Evolution of a Nineteenth Century Atlantic Economy. MIT. Press, Cambridge, MA.

Pagano, M., Volpin, P., 2000. The political economy of corporate governance. Unpublished working paper, Harvard University, Cambridge, MA.

Petersen, M., Rajan, R., 1995. The effect of credit market competition on lending relationships. Quarterly Journal of Economics 110, 407–443.

Rajan, R., Zingales, L., 1998a. Financial dependence and growth. The American Economic Review 88, 559–586.

Rajan, R., Zingales, L., 1998b. Which capitalism? Lessons from the East Asia crisis. Journal of Applied Corporate Finance 11, 40–48.

Rajan, R., Zingales, L., 1999. The politics of financial development. Unpublished working paper, University of Chicago, Chicago.

Rajan, R., Zingales, L., 2003. Saving Capitalism from the Capitalists. Crown Business Division of Random House, New York.

Roe, M., 1994. Strong Managers and Weak Owners: The Political Roots of American Corporate Finance. Princeton University Press, Princeton, NJ.

Roe, M., 1999. Political preconditions to separating ownership from corporate control. Unpublished working paper, Columbia Law School, New York.

Rogowski, R., 1989. Commerce and Coalitions: How Trade Affects Domestic Political Arrangements. Princeton University Press, Princeton, NJ.

Rose, N., 1987. Labor rent sharing and regulation: evidence from the trucking industry. Journal of Political Economy 95, 1146–1178.

Rosenbluth, F., 1989. Financial Politics in Contemporary Japan. Cornell University Press, Ithaca, NY.

Salinger, M., 1984. Tobin's q, unionization, and the concentration-profits relationship. The Rand Journal of Economics 15, 159–170.

Simon, C., 1989. The effect of the 1933 securities act on investor information and the performance of new issues. American Economic Review 79, 295–318.

Stigler, G., 1971. The theory of economic regulation. Bell Journal of Economics and Management Science 2, 3–21.

Stulz, R., Williamson, R., 2001. Culture, openness, and finance. Unpublished Working Paper 8222, NBER, Cambridge, MA.

Svaleryd, H., Vlachos, J., 2002. Market for risk and openness to trade: how are they related? Journal of International Economics 57, 369–395.

Sylla, R., Smith, G., 1995. Information and capital market regulation in Anglo-American finance. In: Bordo, M., Sylla, R. (Eds.), Anglo-American Financial Systems: Institutions and Markets in the Twentieth Century. Irwin Publishers, Burr Ridge, IL.

Tanzi, V., Schuknecht, L., 2000. Public Spending in the twentieth century: a global perspective. Cambridge University Press, Cambridge, England.

Taylor, A., 1998. Argentina and the world capital market: saving, investment, and international capital mobility in the Twentieth Century. Development and Economics 57, 147–184.

Teranishi, J., 1994. Loan syndication in war-time Japan and the origins of the main bank system. In: Aoki, M., Patrick, H. (Eds.), The Japanese Main Bank System: Its Relevance for Developing and Transferring Economies. Oxford University Press, New York.

Tilly, R., 1992. An overview of the role of large German banks up to 1914. In: Cassis, Y. (Ed.), Finance and Financiers in European History 1880–1960. Cambridge University Press, Cambridge, England.

Weber, K., Davis, G., 2000. The global spread of stock exchanges 1980–1998. Unpublished working paper, University of Michigan.

Wei, S., 2000. Natural openness and good government. Unpublished Working Paper 7765, NBER, Cambridge, MA.

[4]

THE COMMON LAW AND ECONOMIC GROWTH: HAYEK MIGHT BE RIGHT

*PAUL G. MAHONEY**

ABSTRACT

Recent finance scholarship finds that countries with legal systems based on the common law have more developed financial markets than civil-law countries. The present paper argues that finance is not the sole, or principal, channel through which legal origin affects growth. Instead, following Hayek, I focus on the common law's association with limited government. I present evidence that common-law countries experienced faster economic growth than civil-law countries during the period 1960–92 and then present instrumental variables results that suggest that the common law produces faster growth through greater security of property and contract rights.

> "[T]he ideal of individual liberty seems to have flourished chiefly among people where, at least for long periods, judge-made law predominated." [FRIEDRICH A. HAYEK, Law, Legislation and Liberty: A New Statement of the Liberal Principles of Justice and Political Economy 94 (1973)]

I. INTRODUCTION

RECENTLY, financial economists have produced evidence that financial markets contribute to economic growth and legal institutions contribute to the growth of financial markets. Robert King and Ross Levine demonstrate that the average rate of increase in per capita gross domestic product (GDP) is greater in countries with more developed financial markets.[1] Rafael La Porta and coauthors show that legal rules protecting creditors and minority shareholders are an important determinant of the cost of external capital.[2] What is also interesting, they find that countries whose legal systems are

* University of Virginia School of Law. I thank Kevin Davis, Ronald Gilson, Barry Ickes, Ross Levine, Julia Mahoney, Katharina Pistor, Andrei Shleifer, Todd Zywicki, two anonymous referees, the editor, Eric Posner, and seminar and conference participants at George Mason University, the University of Michigan, the University of Virginia, the American Law and Economics Association 2000 annual meeting, and the Latin American and Caribbean Law and Economics Association 2000 annual meeting. I am also grateful to Ross Levine for access to some of the data used in the paper.

[1] See Robert G. King & Ross Levine, Finance and Growth: Schumpeter Might Be Right, 108 Q. J. Econ. 717 (1993).

[2] See Rafael La Porta *et al.*, Law and Finance, 106 J. Pol. Econ. 1113 (1998); Rafael La Porta *et al.*, Legal Determinants of External Finance, 52 J. Fin. 1131 (1997).

[*Journal of Legal Studies*, vol. XXX (June 2001)]

derived from the common-law tradition provide superior investor protections on average, particularly in comparison to the French civil-law tradition.

Building on these results, Levine, Norman Loayza, and Thorsten Beck treat legal origin as an instrumental variable for financial development.[3] Legal origin is well suited to the purpose. It is largely exogenous, as most countries obtained their legal systems through colonization or conquest. It also correlates strongly with policies (such as creditor and minority shareholder protections) that on the basis of theory and empirical results should lead to greater financial market development. The principal drawback of the analysis is the lack of a theoretical reason to expect legal origin to be especially relevant to investor protection. Indeed, because corporate and bankruptcy law are generally codified in both common- and civil-law countries, differences in those areas should be small compared to differences in other commercial law fields.

The present paper, by contrast, argues that legal origin does not affect economic growth solely, or even principally, through its effect on financial markets. The major families of legal systems were created as a consequence of debates about government structure, not merely about the rules that should govern particular transactions. A country's legal system accordingly reflects, albeit remotely and indirectly, a set of prior choices about the role of the state and the private sector in responding to change.

Friedrich Hayek provides the most prominent discussion in the economics literature of differences between legal families.[4] He argues vigorously that the English legal tradition (the common law) is superior to the French (the civil law), not because of substantive differences in legal rules, but because of differing assumptions about the roles of the individual and the state. In general, Hayek believed that the common law was associated with fewer government restrictions on economic and other liberties. More recently, La Porta and coauthors revived this argument, positing that "[a] civil legal tradition . . . can be taken as a proxy for an intent to build institutions to further the power of the State. . . . A common law tradition . . . can be taken as a proxy for the intent to limit rather than strengthen the State."[5]

These views are correct as a matter of legal history. Although legal systems are most often acquired involuntarily, they were an object of conscious choice in England and France. English common law developed as it did because landed aristocrats and merchants wanted a system of law that would provide strong protections for property and contract rights and limit the Crown's ability to interfere in markets. French civil law, by contrast, developed as it

---

[3] See Ross Levine, Law, Finance, and Economic Growth, 8 J. Fin. Intermediation 8 (1999); Ross Levine, Norman Loayza, & Thorsten Beck, Financial Intermediation and Growth: Causality and Causes, 46 J. Monetary Econ. 31 (2000).

[4] See Friedrich A. Hayek, The Constitution of Liberty (1960); Friedrich A. Hayek, Law, Legislation and Liberty: A New Statement of the Liberal Principles of Justice and Political Economy (1973).

[5] See La Porta *et al.*, The Quality of Government, 15 J. L. Econ. & Org. 222, 232 (1999).

did because the revolutionary generation, and Napoleon after it, wished to use state power to alter property rights and attempted to ensure that judges could not interfere. Thus, quite apart from the substance of legal rules, there is a sharp difference between the ideologies underlying common and civil law, with the latter notably more comfortable with a centralized and activist government.[6]

The more complex question is whether these differences in origin and ideology translate into institutional differences that could affect economic outcomes today. We are far removed from seventeenth-century England and eighteenth-century France, and most countries did not choose a legal family. Moreover, civil law has not hindered much of continental Europe from developing highly successful economies, and the common law has not guaranteed economic growth and the security of property rights in every former English colony.

Nevertheless, there is evidence that legal origin explains part of the cross-sectional variation in various measures of government intervention, government size, and public sector efficiency.[7] I attempt to tie that observation in with the law and finance results in two ways. First, I discuss in detail the historical origins of the common and civil law and show that they reflect different views about the relative role of the private sector and the state. Second, I note that there are structural differences between common- and civil-law systems, most notably the greater degree of judicial independence in the former and the lower level of scrutiny of executive action in the latter, that provide governments more scope to alter property and contract rights in civil-law countries. Thus, while the explanation does not turn narrowly on the substance of specific investor protection rules, neither does it rely solely on different "cultural" features of common and civil law.

I then report results of cross-country regression analyses for a large set of nonsocialist countries showing an association between the common law and higher rates of real per capita GDP growth. I eliminate socialist countries from the sample in order to focus specifically on differences between common and civil law. Finally, I test the idea that the institutional features of the common law I have identified are an important avenue through which legal origin affects growth. I use legal origin as an instrument for variables measuring the quality of the judiciary and the security of property and contract rights.

Section II provides theoretical background by drawing a link between the role of the judiciary and economic growth. Section III draws on the history of the common- and civil-law traditions to show that the two differ sharply

---

[6] See John Henry Merryman, The Civil Law Tradition: An Introduction to the Legal Systems of Western Europe and Latin America 18 (2d ed. 1985) (describing "[g]lorification of the state" as a central element in the civil-law tradition).

[7] See La Porta *et al.*, *supra* note 5.

in attitudes toward the judicial role and notes ongoing institutional effects. Section IV reports the results of cross-country growth regressions. Section V provides additional evidence that the association between the common law and growth is a consequence of greater judicial protection of property and contract rights from executive interference, and Section VI concludes.

II. THEORETICAL BACKGROUND

Why should legal origin affect economic growth? One possibility is that the average quality of legal rules varies by origin. The finance literature focuses on the association between the common law and superior rules of investor protection. Nevertheless, it is difficult to make out a strong case for the superiority of the rules produced by the common law or the civil law across the board. Although there are substantive differences, each performs well on the most important measures, providing for enforcement of property and contract rights and requiring compensation for certain wrongful (tortious) acts. The creation of a system of enforceable property rights is one of the most important institutional prerequisites to economic growth.[8] The substantive rules of common and civil law provide redress for private actors' interference in property or contracts. One might therefore think that the results obtained by La Porta and coauthors tell us nothing systematic about legal origin—the common law happened, by chance, to produce good corporate governance rules, and good corporate governance rules are especially important for growth.

Some scholars argue that the common law's adversarial adjudication process tends to result in the survival of efficient and the demise of inefficient rules.[9] The unspoken implication is that statutory law is generally less efficient than judge-made law. More recently, however, these claims have come under sustained attack. Legislatures have incentives to create efficient and not merely redistributive rules.[10] Courts, moreover, can and do promote wealth-destroying, rent-seeking litigation, a fact that prompts Gordon Tullock to argue in favor of civil-law codification.[11]

Another possibility is that the average quality of rules is similar, but the common law provides greater stability and predictability. The common-law tradition includes two features—respect for precedent and the power of an appellate court to reverse the legal conclusions of a lower court—that should

---

[8] See Douglass Cecil North, Structure and Change in Economic History (1981).

[9] See, for example, Richard A. Posner, Economic Analysis of Law 399–427 (2d ed. 1977); George L. Priest & Benjamin Klein, The Selection of Disputes for Litigation, 13 J. Legal Stud. 1 (1984); George L. Priest, The Common Law Process and the Selection of Efficient Rules, 6 J. Legal Stud. 65 (1977); Paul H. Rubin, Why Is the Common Law Efficient? 6 J. Legal Stud. 51 (1977).

[10] See Jürgen G. Backhaus, Efficient Statute Law, in 2 The New Palgrave Dictionary of Economics and the Law (Peter Newman ed. 1997).

[11] See Gordon Tullock, The Case against the Common Law (1997).

result in more predictable outcomes.[12] These features are nominally lacking in the civil law. Only the code itself—not prior judicial decisions or the pronouncement of a superior tribunal—counts as binding law in the civil-law tradition. Legislatures, unlike common-law courts, are not bound by precedent. The differences are not, however, as sharp in practice as in theory. Civil-law courts in fact consult precedents and the decisions of higher courts.

A final possibility is that the economic significance of the distinction between the common and civil law derives principally from their distinct ideological and constitutional content, not in their substantive rules. As I show below, the common law is historically connected to strong protection for property rights against state action, whereas the civil law is connected to a strong and less constrained central government. The distinction not only is ideological, however, but leads to an important structural difference—the role of the judiciary. In the common-law system, the judge is an independent policy maker occupying a high-status office, whereas in the civil-law system, the judge is a (relatively) low-status civil servant without independent authority to create legal rules.

This difference in the judicial role fragments power more in a common-law system than in a civil-law system. A recent literature focuses on self-enforcing limits on governmental power as a critical feature of a stable and prosperous state.[13] One important form of self-enforcing limitations consists of the fragmentation of governmental power. Fragmentation limits the ability of government actors to grant, and therefore of interest groups to obtain, rents because it is more difficult to coordinate the decisions and actions of multiple government actors.[14] Federalism, or the vertical dispersion of governmental authority among different levels, is an example. Another is the horizontal separation of legislative, executive, and judicial powers. Recent theoretical and empirical scholarship shows that the horizontal dispersion of power produces less redistribution.[15] The fundamental structural distinction between the common law and civil law lies in the judiciary's greater power to act as a check on executive and legislative action in a common-law system. Thus, although both the common and civil law provide strong protections for property and contract rights against other private actors, those rights may be more secure against the government itself in a common-law system.

---

[12] See Henry G. Manne, The Judiciary and Free Markets, 21 Harv. J. L. & Pub. Pol. 11 (1997).

[13] See, for example, Barry R. Weingast, The Political Foundations of Democracy and the Rule of Law, 91 Am. Pol. Sci. Rev. 245 (1997); Barry R. Weingast, The Economic Role of Political Institutions: Market-Preserving Federalism and Economic Development, 11 J. L. Econ. & Org. 1 (1995); Barry R. Weingast, Constitutions as Governance Structures: The Political Foundations of Secure Markets, 149 J. Inst. & Theoretical Econ. 286 (1993).

[14] See Weingast, Constitutions as Governance Structures, *supra* note 13; Thorsten Persson, Gerard Roland, & Guido Tabellini, Comparative Politics and Public Finance, 108 J. Pol. Econ. 1121 (2000).

[15] See Persson, Roland, & Tabellini, *supra* note 14.

THE JOURNAL OF LEGAL STUDIES

III.   Ideological and Constitutional Distinctions

A.   *Individual versus Collective Liberty*

The substantive rules of most common-law and civil-law jurisdictions evolved from a combination of Roman law concepts and local practices and share many substantive traits. The common law and civil law also played important roles in the creation of the modern English and French constitutional arrangements. Those roles were sharply divergent, however, and as a consequence each system has an ideological content distinct from the substance of particular legal rules.

England's constitutional structure, including the role of the judiciary, took its modern shape as a result of conflicts between Parliament and the Crown in the seventeenth century. During that period, the common law became strongly associated with the idea of economic freedom and, more generally, the subject's liberty from arbitrary action by the Crown. While that association came about partly by chance—because judges opposed the Crown and sided with Parliament—it had substantial consequences for the future role of the judiciary.

Over the course of several centuries, England's large landowners pried their land loose from the feudal system and became in practice owners rather than tenants of the king. Because landowners served as local justices of the peace and the landowning nobility as judges of last resort, the judges unsurprisingly developed legal rules that treated them as owners with substantial rights. The common law they created was principally a law of property. Thus the first of Sir Edward Coke's *Institutes of the Laws of England* is an extensive treatise on the law of real property, structured as a commentary on Littleton's earlier treatise that itself is devoted entirely to property law.[16] William Blackstone describes the Court of Common Pleas, which resolved disputes between subjects, as "the grand tribunal for disputes of property."[17]

During the seventeenth century, however, the Stuart kings attempted to reassert feudal prerogatives as a means of raising revenue.[18] The Crown responded to a budgetary crisis by coercing merchants to grant it loans, using claims of feudal rights to appropriate land and goods, and selling monopoly rights. Disputes over the security of property and executive intervention in

---

[16] See Sir Edward Coke, The First Part of the Institutes of the Laws of England (1979) (1628). See also Thomas Littleton, Tenures in English (1903) (1481).

[17] See William Blackstone, 1 Commentaries on the Laws of England 22 (1765). David Hume sounds a similar note when he defines a judge as one "who in all disputed cases can fix by his opinion the possession or property of any thing." See David Hume, A Treatise of Human Nature 60 (1969).

[18] See Douglass C. North & Barry R. Weingast, Constitutions and Commitment: The Evolution of Institutions Governing Public Choice in Seventeenth-Century England, 49 J. Econ. Hist. 803 (1989).

the economy played a central role in both the English Civil War and the Glorious Revolution.

Indeed, as Richard Pipes argues, the equation of good government with secure property rights reached a high-water mark in English seventeenth-century political thought.[19] Commentators such as James Harrington, Henry Neville, and John Locke described the foremost function of government as the protection of property.[20] They also championed the concept of the rule of law as a superior organizational principle to royal absolutism.

In the dispute between property owners and the Crown, the common-law courts and Parliament took the side of economic freedom and opposed the Crown. For example, in the *Case of Monopolies*, the Court of King's Bench decided that the king's sale of monopoly rights violated the common law.[21] This decision and others challenging the king's right to alter property rights drew the courts, led by Chief Justice Coke, into confrontation with James I, who insisted that the unconstrained royal power trumped the common law. Coke's insistence that the common law bound even the king led James I to dismiss him and like-minded judges. Thus Coke, his successor Matthew Hale, and other common-law judges came to stand for the protection of the rule of law and economic rights against royal power.

Unable to control the ordinary courts, the Stuarts brought politically sensitive cases in a separate body of prerogative courts, such as the Star Chamber, that were under the Crown's direct control and could be counted on to uphold royal authority. After Parliament prevailed in the Civil War, it abolished the prerogative courts. It also rewarded common-law judges with tenure during good behavior and a salary sufficient to make the potential loss of office a substantial disincentive to corruption.[22]

The French experience was very different. Judges were villains, not heroes, in French constitutional development. While security of economic rights was the motivating force in the development of English common law, security of executive power from judicial interference was the motivating force in the post-Revolution legal developments that culminated in the *Code Napoleon*.

The highest courts in pre-Revolutionary France, the *parlements*, were very different from the common-law courts in England. They were part court, part legislature, and part administrative agency. They decided cases, promulgated

[19] See Richard Pipes, Property and Freedom 30–38 (1999).

[20] See James Harrington, The Commonwealth of Oceana (1992) (1656); Henry Neville, Plato Redivivus (1681); John Locke, Two Treatises of Government (1988) (1690).

[21] See Darcy v. Allen (The Case of Monopolies), 11 Co. Rep. 84b, 77 Eng. Rep. 1260 (1603). Coke did not publish the case report until 1615, and he may have embellished it to make a stronger statement against royal power than he had in fact done in 1603. See Jacob Corre, The Argument, Decision and Reports of *Darcy v. Allen*, 45 Emory L. Rev. 1261 (1996). This would not be surprising, as Coke's resistance to James I grew during the 1610s.

[22] See Christopher Hill, The Century of Revolution, 1603–1714 (2d ed. 1980).

regulations, and had partial veto power over royal legislation. As a practical matter, judicial offices were salable and inheritable. The purchase of a judge-ship or other royal office automatically conveyed noble status and qualified the purchaser and his descendants for entry into the *parlements*.[23] The return on the investment was straightforward; in addition to obtaining prestige and various exemptions from taxation that accompanied noble status, judges en-forced the rigidly controlled system of guilds and monopolies that charac-terized Bourbon France.[24]

Like the Stuarts in seventeenth-century England, the Bourbons faced a fiscal crisis in eighteenth-century France. Having sold monopoly rights over nearly every trade possible and raised taxes on the peasantry to levels that could not easily be sustained, continuance of royal consumption and war making required new sources of revenue. Louis XV's and Louis XVI's min-isters attempted to address the situation by increasing the role of royal ad-ministrators, the *intendents*, in the profitable business of enforcing guild and monopoly rights at the expense of the *parlements*. This was partly successful, judging from the fact that the prices of judicial offices declined on average throughout most of the century.[25] The Crown also attempted to increase the tax base by eliminating some aristocratic privileges. The *parlements*, not surprisingly, strongly resisted these strategies, and the resulting conflict be-tween king and *parlements* helped ignite the Revolution.

A central goal of post-Revolution legal reform, then, was to prevent a return of "government by judges."[26] A law of 1790 forbade the judiciary to review any act of the executive.[27] The *parlements* themselves were shortly thereafter abolished and replaced with courts of drastically reduced authority. The Civil Code was accordingly much more than a simplification and cod-ification of legal rules. As the code's principal drafter explained, it was also the expression of an "overriding desire to sacrifice all rights to political ends and no longer consider anything but the mysterious and variable interests of the State."[28] This assertion of the primacy of politics over law later dovetailed nicely with Napoleon's goal of centralizing power in the executive.

The English experience was that dispersion of authority to judges helped to secure desirable political and economic outcomes. The French experience

[23] See Bailey Stone, The French Parlements and the Crisis of the Old Regime (1986).

[24] See Robert B. Ekelund, Jr., & Robert D. Tollison, Politicized Economies: Monarchy, Monopoly, and Mercantilism (Texas A&M Econ. Ser. 14, 1997).

[25] See Stone, *supra* note 23, at 56–58.

[26] See Merryman, *supra* note 6, at 28–29.

[27] See L. Neville Brown, John S. Bell, & Jean-Michel Galabert, French Administrative Law 46 (5th ed. 1998).

[28] See Discours préliminaire prononcé par Portalis, le 24 thermidor an 8, lors de la présentation du projet arrêté par las commission du gouvernement, in P. A. Fenet, Recueil Complet des Travaux Preparatoires du Code Civil 465 (1968) (1827): "le désir exalté de sacrificier violemment tous les droits à un but politique, et de ne plus admettre d'autre considération que celle d'un mystérieux et variable intérêt d'état." I thank John Portman for the translation in the text.

was just the opposite. The authority of the *parlements* stalled needed reforms in *ancien régime* taxation, and the lesson drawn was that economic and political progress required the centralization of power. The civil law and common law, then, are closely connected to the more centralizing tendency of French political thought and the decentralized, individualistic tradition of English political thought, respectively. Hayek argued that English and French concepts of law stemmed from English and French models of liberty, the first (derived from Locke and Hume) emphasizing the individual's freedom to pursue individual ends and the second (derived from Hobbes and Rousseau) emphasizing the government's freedom to pursue collective ends.[29]

In this, Hayek echoed many nineteenth- and early twentieth-century writers. Francis Lieber argued that "Gallican liberty is sought in the *government*, and according to an Anglican point of view, it is looked for in a wrong place, where it cannot be found. Necessary consequences of the Gallican view are, that the French look for the highest degree of political civilization in *organization*, that is, in the highest degree of interference by public power. The question whether this interference be despotism or liberty is decided solely by the fact *who* interferes, and for the benefit of which class the interference takes place, while according to the Anglican view this interference would always be either absolutism or aristocracy."[30]

More recently, Pipes described the French eighteenth century as a period of intellectual "assault" on property.[31] A part of the French intellectual heritage is a concept of law that is more congenial to economic intervention and redistribution as acts of the "general will."

B.   Structural Consequences

The common law and civil law continue to reflect their intellectual heritage and, as a consequence, legal origin is relevant both to the ideological background and the structural design of government. At an ideological or cultural level, the civil-law tradition assumes a larger role for the state, defers more to bureaucratic decisions, and elevates collective over individual rights. It casts the judiciary into an explicitly subordinate role. In the common-law tradition, by contrast, judicial independence is viewed as essential to the protection of individual liberty.[32] These ideological distinctions may be particularly important given the prevalence of lawyers in government in many countries.

At a structural level, the two systems' different attitudes about the judicial

---

[29] See Hayek, *supra* note 4, at 54–70.

[30] Francis Lieber, Anglican and Gallican Liberty, in 2 Miscellaneous Writings 369, 382–83 (Daniel Coit Gilman ed. 1881) (emphasis in original). The essay was originally published in 1848.

[31] See Pipes, *supra* note 19, at 39–44.

[32] Note that George III's undermining of the independence of colonial judges was one of the grievances listed in the Declaration of Independence.

role have produced distinct institutional arrangements, including a difference in the authority of judges to review executive action. A central feature of the civil law is a sharp distinction between "private" law (the law that governs relations between citizens) and "public" law (the law that governs relations between the citizen and the state). The ways in which private and public rights are protected differ both procedurally and substantively, and in general, public law in a civil-law system puts light restraints on public officials compared to a common-law system.[33]

Procedurally, the ordinary courts in a civil-law jurisdiction typically have no authority to review government action. In France, the relevant statute remains unchanged from 1790: "It shall be a criminal offence for the judges of the ordinary courts to interfere in any manner whatsoever with the operation of the administration, nor shall they call administrators to account before them in respect of the exercise of their official functions."[34] France eventually developed a system of specialized administrative courts authorized to review administrative decisions. These courts, however, are under the direct supervision of the executive. Its judges are trained at the administrative schools alongside the future civil servants whose decisions they will oversee.[35]

Substantive administrative law in a civil-law system insists that the courts intrude as little as possible in the administration's pursuit of the public interest.[36] The strong emphasis on property and contract that characterizes private law gives way in public law to a concern for preserving the government's freedom to pursue collective ends.[37]

Under the common law, by contrast, there is no sharp distinction between private and public law. As described by the United Kingdom's highest court, the House of Lords, the same principles apply to deprivations of property by private and public actors.[38] The same judges who enforce private rights, moreover, review administrative action. Although some common-law jurisdictions (such as the United States) have administrative courts, their decisions are subject to review by the ordinary courts.

Long after the English and French revolutions, commentators have described these differences in judicial review of administrative action as a proxy for restrictions on the executive's freedom of action. A recent comparative law text argues that the common law's hostility to specialized courts stems

---

[33] See René David & John E. C. Brierley, Major Legal Systems in the World Today: An Introduction to the Comparative Study of Law (3d ed. 1985).

[34] Loi des 16–24.8.1790, Article 13, quoted in Brown, Bell, & Galabert, *supra* note 27, at 46.

[35] See Charles Szladits, The Civil Law System, in 2 International Encyclopedia of Comparative Law 15, 41 (René David ed. 1974).

[36] See Brown, Bell, & Galabert, *supra* note 27, at 176.

[37] See Szladits, *supra* note 35, at 48–49.

[38] See Davy v. Spelthorne Borough Council, [1983] 3 All Eng. Rep. 278, 285 (opinion of Lord Wilberforce).

from the controversy over prerogative courts in the seventeenth century.[3] A. V. Dicey notoriously argued that France did not possess the "rule of law' because ordinary courts are not permitted to review administrative action touching off a debate among comparative law scholars that continues to the present day.[40]

C.　The Problem of Germany and Scandinavia

German and Scandinavian civil law are distinct traditions that developed separately from French civil law. This complicates the task of drawing general distinctions between common- and civil-law systems. On several dimensions, German and Scandinavian civil law can be grouped together with French civil law without difficulty. All rely on legislative rather than judge-made rules, and in all the judiciary occupies a lower status than in a common-law system. Both the French and German civil codes are associated with the development of a powerful central government.

There are also important differences. Codification was not part of a general upheaval, but rather a gradual process, in the various German states and in Scandinavia from the time of rediscovery of Roman law in the Middle Ages. More important, the development of separate administrative courts in Germany did not, as in France, stem from a fear of judicial interference with the bureaucracy—rather, Germany's administrative court system proceeded from a desire to subject administrators to external control.[41] In order to prevent executive or legislative interference, Germany's constitution provides for the independence of judges, who cannot be reassigned without their consent.[42] For these reasons, Hayek found the German civil-law system more conducive to individual liberty than its French counterpart.[43] Much of the prior law and finance literature treats German and Scandinavian civil law as separate categories.[44]

Drawing a sharp distinction between the civil-law subfamilies, however, might appear to a skeptical observer to be post hoc rationalization. The handful of countries outside western Europe that have adopted German civil law include Japan and South Korea, which have had extremely successful

---

[39] See Peter de Cruz, Comparative Law in a Changing World (2d ed. 1999).

[40] See A. V. Dicey, Lectures Introductory to the Study of the Law of the Constitution 178–79 (1886); Brown, Bell, & Galabert, *supra* note 27, at 4–5.

[41] See Thorsten Beck, Asli Demirgüç-Kunt, & Ross Levine, Law, Politics and Finance 13–14 (unpublished manuscript 2001) (available at http://www.csom.umn.edu/wwwpages/faculty/rlevine); Szladits, *supra* note 35, at 35.

[42] Grundgesetz, Article 97.

[43] See Hayek, *supra* note 4, at 193–204.

[44] See, for example, La Porta *et al.*, Law and Finance, *supra* note 2; La Porta *et al.*, Legal Determinants of External Finance, *supra* note 2.

economies in the postwar period.[45] Most of the remaining German, and all Scandinavian, civil-law countries are in economically advanced western Europe. In order to avoid this concern, I treat all civil-law countries as a single category except as otherwise noted. Any bias, then, would be in the direction of making the civil law look better.

IV.   LAW AND GROWTH: CROSS-COUNTRY EVIDENCE

In the tradition of cross-country growth studies, I examine differences in average annual growth in real per capita GDP. The sample consists of 102 countries (see Appendix A) covered by the Penn World Tables, Mark 5.6.[46] Growth rates are averaged over the period 1960–92, and I eliminate any country for which real per capita GDP data are missing for more than 3 years of that period. Following the prior literature, I take the description of legal systems from Thomas Reynolds and Arturo Flores.[47] For all but a handful of countries, assignment to a legal family is straightforward.[48] There are a few countries in east Asia and Africa that have had both English and French influence. However, for several of these, the Privy Council in England remains the highest court of appeal. Given my focus on the common law as a constitutional arrangement, I assign these to the common-law family.[49] I eliminate only Cameroon from the sample on the basis that French and English influences are too mixed to make a choice. I also exclude some Middle Eastern countries whose legal systems are almost entirely based on Islamic law (such as Saudi Arabia and Oman) and a few countries whose legal systems have been largely free of European influence (such as Ethiopia and Iceland). Finally, all socialist countries are eliminated in order to focus strictly on differences between the common and civil law.

I test the effect of the common law using ordinary least squares regressions with the average annual rate of real per capita GDP growth (GROW) as the dependent variable (see Appendix B). The independent variable of interest is a dummy (COMMONLAW) that takes on the value one for common-law countries and zero otherwise. I begin with a "base" regression that includes

[45] There have been some much less successful adopters, such as Russia and much of eastern Europe, but these countries are socialist during my sample period and therefore excluded from the sample.

[46] For a description of the Penn World Tables, see Robert Summers & Alan Heston, The Penn World Tables (Mark 5): An Expanded Set of International Comparisons, 1950–1988, 106 Q. J. Econ. 327 (1991).

[47] See Thomas H. Reynolds & Arturo A. Flores, Foreign Law: Current Sources of Codes and Basic Legislation in Jurisdictions of the World (1989).

[48] See de Cruz, *supra* note 39, at 34–36.

[49] This results in one difference between my assignments and that of some of the law and finance literature. I include Mauritius, a Commonwealth country that recognizes the jurisdiction of the Judicial Committee of the Privy Council, in the common-law category, whereas some studies assign it to the civil-law category.

TABLE 1

DESCRIPTIVE STATISTICS, COMMON- AND CIVIL-LAW COUNTRIES

A. FULL SAMPLE ($n = 102$)				
Variable	Mean	Standard Deviation	Minimum	Maximum
GROW	2.06	1.71	−2.00	7.03
PCG60	2421.98	2309.97	313.00	9895.00
PRI60	.75	.34	.05	1.44
GPO	2.11	1.00	.17	4.08
INV	16.34	7.94	1.40	34.43
B. COMMON-LAW COUNTRIES ($n = 38$)				
Variable	Mean	Standard Deviation	Minimum	Maximum
GROW	2.44	1.81	−.83	6.67
PCG60	2274.89	2504.96	313.00	9895.00
PRI60	.72	.33	.09	1.26
GPO	2.18	.96	.17	3.71
INV	15.83	7.66	1.47	31.18
C. CIVIL-LAW COUNTRIES ($n = 64$)				
Variable	Mean	Standard Deviation	Minimum	Maximum
GROW	1.83	1.61	−2.00	7.03
PCG60	2509.31	2201.92	367.00	9409.00
PRI60	.76	.35	.05	1.44
GPO	2.07	1.03	.24	4.08
INV	16.64	8.14	1.40	34.43

NOTE.—The variables are the average annual rate of real per capita GDP growth (GROW), the initial real per capita GDP (PCG60), the initial rate of enrollment in primary education (PRI60), the average annual rate of population growth during the sample period (GPO), and the average investment share of GDP over the sample period (INV).

prevalent conditioning variables from the cross-country growth literature.[50] The variables are initial real per capita GDP (PCG60), the initial rate of enrollment in primary education (PRI60), the average annual rate of population growth during the sample period (GPO), and the average investment share of GDP over the sample period (INV). Table 1 provides descriptive statistics for each variable in the base regression for the full sample and the common- and civil-law subsamples.

The first column of Table 2 reports results for the base regression (Model 1). All of the conditioning variables enter with the signs we would predict from theory and prior empirical studies. Initial per capita GDP and the rate of population growth are both negatively related to growth, and initial enrollment in primary education and average investment share of GDP are

---

[50] See Ross Levine & David Renelt, A Sensitivity Analysis of Cross-Country Growth Regressions, 82 Am. Econ. Rev. 942 (1992), for a survey. Xavier Sala-i-Martin argues that a less restrictive test finds a larger set of robust variables. See Xavier X. Sala-i-Martin, I Just Ran Two Million Regressions, 87 Am. Econ. Rev. Papers & Proc. 178 (1997). I use some of these additional variables in robustness checks described below.

TABLE 2

COMMON LAW AND GROWTH, 1960–92

Variable	Model 1	Model 2
COMMONLAW	.714**	.768**
	(.261)	(.258)
PCG60	−.0004**	−.0005**
	(.000)	(.000)
PRI60	1.790**	1.546**
	(.531)	(.527)
GPO	−.300*	−.092
	(.145)	(.134)
INV	.121**	.113**
	(.028)	(.029)
ETHNIC		−1.405**
		(.504)
SEC60		.719
		(.944)
INFLATION		−.002⁺
		(.001)
EXPORT		1.074⁺
		(.599)
R^2	.54	.59
N	102	97

NOTE.—The dependent variable for all regressions is GROW. For variable definitions, see Appendix B. White-corrected standard errors are in parentheses.
  ⁺ Significant at the 10 percent level.
  * Significant at the 5 percent level.
  ** Significant at the 1 percent level.

positively related to growth. The coefficient on the common-law dummy variable is both economically and statistically significant. Controlling for the other variables, the common-law countries grew, on average, .71 percent per year faster than the civil-law countries ($p = .007$).

I also estimate an extended model that includes other variables that have been found to be significantly related to growth but that should not be related to legal origin. The additional variables are the initial rate of secondary school enrollment (SEC60), William Easterly and Levine's ethnoliguistic fractionalization index (ETHNIC),[51] the average annual rate of change in the GDP deflator (INFLATION), and the average export share of GDP over the sample period (EXPORT).

Results for the extended model are reported as Model 2 in Table 2. Each of the new variables enters with the expected sign. The estimated coefficient on the common-law dummy is little changed from Model 1 and remains significant at the 1 percent level. As found in other studies, initial per capita

[51] See William Easterly & Ross Levine, Africa's Growth Tragedy: Policies and Ethnic Divisions, 112 O. J. Econ. 1203 (1997).

TABLE 3

SENSITIVITY: REGION AND RELIGION

Variable	Model 3	Model 4
COMMONLAW	.561*	.557*
	(.266)	(.241)
PCG60	−.0005**	−.0004**
	(.000)	(.000)
PRI60	1.967**	2.064**
	(.617)	(.680)
GPO	−.155	−.234
	(.141)	(.145)
INV	.086**	.085**
	(.029)	(.028)
AFRICA	−1.293**	
	(.375)	
LATINAM	−1.321**	
	(.352)	
PROTESTANT		−.197*
		(.099)
CATHOLIC		−.0001
		(.004)
MUSLIM		1.432**
		(.448)
CONFUCIAN		7.646**
		(1.42)
BUDDHIST		1.289+
		(.759)
R^2	.64	.70

NOTE.—The dependent variable for all regressions is GROW. For variable definitions, see Appendix B. White-corrected standard errors are in parentheses.
+ Significant at the 10 percent level.
* Significant at the 5 percent level.
** Significant at the 1 percent level.

GDP and the investment share of GDP are the most robust predictors. The common-law dummy, however, performs quite well.

Table 3 reports the results of regressions that attempt to meet two possible objections to the analysis thus far. Sub-Saharan Africa and Latin America were notably poor performers during the period of interest. Latin America consists almost entirely of civil-law countries. Any omitted variable causing low growth in Latin America could, therefore, lead to a mistaken conclusion that the civil law is to blame. Africa is unusual on many accounts during the period of interest.[52] I accordingly estimate the base regression after adding in dummy variables for sub-Saharan Africa and Latin America. The results are reported as Model 3 in Table 3. The common-law dummy is still associated with higher growth, although the magnitude is lower and the significance level is 5 percent.

One might also wonder whether common-law versus civil-law origin, for part of the world, is merely a proxy for Protestant versus Catholic religious heritage. The package of endowments received by many former colonies includes, along with the common or civil law, the English, French, Spanish, or Portuguese language and Protestantism or Catholicism. Max Weber famously argued that Protestant (particularly Calvinist) doctrine encouraged vigorous worldly pursuits as a means of demonstrating one's faith and thereby unleashed a "heroic age" of capitalism.[53] I therefore estimate the base regression together with a set of religion variables previously used by Robert Barro.[54] These variables measure the percentage of the population that practices some form of Protestantism, Roman Catholicism, Islam, Buddhism, or Confucianism.[55] The results are reported as model 4 in Table 3. Estimated coefficients on all religion variables other than the percentage of Catholics are significant, and those on the Confucianism, Buddhism, and Islam variables are large. The estimated coefficient and significance level for the common-law dummy, however, are almost unchanged from model 3.

The variables I have used to this point are drawn principally from Levine and David Renelt's study of variables whose estimated coefficients are highly robust to different specifications of the growth equation.[56] In regressions not reported here, I added to the base regression groups of variables from Xavier Sala-i-Martin's 1997 survey of empirical growth research.[57] Using a less restrictive approach than Levine and Renelt, Sala-i-Martin found 22 variables from the prior literature that are robust. In addition to those already reported herein, these include equipment investment,[58] the number of years an economy was open between 1950 and 1992,[59] the capital city's distance from the equator,[60] the average number of revolutions and coups per unit time,[61] the fraction of GDP in mining,[62] and several policy-related variables. Although

---

[53] See Max Weber, The Protestant Ethic and the Spirit of Capitalism (1958).

[54] See Robert J. Barro, Determinants of Economic Growth: A Cross-Country Empirical Study (1997). I obtained the data from Sala-i-Martin's Web page (http://www.columbia.edu/~xs23/data.htm).

[55] These are the only religion variables that are robustly associated with growth. See Sala-i-Martin, *supra* note 50, at 181.

[56] See Levine & Renelt, *supra* note 50.

[57] See *id.*

[58] See J. Bradford De Long & Lawrence H. Summers, Equipment Investment and Economic Growth, 106 Q. J. Econ. 445 (1991).

[59] See Jeffrey Sachs & Andrew Warner, Economic Reform and the Process of Global Integration: Comments and Discussion, 1995 Brookings Papers Econ. Activity 1.

[60] See Robert J. Barro & Jong-Wha Lee, International Comparisons of Educational Attainment, 32 J. Monetary Econ. 363 (1993).

[61] See Robert J. Barro, Economic Growth in a Cross-Section of Countries, 106 Q. J. Econ. 407 (1991).

[62] See Robert E. Hall & Charles I. Jones, Why Do Some Countries Produce So Much More Output per Worker than Others? 114 Q. J. Econ. 83 (1999).

I did not use every possible specification, I employed each of the additional "robust" Sala-i-Martin variables in small groups in additional regressions and found that the estimated coefficient on the common-law dummy remains in the range of .5–.7 and is statistically significant in all specifications. The estimated coefficient becomes unstable when using large numbers of variables and regional dummies. However, the coefficients on all of the variables (including the investment variable) are unstable in these specifications.

As discussed above, the German and Scandinavian civil-law families can be viewed as distinct from the French law tradition. There are not enough German and Scandinavian civil-law countries to include separate dummies for each and expect significant results. I did, however, estimate all of the regressions using a dummy for French civil law in place of the common-law dummy, in effect grouping German and Scandinavian origin countries with the common-law countries. The absolute values of the coefficients were slightly higher on average compared to those in the regressions estimated with a common-law dummy. The result, although far from conclusive, is consistent with the notion that German and Scandinavian law fit somewhere between French law and common law.

V. TESTING THE INTERVENTION HYPOTHESIS

The results so far confirm directly what Levine finds using legal origin as an instrument for financial market development.[63] The existing literature focuses on variation in minority shareholder and creditor rights and their effects on financial markets as the causal link between legal origin and growth.

I suggest a different and broader link from legal origin to more dispersed governmental power and from there to superior protections for property and contract rights. I therefore examine measures of judicial power, security of property rights, and contract enforcement and use legal origin as an instrument for those variables.

The economic growth literature provides measures, albeit imperfect, for each of these phenomena. Paolo Mauro uses Business International Corporation's (BIC's) index of judicial quality, a survey-based assessment of the "efficiency and integrity" of the judiciary.[64] I expect judges in common-law countries, who occupy a higher-prestige office (and therefore have more to lose) relative to their civil-law counterparts, and who have more authority to redress adverse actions by other governmental actors, to score more highly on this index. Kim Holmes and coauthors develop an index of the security of property rights.[65] Christopher Clague and coauthors define "contract in-

---

[63] See Levine, *supra* note 3.

[64] See Paolo Mauro, Corruption and Growth, 110 Q. J. Econ. 681 (1995).

[65] See 1997 Index of Economic Freedom (Kim R. Holmes, Bryan T. Johnson, & Melanie Kirkpatrick eds. 1997).

tensive money" (CIM) as the ratio of broad money (M2) minus currency to M2 and argue that CIM is a measure of the extent to which contracts are enforced.[66] They reason that CIM, unlike currency, represents a contract right, such as the right of the payee of a check to obtain money from the drawee bank. Second, although currency is well suited to simultaneous exchange, long-term contracting more frequently relies on CIM. The use of CIM in preference to currency, therefore, reflects confidence in the system of contract enforcement.

For the sake of completeness, I examine other measures of state intervention in the economy. Mauro uses BIC's "red-tape" index that assesses the prevalence of bureaucratic obstacles to business activity.[67] Stephan Knack and Philip Keefer use the International Country Risk Guide's "rule of law" index that assesses adherence to legal procedures and "expropriation risk" index that assesses the risk of confiscation or nationalization of business assets.[68] In addition to the property rights measure, Holmes and coauthors provide a "business regulation" index that seeks to capture the extent of regulatory burdens on business activity.[69] Barro employs an index of civil liberties that assesses rights of speech and assembly and personal autonomy in matters such as religion, education, and physical movement.[70] James Gwartney and coauthors derive several measures of government involvement in the economy, including government consumption as a percentage of GDP, an index of the importance of state-owned enterprises in the national economy, government transfers and subsidies as a percentage of GDP, and top marginal tax rates.[71]

Each of these measures has some drawbacks. Many are survey based and accordingly subjective. Because the surveys are in all cases compiled by Anglophone firms or researchers, the compilers could be biased in favor of more familiar legal arrangements. The CIM ratio is a helpful addition because it is an objective measure, but it may reflect phenomena other than contract

---

[66] See Christopher Clague *et al.*, Contract-Intensive Money: Contract Enforcement, Property Rights, and Economic Performance, 4 J. Econ. Growth 187 (1999).

[67] See Mauro, *supra* note 64.

[68] See Stephan Knack & Philip Keefer, Institutions and Economic Performance: Cross-Country Tests Using Alternative Institutional Measures, 7 Econ. & Pol. 207 (1995); see also Levine, *supra* note 3. The rule-of-law measure might seem to be at least as relevant as the property and contract enforcement measures. However, the rule-of-law assessment is problematic because, following the dominant intellectual trend in legal theory, the compilers focus only on whether the government acts with a high degree of procedural regularity. Thus the former Soviet Union and its client states, for example, score relatively high on this measure. Hayek frequently criticized legal positivists for their insistence that "legality" consists only in adherence to appropriate procedures, as opposed to respect for individual rights.

[69] See 1997 Index of Economic Freedom, *supra* note 65.

[70] See Barro, *supra* note 54, at 55–58. The data come from Raymond D. Gastil, Freedom in the World (various years).

[71] See James D. Gwartney, Robert Lawson, & Walter Block, Economic Freedom of the World, 1975–1995 (1996).

TABLE 4

PARTIAL CORRELATIONS WITH COMMON LAW

Variable	Partial Correlation Coefficient	p-Value
JUDIC	.296	.021
PROP	.218	.044
CIM	.303	.003
REDTAPE	.168	.196
RULELAW	.164	.124
EXPROP	.078	.604
CIVLIB	−.267	.007
BUSREG	.181	.096
MARG	−.124	.314
GOVCONS	.125	.264
SOE	−.104	.358
TRANSUB	−.107	.361

NOTE.—All partial correlations control for starting real per capita GDP (PCG60 or PCG80, depending on the period for which the relevant variable is measured). The variable CIVLIB is defined so that a lower score implies more civil liberties. All other survey-based measures (JUDIC, PROP, REDTAPE, RULELAW, EX-PROP, and BUSREG) are defined so that a higher score is better. For variable definitions, see Appendix B.

enforcement. The judicial quality, red-tape, rule-of-law, and expropriation risk measures were compiled for use by foreign businesses and are therefore concerned principally with the government's treatment of foreign firms rather than domestic firms and citizens. The measures of government size are noisy measures of intervention because governments can choose to engage in commercial activities directly or to heavily regulate the private sector. Either may have a retarding effect on growth, but the former would tend to produce larger measures of government spending and employment.

It is also obvious by inspection that rich countries score better than poor ones, on average, on each of these measures. I therefore begin by examining the partial correlations between each of these measures and the common-law dummy, controlling for starting real per capita GDP. These partial correlations are reported in Table 4. As predicted, there are statistically significant partial correlations between the common law and the judicial quality, property rights, and contract rights (CIM) measures. The common law's partial correlation with the civil liberties measure is also large and significant. The common-law countries perform better (that is, the sign of the correlation coefficient is consistent with less intervention) for each measure except government consumption. Using multivariate analysis, La Porta and coauthors find a strong association between common-law origin and less interventionist government using several of these measures.[72]

On the basis of these results, I use legal origin as an instrumental variable for judicial quality, the security of property rights, and contract enforcement.

[72] See La Porta *et al.*, *supra* note 5, at 246–50.

TABLE 5

COMMON LAW AND GROWTH: INSTRUMENTAL VARIABLES

		A. SIMPLE CONDITIONING SET				
Variable	Estimated Coefficient	(White-Corrected) Standard Error	P-Value	N	J-Statistic	P-Value, OIR
JUDIC	.430	.128	.001	60	.032	.381
PROP	1.798	.372	.000	85	.004	.848
CIM	.116	.039	.004	91	.036	.193
		B. EXTENDED CONDITIONING SET				
Variable	Estimated Coefficient	(White-Corrected) Standard Error	P-Value	N	J-Statistic	P-Value, OIR
JUDIC	.270	.273	.328	60	.069	.127
PROP	1.756	.621	.006	85	.005	.807
CIM	.093	.031	.004	91	.019	.410

NOTE.—OIR = overidentifying restrictions. The dependent variable for all regressions is GROW. The simple conditioning set includes PCG60, PRI60, and ETHNIC. The extended conditioning set includes, in addition, GPO and INV. The instruments are COM, FRCIV, and GERCIV. For variable definitions, see Appendix B.

I compute generalized method of moments (GMM) estimates for three regression equations using the BIC judicial quality index (JUDIC), the Holmes et al. property rights index (PROP), and the CIM ratio (CIM) of Clague and coauthors as endogenous variables. In order to have sufficient degrees of freedom to test for overidentifying restrictions, I use dummy variables for common law, French civil law, and German civil law as instruments (Scandinavian civil law is the omitted category).

I first estimate the GMM coefficients using a simple set of additional conditioning information consisting of initial per capita GDP, primary school enrollment, and ethnic fractionalization.[73] I then reestimate with an extended conditioning set that includes population growth and average investment. In each case, after computing the GMM estimates, I test for overidentifying restrictions by using a Lagrange multiplier test. As a check, I also estimate the same regressions using two-stage least squares and obtain consistent results.

Table 5 reports results for the instrumental variables regressions. Using the simple conditioning set, the judicial quality, property rights, and contract enforcement variables each enters significantly at the 1 percent level. With the extended conditioning set, the estimated coefficient on the judicial quality index loses significance (when estimated using two-stage least squares, it is significant at the 10 percent level). The coefficients on the other two variables

[73] The procedure tracks Levine. *supra* note 3, at 26–31.

are slightly reduced and remain significant at the 1 percent level. The weaker results in the extended regression may reflect the fact that judicial quality (in particular), property rights, and contract enforcement may affect growth in part directly and in part indirectly through investment. The investment variable is highly correlated with each of the three endogenous variables.

Looking at the Lagrange multiplier test for overidentifying restrictions, in no case can we reject the hypothesis that legal origin affects growth solely through its effect on the endogenous variables (in other words, that the legal origin variables are uncorrelated with the error term). Levine reaches a similar conclusion with respect to a set of endogenous variables that measure financial development.[74] The inability to reject the null hypothesis in any of these cases suggests that the overidentifying restrictions test has low power with the sample sizes typical in cross-country growth studies. More important, the results support the hypothesis that legal origin affects growth through channels other than finance.

The data, then, are consistent with the notion that the common law produces improvements in property rights and contract enforcement that in turn speed economic growth. The instrumental variables results also suggest that the strong association between secure property and contract rights and growth is causal, and not simply a consequence of simultaneity.

VI. Conclusion

Common and civil lawyers have long debated the relative merits of the two legal traditions. These discussions, like the law and finance literature, focus on differences in substantive rules. An alternative view, associated most notably with Hayek, focuses on legal tradition as a reflection of different philosophies of government. The common law and civil law, in this view, proceed from different views about the relative role of collective and individual action. These associations have to do with possibly chance connections between the judiciary and specific political problems of seventeenth-century England and eighteenth-century France, but once established, they have had continuing effects on institutional arrangements. Judges are invested with greater prestige and insulated more from political influence in common-law systems. Administrative bodies are insulated more from judicial influence in civil-law systems. These differences result in stricter protection for property and contract rights against government action in the common-law tradition.

This paper's results suggest that the association between common law and growth is not an artifact of different rules of investor protection. Rather, it stems from a more fundamental divergence between the security of property and contract rights in the two systems.

[74] See *id.* at 29–31.

APPENDIX A

SAMPLE OF COUNTRIES

I. COMMON-LAW COUNTRIES

Australia, Bangladesh, Barbados, Botswana, Canada, Cyprus, Gambia, Ghana, Hong Kong, India, Ireland, Israel, Jamaica, Kenya, Lesotho, Liberia, Malawi, Malaysia, Malta, Mauritius, Nepal, New Zealand, Nigeria, Pakistan, Papua New Guinea, Sierra Leone, Singapore, South Africa, Sri Lanka, Swaziland, Tanzania, Thailand, Trinidad and Tobago, Uganda, United Kingdom, United States, Zambia, Zimbabwe

II. CIVIL-LAW COUNTRIES

Algeria, Argentina, Austria, Belgium, Benin, Bolivia, Brazil, Burkina Faso, Burundi, Central African Republic, Chad, Chile, Colombia, Congo, Costa Rica, Côte d'Ivoire, Denmark, Dominican Republic, Ecuador, Egypt, El Salvador, Finland, France, Gabon, Germany, Greece, Guatemala, Guinea-Bissau, Haiti, Honduras, Indonesia, Iran, Iraq, Italy, Japan, Jordan, Luxembourg, Madagascar, Mali, Mauritania, Mexico, Morocco, Netherlands, Nicaragua, Niger, Norway, Panama, Paraguay, Peru, Philippines, Portugal, Rwanda, Senegal, South Korea, Spain, Suriname, Sweden, Switzerland, Syria, Togo, Tunisia, Turkey, Uruguay, Venezuela

APPENDIX B

VARIABLE DEFINITION AND SOURCES

AFRICA: Dummy for Sub-Saharan African countries (Oxford Atlas of the World (2d ed. 1994))

BUDDHIST: Buddhists as percent of population (Xavier X. Sala-i-Martin, I Just Ran Two Million Regressions, 87 Am. Econ. Rev. Papers & Proc. 178 (1997); data obtained from http://www.columbia.edu/~xs23/data.htm)

BUSREG: Business regulation index (Kim Holmes, Bryan Johnson, & Melanie Kirkpatrick, 1997 Index of Economic Freedom (1997))

CATHOLIC: Roman Catholics as percent of population (Xavier X. Sala-i-Martin, I Just Ran Two Million Regressions, 87 Am. Econ. Rev. Papers & Proc. 178 (1997); data obtained from http://www.columbia.edu/~xs23/data.htm)

CIM: Average ratio of broad money (M2) less currency to M2, 1969–90 (Christopher Clague et al., Contract-Intensive Money: Contract Enforcement, Property Rights, and Economic Performance, 4 J. Econ. Growth 187 (1999))

CIVLIB: Index of civil liberties (Raymond D. Gastil, Freedom in the World (various years))

COMMONLAW: Dummy for common-law origin (Thomas H. Reynolds & Arturo A. Flores, Foreign Law: Current Sources of Codes and Basic Legislation in Jurisdictions of the World (1989))

CONFUCIAN: Adherents to Confucianism as percent of population (Xavier X. Sala-i-Martin, I Just Ran Two Million Regressions, 87 Am. Econ. Rev. Papers & Proc. 178 (1997); data obtained from http://www.columbia.edu/~xs23/data.htm)

ETHNIC: Ethnolinguistic fractionalization (William Easterly & Ross Levine, Africa's Growth Tragedy: Policies and Ethnic Divisions, 112 Q. J. Econ. 1203 (1997))

EXPORT: Average export share of GDP, 1960–89 (Ross Levine & David Renelt, A Sensitivity Analysis of Cross-Country Growth Regressions, 82 Am. Econ. Rev. 942 (1992); data obtained from Ross Levine)

EXPROP: Expropriation risk index (International Country Risk Guides (various years))

FRCIV: Dummy for French civil-law origin (Thomas H. Reynolds & Arturo A. Flores, Foreign Law: Current Sources of Codes and Basic Legislation in Jurisdictions of the World (1989))

GERCIV: Dummy for German civil-law origin (Thomas H. Reynolds & Arturo A. Flores, Foreign Law: Current Sources of Codes and Basic Legislation in Jurisdictions of the World (1989))

GOVCONS: Government consumption as percent of GDP (James Gwartney, Robert Lawson, & Walter Block, Economic Freedom of the World, 1975–1995 (1996))

GPO: Average annual population growth, 1960–89 (Ross Levine & David Renelt, A Sensitivity Analysis of Cross-Country Growth Regressions, 82 Am. Econ. Rev. 942 (1992); data obtained from Ross Levine)

GROW: Average annual growth in real per capita GDP, 1960–92 (Penn World Tables, Mark 5.6)

INFLATION: Average rate of change of GDP deflator, 1960–89 (Ross Levine & David Renelt, A Sensitivity Analysis of Cross-Country Growth Regressions, 82 Am. Econ. Rev. 942 (1992); data obtained from Ross Levine)

INV: Average investment share of GDP, 1960–92 (Penn World Tables, Mark 5.6)

JUDIC: Judicial quality index (Paolo Mauro, Corruption and Growth, 110 Q. J. Econ. 681 (1995))

LATINAM: Dummy for Latin American countries (Oxford Atlas of the World (2d ed. 1994))

MARG: Scaled measure of top marginal tax rates (James Gwartney, Robert Lawson, & Walter Block, Economic Freedom of the World, 1975–1995 (1996))

MUSLIM: Muslims as percent of population (Xavier X. Sala-i-Martin, I Just Ran Two Million Regressions, 87 Am. Econ. Rev. Papers & Proc. 178 (1997); data obtained from http://www.columbia.edu/~xs23/data.htm)

PCG60: Real per capita gross domestic product, 1960 (Penn World Tables, Mark 5.6)

PCG80: Real per capita gross domestic product, 1980 (Penn World Tables, Mark 5.6)

PROP: Property rights index (Kim Holmes, Bryan Johnson, & Melanie Kirkpatrick, 1997 Index of Economic Freedom (1997))

PROTESTANT: Protestants as percent of population (Xavier X. Sala-i-Martin, I Just Ran Two Million Regressions, 87 Am. Econ. Rev. Papers & Proc. 178 (1997); data obtained from http://www.columbia.edu/~xs23/data.htm)

PRI60: Gross enrollment rate in primary education, 1960 (Ross Levine & David Renelt, A Sensitivity Analysis of Cross-Country Growth Regressions, 82 Am. Econ. Rev. 942 (1992); data obtained from Ross Levine)

REDTAPE: Bureaucratic delay index (Paolo Mauro, Corruption and Growth, 110 Q. J. Econ. 681 (1995))

RULELAW: Index of law and order (International Country Risk Guides (various years))

SEC60: Gross enrollment rate in secondary education, 1960 (Ross Levine & David Renelt, A Sensitivity Analysis of Cross-Country Growth Regressions, 82 Am. Econ. Rev. 942 (1992); data obtained from Ross Levine)

SOE: Index of importance of state-owned enterprises (James Gwartney, Robert Lawson, & Walter Block, Economic Freedom of the World, 1975–1995 (1996))

TRANSUB: Government transfers and subsidies as percent of GDP (James Gwartney, Robert Lawson, & Walter Block, Economic Freedom of the World, 1975–1995 (1996))

[5]

The End of History for Corporate Law

HENRY HANSMANN* AND REINIER KRAAKMAN**

INTRODUCTION

Much recent scholarship has emphasized institutional differences in corporate governance, capital markets, and law among European, American, and Japanese companies.[1] Despite very real differences in the corporate systems, the deeper tendency is toward convergence, as it has been since the nineteenth century. The basic law of corporate governance—indeed, most of corporate law—has achieved a high degree of uniformity across developed market jurisdictions, and continuing convergence toward a single, standard model is likely. The core legal features of the corporate form were already well established in advanced jurisdictions one hundred years ago, at the turn of the twentieth century. Although there remained considerable room for variation in governance practices and in the fine structure of corporate law throughout the twentieth century, the pressures for further convergence are now rapidly growing. Chief among these pressures is the recent dominance of a shareholder-centered ideology of corporate law among the business, government, and legal elites in key commercial jurisdictions. There is no longer any serious competitor to the view that corporate law should principally strive to increase long-term shareholder value. This emergent consensus has already profoundly affected corporate governance practices throughout the world. It is only a matter of time before its influence is felt in the reform of corporate law as well.

I. CONVERGENCE PAST: THE RISE OF THE CORPORATE FORM

We must begin with the recognition that the law of business corporations had already achieved a remarkable degree of worldwide convergence at the end of the nineteenth century. By that time, large-scale business enterprise in every major commercial jurisdiction had come to be organized in the corporate form, and the core functional features of that form were essentially identical across these jurisdictions. Those features, which continue to characterize the corporate form today, are: (1) full legal personality, including well-defined authority to

---

* Professor, Yale Law School.

** Professor, Harvard Law School.

1. *See, e.g.*, Bernard S. Black & John C. Coffee, Jr., *Hail Britannia?: Institutional Investor Behavior Under Limited Regulation*, 92 MICH. L. REV. 1997 (1994); Ronald J. Gilson & Mark J. Roe, *Understanding the Japanese Keiretsu: Overlaps Between Corporate Governance and Industrial Organization*, 102 YALE L.J. 871 (1993); Mark J. Roe, *Some Differences in Company Structure in Germany, Japan, and the United States*, 102 YALE L.J. 1927 (1993).

bind the firm to contracts and to bond those contracts with assets that are the property of the firm, as distinct from the firm's owners;[2] (2) limited liability for owners and managers; (3) shared ownership by investors of capital; (4) delegated management under a board structure; and (5) transferable shares.

These core characteristics, both individually and in combination, offer important efficiencies in organizing the large firms with multiple owners that have come to dominate developed market economies. We explore those efficiencies in detail elsewhere.[3] What is important to note here is that while those characteristics and their associated efficiencies are now commonly taken for granted, prior to the beginning of the nineteenth century there existed only a handful of specially chartered companies that combined all five of these characteristics. The joint stock company with tradeable shares was not made generally available for business activities in England until 1844, and limited liability was not added to the form until 1855.[4] While some American states developed the form for general use a few years earlier, all general business corporation statutes appear to date from well after 1800. By around 1900, however, every major commercial jurisdiction appears to have provided for at least one standard-form legal entity with the five characteristics listed above as the default rules, and this has remained the case ever since. Thus there was already strong and rapid convergence a century ago regarding the basic elements of the law of business corporations. It is, in general, only in the more detailed structure of corporate law that jurisdictions have varied significantly since then.

The five basic characteristics of the corporate form provide, by their nature, for a firm that is strongly responsive to shareholder interests. They do not, however, necessarily dictate how the interests of other participants in the firm—such as employees, creditors, other suppliers, customers, or society at large—will be accommodated. Nor do they dictate the way in which conflicts of interest among shareholders themselves—and particularly between controlling and noncontrolling shareholders—will be resolved. Throughout most of the twentieth century there has been debate over these issues and experimentation with alternative approaches to them.

II. THE SHAREHOLDER-ORIENTED (OR "STANDARD") MODEL

Recent years, however, have brought strong evidence of a growing consensus on these issues among the academic, business, and governmental elites in leading jurisdictions. The principal elements of this emerging consensus are that ultimate control over the corporation should rest with the shareholder class; the

---

2. *See* Henry Hansmann & Reinier Kraakman, *The Essential Role of Organizational Law*, YALE L.J. (forthcoming 2000).

3. *See* HENRY HANSMANN, THE OWNERSHIP OF ENTERPRISE (1996); Henry Hansmann & Reinier Kraakman, *What Is Corporate Law?*, *in* THE ANATOMY OF CORPORATE LAW: A COMPARATIVE AND FUNCTIONAL APPROACH (Reinier Kraakman et al. eds., forthcoming 2001).

4. *See* PHILLIP BLUMBERG, THE LAW OF CORPORATE GROUPS: SUBSTANTIVE LAW 9-20 (1988).

managers of the corporation should be charged with the obligation to manage the corporation in the interests of its shareholders; other corporate constituencies, such as creditors, employees, suppliers, and customers, should have their interests protected by contractual and regulatory means rather than through participation in corporate governance; noncontrolling shareholders should receive strong protection from exploitation at the hands of controlling shareholders; and the market value of the publicly traded corporation's shares is the principal measure of its shareholders' interests. For simplicity, we shall refer to the view of the corporation comprised by these elements as the "standard shareholder-oriented model" of the corporate form (or, for brevity, simply "the standard model"). To the extent that corporate law bears on the implementation of this standard model—as to an important degree it does—this consensus on the appropriate conduct of corporate affairs is also a consensus as to the appropriate content of corporate law, and it is likely to have profound effects on the structure of that law.

A. IN WHOSE INTEREST?

As we argue in Part IV, there is today a broad normative consensus that shareholders alone are the parties to whom corporate managers should be accountable, resulting from widespread disenchantment with a privileged role for managers, employees, or the state in corporate affairs. This is not to say that there is agreement that corporations should be run in the interests of shareholders alone—much less that the law should sanction that result. All thoughtful people believe that corporate enterprise should be organized and operated to serve the interests of society as a whole, and that the interests of shareholders deserve no greater weight in this social calculus than do the interests of any other members of society. The point is simply that now, as a consequence of both logic and experience, there is convergence on a consensus that the best means to this end (that is, the pursuit of aggregate social welfare) is to make corporate managers strongly accountable to shareholder interests and, at least in direct terms, only to those interests. It follows that even the extreme proponents of the so-called "concession theory" of the corporation can embrace the primacy of shareholder interests in good conscience.[5]

---

5. In a hoary debate that cuts across jurisdictional boundaries, proponents of the view that corporations exist by virtue of a state "concession" or privilege have also been associated with the view that corporations ought to be governed in the interests of society—or all corporate constituencies—rather than in the private interest of shareholders alone. *See, e.g.,* E. Merrick Dodd, Jr., *For Whom Are Corporate Managers Trustees?*, 45 HARV. L. REV. 1145, 1148-50 (1932); PAUL G. MAHONEY, CONTRACT OR CONCESSION? A HISTORICAL PERSPECTIVE ON BUSINESS CORPORATIONS (University of Virginia School of Law, Working Paper, 1999) (on file with author). Conversely, proponents of the view that the corporation is at bottom a contract among investors have tended to advance the primacy of shareholder interests in corporate governance.

In our view the traditional debate between concession and contract theorists is simply confused. On the one hand, corporations—whether "concessions" or contracts—should be regulated when it is in the

Of course, asserting the primacy of shareholder interests in corporate law does not imply that the interests of corporate stakeholders must or should go unprotected. It merely indicates that the most efficacious legal mechanisms for protecting the interests of nonshareholder constituencies—or at least all constituencies other than creditors—lie outside of corporate law. For workers, this includes the law of labor contracting, pension law, health and safety law, and antidiscrimination law. For consumers, it includes product safety regulation, warranty law, tort law governing product liability, antitrust law, and mandatory disclosure of product contents and characteristics. For the public at large, it includes environmental law and the law of nuisance and mass torts.

Creditors, to be sure, are to some degree an exception. There remains general agreement that corporate law should directly regulate some aspects of the relationship between a business corporation and its creditors. Conspicuous examples include rules governing veil-piercing and limits on the distribution of dividends in the presence of inadequate capital. The reason for these rules, however, is that there are unique problems of creditor contracting that are integral to the corporate form, owing principally to the presence of limited liability as a structural characteristic of that form. These types of rules, however, are modest in scope. Outside of bankruptcy, they do not involve creditors in corporate governance, but rather are confined to limiting shareholders' ability to use the characteristics of the corporate form opportunistically to exploit creditors.

B. WHICH SHAREHOLDERS?

The shareholder-oriented model does more than assert the primacy of shareholder interests, however. It asserts the interests of *all* shareholders, including minority shareholders. More particularly, it is a central tenet in the standard model that minority or noncontrolling shareholders should receive strong protection from exploitation at the hands of controlling shareholders. In publicly traded firms, this means that all shareholders should be assured an essentially equal claim on corporate earnings and assets.

There are two conspicuous reasons for this approach, both of which are rooted in efficiency concerns. One reason is that, absent credible protection for noncontrolling shareholders, business corporations will have difficulty raising capital from the equity markets. The second reason is that the devices by which controlling shareholders divert to themselves a disproportionate share of corporate benefits commonly involve inefficient investment choices and management policies.

---

public interest to do so. On the other hand, the standard model is, in effect, an assertion that social welfare is best served by encouraging corporate managers to pursue shareholder interests.

C. THE IMPORT OF OWNERSHIP STRUCTURE

It is sometimes said that the shareholder-oriented model of corporate law is well suited only to those jurisdictions in which one finds large numbers of firms with widely dispersed share ownership, such as the United States and the United Kingdom. A different model is appropriate, it is said, for those jurisdictions in which ownership is more concentrated, such as the nations of continental Europe. This view, however, is unconvincing.

Closely held corporations, like publicly held corporations, operate most efficiently when the law helps assure that managers are primarily responsive to shareholder interests and that controlling shareholders do not opportunistically exploit noncontrolling shareholders. The shareholder primacy model does not logically privilege any particular ownership structure. Indeed, both concentrated and dispersed shareholdings have been celebrated, at different times and by different commentators, for their ability to advance shareholder interests in the face of serious agency problems.

Equally important, every jurisdiction includes a range of corporate ownership structures. While both the U.S. and U.K. have many large firms with dispersed ownership, both countries also contain a far larger number of corporations that are closely held. Similarly, every major continental European jurisdiction has at least a handful of firms with dispersed ownership, and the number of such firms is evidently growing. It follows that every jurisdiction must have a system of corporate law that is adequate to handle the full range of ownership structures.

Thus, just as there was rapid crystallization of the core features of the corporate form in the late nineteenth century, at the beginning of the twenty-first century we are witnessing rapid convergence on the standard shareholder-oriented model as a normative view of corporate structure and governance. We should also expect this normative convergence to produce substantial convergence in the practices of corporate governance and in corporate law.

III. FORCES OF IDEOLOGICAL CONVERGENCE

There are three principal factors driving consensus on the standard model: the failure of alternative models; the competitive pressures of global commerce; and the shift of interest group influence in favor of an emerging shareholder class. We consider these developments here in sequence.

A. THE FAILURE OF ALTERNATIVE MODELS

Debate and experimentation concerning the basic structure of corporate law during the twentieth century centered on the ways in which that law should accommodate the interests of nonshareholder constituencies. In this regard, three principal alternatives to a shareholder-oriented model were the traditional foci of attention. We term these the manager-oriented, labor-oriented, and state-oriented models of corporate law. Although each of these three alternative models has, at various points and in various jurisdictions, achieved some

444   THE GEORGETOWN LAW JOURNAL   [Vol. 89:439

success both in practice and in received opinion, all three have ultimately lost much of their normative appeal.

1. The Manager-Oriented Model

In the United States, there existed an important strain of normative thought from the 1930s through the 1960s that extolled the virtues of granting substantial discretion to the managers of large business corporations. Merrick Dodd and John Kenneth Galbraith, for example, were conspicuously identified with this position, and Adolph Berle came to it late in life.[6] At the core of this view was the belief that professional corporate managers could serve as disinterested technocratic fiduciaries who would guide business corporations to perform in ways that would serve the general public interest. The corporate social responsibility literature of the 1950s can be seen as an embodiment of these views.[7]

The normative appeal of this view arguably provided part of the rationale for the various legal developments in U.S. law in the 1950s and 1960s that tended to reinforce the discretionary authority of corporate managers, such as the SEC proxy rules and the Williams Act. The collapse of the conglomerate movement in the 1970s and 1980s, however, largely destroyed the normative appeal of the managerialist model. It is now the conventional wisdom that, when managers are given great discretion over corporate investment policies, they tend to serve disproportionately their own interests, however well-intentioned managers may be. While managerial firms may be in some ways more efficiently responsive to nonshareholder interests than are firms that are more dedicated to serving their shareholders, the price paid in inefficiency of operations and excessive investment in low-value projects is now considered too great.

2. The Labor-Oriented Model

Large-scale enterprise clearly presents problems of labor contracting. Simple contracts and the basic doctrines of contract law are inadequate in themselves to govern the long-term relationships between workers and the firms that employ them—relationships that may be afflicted by, among other things, substantial transaction-specific investments and asymmetries of information.

---

6. Dodd and Berle conducted a classic debate on the subject in the 1930s, in which Dodd pressed the social responsibility of corporate managers while Berle championed shareholder interests. *See* Adolph A. Berle, *Corporate Powers as Powers in Trust*, 44 HARV. L. REV. 1049, 1049 (1931); Adolph A. Berle, *For Whom Corporate Managers Are Trustees: A Note*, 45 HARV. L. REV. 1365, 1367-68 (1932); Dodd, *supra* note 5, at 1145. By the 1950s, Berle seemed to have come around to Dodd's celebration of managerial discretion as a positive virtue that permits managers to act in the interests of society as a whole. *See* ADOLPH A. BERLE, JR., POWER WITHOUT PROPERTY: A NEW DEVELOPMENT IN AMERICAN POLITICAL ECONOMY 107-10 (1959) [hereinafter BERLE, POWER WITHOUT PROPERTY]. John Kenneth Galbraith takes a similar position in *The New Industrial State*. *See* JOHN KENNETH GALBRAITH, THE NEW INDUSTRIAL STATE (1967).

7. *See, e.g.*, BERLE, POWER WITHOUT PROPERTY, *supra* note 6; GALBRAITH, *supra* note 6. For an important collection of essays arguing both sides of the question of managerial responsibility to the broader interests of society, see THE CORPORATION IN MODERN SOCIETY (Edward Mason ed., 1959).

Collective bargaining via organized unions has been one approach to those problems—an approach that lies outside corporate law, since it is not dependent on the organizational structure of the firms with which the employees bargain. Another approach, and one that importantly involves corporate law, has been to involve employees directly in corporate governance by, for example, providing for employee representation on the firm's board of directors. Although serious attention was given to employee participation in corporate governance in Germany as early as the Weimar Republic, unionism was the dominant approach everywhere until the Second World War. Then, after the War, serious experimentation with employee participation in corporate governance began in Europe. The results of this experimentation are most conspicuous in Germany, where, under legislation initially adopted for the coal and steel industries in 1951 and extended by stages to the rest of German industry between 1952 and 1976, employees are entitled to elect half of the members of the (upper-tier) board of directors in all large German firms. This German form of "codetermination" has been the most far-reaching experiment with employee participation. It is not unique, however. A number of other European countries have experimented in more modest ways, typically requiring between one and three labor representatives on the boards of large corporations. Moreover, the Dutch have adopted a wholly unique model for larger domestic companies that combines elements of the manager-, labor-, and state-oriented models. Under the Dutch "structure" regime, supervisory boards are self-appointing, although both labor and shareholders retain the right to object to the board appointments. In the event of an objection, the commercial court decides.

Enthusiasm for employee participation crested in the 1970s with the radical expansion of codetermination in Germany and the drafting of the European Community's proposed Fifth Directive on Company Law,[8] under which German-style codetermination would be extended throughout Europe. Employee participation also attracted considerable attention in the United States during that period, as adversarial unionism began to lose its appeal as a means of dealing with problems of labor contracting and, in fact, began to disappear from the industrial scene. Since then, worker participation in corporate governance has steadily lost power as a normative ideal. Despite repeated dilution, Europe's Fifth Directive has never become law, and it now seems highly unlikely that German-style codetermination will ever be adopted elsewhere.

The growing view today is that meaningful direct worker voting participation in corporate affairs tends to produce inefficient decisions, paralysis, or weak boards, and that these costs are likely to exceed any potential benefits that worker participation might bring. The problem, at root, seems to be one of governance. While direct employee participation in corporate decisionmaking

---

8. Amended Proposal for a Fifth Directive Founded on Article 54(3)(G) of the Treaty Concerning the Structure of Public Limited Companies and the Powers and Obligations of their Organs, 1983 O.J. (C 240) 2.

446   THE GEORGETOWN LAW JOURNAL   [Vol. 89:439

may mitigate some of the inefficiencies that can beset labor contracting, the workforce in typical firms is too heterogeneous in its interests to form an effective governing body—and the problems are magnified greatly when employees must share governance with investors, as in codetermined firms. In general, contractual devices, whatever their weaknesses, are (when supplemented by appropriate labor market regulation) evidently superior to voting and other collective choice mechanisms in resolving conflicts of interest among and between a corporation's investors and employees.[9]

Today, even inside Germany, few commentators argue for codetermination as a general model for corporate law in other jurisdictions. Rather, codetermination now tends to be defended in Germany as, at most, a workable adaptation to local interests and circumstances or, even more modestly, an experiment that, though of questionable value, would now be politically difficult to undo.[10]

3. The State-Oriented Model

Both before and after the Second World War, there was widespread support for a corporatist system in which the government would play a strong direct role in the affairs of large business firms to provide some assurance that private enterprise would serve the public interest. Technocratic government bureaucrats, the theory went, would help to avoid the deficiencies of the market through the direct exercise of influence in corporate affairs. This approach was most extensively realized in postwar France and Japan. In the United States, though there was little actual experimentation with this approach outside of the defense industries, the model attracted considerable intellectual attention. Perhaps the most influential exposition of the state-oriented model in the Anglo-American world was Andrew Shonfield's 1968 book, *Modern Capitalism*, with its admiring description of French and Japanese style "indicative planning."[11] The strong performance of the Japanese economy, and subsequently of other state-guided Asian economies, lent substantial credibility to this model even through the 1980s.

The principal instruments of state control over corporate affairs in corporatist economies generally lie outside of corporate law. They include, for example,

---

9. *See* HANSMANN, *supra* note 3, at 89-119; Henry Hansmann, *Probleme von Kollektiventscheidungen und Theorie der Firma—Folgerungen für die Arbeitnehmermitbestimmung, in* OKONOMISCHE ANALYSE DES UNTERNEHMENSRECHTS 287-305 (Claus Ott & Hans-Bernd Schäfer eds., 1993); Henry Hansmann, *Worker Participation and Corporate Governance*, 43 U. TORONTO L.J. 589, 589-606 (1993). On the weaknesses of German boards, see, for example, Mark Roe, *German Securities Markets and German Codetermination*, 1998 COLUM. BUS. L. REV. 167.

10. Some commentators, of course, continue to see codetermination as a core element of a unique Northern European form of corporate governance. *See, e.g.,* MICHEL ALBERT, CAPITALISM VS. CAPITALISM (1993) (asserting generally the superiority of the "Rhine Model" of capitalism over the "Anglo-Saxon Model"). Even Albert concedes, however, the growing ideological power of shareholder-oriented corporate governance. *See id.* at 169-90.

11. ANDREW SHONFIELD, MODERN CAPITALISM: THE CHANGING BALANCE OF PUBLIC AND PRIVATE POWER 84-85 (1968).

substantial discretion in the hands of government bureaucrats over the allocation of credit, foreign exchange, licenses, and exemptions from anticompetition
rules. Nevertheless, corporate law also plays a role by, for example, weakening
shareholder control over corporate managers (to reduce pressures on managers
that might operate counter to the preferences of the state) and employing
state-administered criminal sanctions rather than shareholder-controlled civil
lawsuits as the principal sanction for managerial malfeasance (to give the state
strong authority over managers that could be exercised at the government's
discretion).

The state-oriented model, however, has now also lost most of its attraction.
One reason is the move away from state socialism in general as a popular
intellectual and political model. Important landmarks on this path include the
rise of Thatcherism in England in the 1970s, Mitterand's abandonment of state
ownership in France in the 1980s, and the sudden collapse of communism
nearly everywhere in the 1990s. The relatively poor performance of the Japanese corporate sector after 1989, together with the more recent collapse of other
Asian economies that were organized on state corporatist lines, has now discredited this model even further. Today, few would assert that giving the state a
strong direct hand in corporate affairs has much normative appeal.

4. Stakeholder Models

Over the past decade, the literature on corporate governance and corporate
law has sometimes advocated "stakeholder" models as a normatively attractive
alternative to a strongly shareholder-oriented view of the corporation. The
stakeholders involved may be employees, creditors, customers, merchants in a
firm's local community, or even broader interest groups such as beneficiaries of
a well-preserved environment. The stakeholders, it is argued, will be subject to
opportunistic exploitation by the firm and its shareholders if corporate managers
are accountable only to the firm's shareholders; corporate law must therefore
ensure that managers are responsive to stakeholder interests as well.

While stakeholder models start with a common problem, they posit two
different kinds of solutions. One group of stakeholder models looks to what we
term a "fiduciary" model of the corporation, in which the board of directors
functions as a neutral coordinator of the contributions and returns of all stakeholders in the firm. Under this model, only investors are given direct representation
on the corporate board. Other stakeholders are protected by relaxing the board's
duty or incentive to represent only the interests of shareholders, thus giving the
board greater discretion to look after other stakeholders' interests.

The fiduciary model finds its most explicit recognition in U.S. law in the
form of constituency statutes that permit boards to consider the interests of
constituencies other than shareholders in mounting takeover defenses. Margaret
Blair and Lynn Stout, sophisticated American advocates of the fiduciary model,
also claim to find support for this normative model in other, broader aspects of

U.S. corporate law.[12] In the U.K., the fiduciary model is a key element in the ongoing debate over the duties of corporate directors.[13]

The second group of stakeholder models substitutes direct stakeholder representatives for fiduciary directors. In this "representative" model of the corporation, two or more stakeholder constituencies appoint representatives to the board of directors, which then elaborates policies that maximize the joint welfare of all stakeholders, subject to the bargaining leverage that each group brings to the boardroom table. The board functions ideally then as a kind of collective fiduciary, even though its individual members remain partisan representatives. The board of directors (or supervisory board) then becomes an unmediated "coalition of stakeholder groups" and functions as "an arena for cooperation with respect to the function of monitoring the management," as well as an arena for resolving "conflicts with respect to the specific interests of different stakeholder groups."[14]

Neither the fiduciary nor the representative stakeholder models, however, constitute at bottom a new approach to the corporation. Rather, despite the new rhetoric with which the stakeholder models are presented, and the more explicit economic theorizing that sometimes accompanies them, they are at heart just variants on the older manager-oriented and labor-oriented models. Stakeholder models of the fiduciary type are in effect just reformulations of the manager-oriented model, and they suffer the same weaknesses. While untethered managers may better serve the interests of some classes of stakeholders, such as a firm's existing employees and creditors, the managers' own interests will often come to have disproportionate prominence in their decisionmaking, with costs to some interest groups—such as shareholders, customers, and potential *new* employees and creditors—that outweigh any gains to the stakeholders who benefit. Moreover, the courts are evidently incapable of formulating and enforcing fiduciary duties of sufficient refinement to ensure that managers behave more efficiently and fairly.

Stakeholder models of the representative type closely resemble yesterday's labor-oriented model, though generalized to extend to other stakeholders as well, and are again subject to the same weaknesses. The mandatory inclusion of

---

12. *See* Margaret M. Blair & Lynn A. Stout, *A Team Production Theory of Corporate Law*, 85 Va. L. Rev. 247, 287-319 (1999).

13. *See* COMPANY LAW REFORM STEERING GROUP, MODERN COMPANY LAW FOR A COMPETITIVE ENVIRONMENT: THE STRATEGIC FRAMEWORK 39-46 (1999) (setting forth the alternatives of maintaining the existing directorial duty of following enlightened shareholder interest or reformulating a "pluralist" duty to all major stakeholders in order to encourage firm-specific investment). After comment and discussion, however, the U.K. Company Law Reform Steering Group has chosen to propose the shareholder primacy norm, in accordance with the emerging consensus of legal scholars and practitioners everywhere. *See* COMPANY LAW REFORM STEERING GROUP, MODERN COMPANY LAW FOR A COMPETITIVE ECONOMY: DEVELOPING THE FRAMEWORK 29-31 (2000) (directors must act for the benefit of "members as a whole," that is, shareholders).

14. REINHARD H. SMITH & GERALD SPINDLER, PATH DEPENDENCE, CORPORATE GOVERNANCE AND COMPLEMENTARITY—A COMMENT ON BEBCHUK AND ROE 14, (Johann Wolfgang Goethe-Universitat Working Paper Series: Finance and Accounting No. 27, 1999).

any set of stakeholder representatives on the board is likely to impair corporate decisionmaking processes with costly consequences that outweigh any gains to the groups that obtain representation. Thus, the same forces that have been discrediting the older models are also undermining the stakeholder model as a viable alternative to the shareholder-oriented model.

B. COMPETITIVE PRESSURES TOWARD CONVERGENCE

The shareholder-oriented model has emerged as the normative consensus not just because of the failure of the alternatives, but because important economic forces have made the virtues of that model increasingly salient. There are, broadly speaking, three ways in which a model of corporate governance can come to be recognized as superior: by force of *logic*, by force of *example*, and by force of *competition*. The emerging consensus in favor of the standard model has, in recent years, been driven with increasing intensity by each of these forces. We examine them here in turn.

1. The Force of Logic

An important source of the success of the standard model is that, in recent years, scholars and other commentators in law, economics, and business have developed persuasive reasons, which we have already explored above, to believe that this model offers greater efficiencies than the principal alternatives. One of these reasons is that, in most circumstances, the interests of equity investors in the firm—the firm's residual claimants—cannot adequately be protected by contract. Rather, to protect their interests, they must be given the right to control the firm. A second reason is that, if the control rights granted to the firm's equity-holders are exclusive and strong, they will have powerful incentives to maximize the value of the firm. A third reason is that the interests of participants in the firm other than shareholders can generally be given substantial protection by contract and regulation, so that maximization of the firm's value by its shareholders complements the interests of those other participants rather than competing with them. A fourth reason is that, even where contractual and regulatory devices offer only imperfect protection for nonshareholder interests, adapting the firm's governance structure to make it directly responsible to those interests creates more difficulties than it solves.

This reasoning is today reflected in much of the current literature on corporate finance and the economics of the firm—a literature that is becoming increasingly international. The consequence is to highlight the economic case for the shareholder-oriented model of governance. In addition, the persuasive power of the standard model has been amplified through its acceptance by a worldwide network of corporate intermediaries, including international law firms, the big five accounting firms, and the principal investment banks and consulting firms—a network whose rapidly expanding scale and scope give it exceptional influence in diffusing the standard model of shareholder-centered corporate governance.

2. The Force of Example

The second source of the success of the standard model of corporate governance is the economic performance of jurisdictions in which it predominates. A simple comparison across countries adhering to different models—at least in very recent years—lends credence to the view that adherence to the standard model promotes better economic outcomes. The developed common-law jurisdictions have performed well in comparison to the principal East Asian and continental European countries, which are less in alignment with the standard model. The main examples include, of course, the strong performance of the American economy in comparison with the weaker economic performance of the German, Japanese, and French economies.

One might surely object that the success of the shareholder-oriented model is quite recent and will perhaps prove to be ephemeral, and that the apparent normative consensus based on that success will be ephemeral as well. After all, only fifteen years ago many thought that Japanese and German firms, which were clearly not organized on the shareholder-oriented model, were winning the competition, and that this was because they had adopted a superior form of corporate governance.[15] However, this is probably a mistaken interpretation of the nature of the economic competition in recent decades, and it is surely at odds with today's prevailing opinion. The competition of the 1960s, '70s, and early '80s was in fact among Japanese state-oriented corporations, German labor-oriented corporations, and American manager-oriented corporations. It was not until the late 1980s that one could speak of widespread international competition from shareholder-oriented firms.

3. The Force of Competition

The increasing internationalization of both product and financial markets has brought individual firms from jurisdictions adhering to different models into direct competition. It is now widely thought that firms organized and operated according to the shareholder-oriented model have had the upper hand in these more direct encounters as well.[16] Such firms can be expected to have important competitive advantages over firms adhering more closely to other models. These advantages include access to equity capital at lower cost (including,

---

15. To be fair, however, American commentators tended to praise corporate governance in Germany and Japan in the name of the shareholder model. Thus, it was the purported ability of German banks to monitor managers and correctly value long-term business projects that caught the eye of American commentators after the 1970s, not codetermination or the labor-oriented model of the firm. *See, e.g.,* MICHAEL T. JACOBS, SHORT-TERM AMERICA: THE CAUSES AND CURES OF OUR BUSINESS MYOPIA 69-71 (1991).

16. Indirect evidence to this effect comes from international surveys such as a recent poll of top managers conducted by *The Financial Times* to determine the world's most respected companies. Four of the top five most respected companies were American and hence operated under the shareholder model (the fifth was DaimlerChrysler, which is "almost" American for these purposes). Similarly, twenty-nine of the top forty firms were either American or British. *See Annual Review, World's Most Respected Companies,* FIN. TIMES (LONDON), Dec. 7, 1999.

conspicuously, start-up capital), more aggressive development of new product markets,[17] stronger incentives to reorganize along lines that are managerially coherent, and more rapid abandonment of inefficient investments.

These competitive advantages do not always imply that firms governed by the standard model will displace those governed by an alternative model in the course of firm-to-firm competition, for two reasons. First, firms operating under the standard model may be no more efficient than other firms in many respects. For example, state-oriented Japanese and Korean companies have demonstrated great efficiency in the management and expansion of standardized production processes, while German and Dutch firms such as Daimler Benz and Philips (operating under labor- and management-oriented models, respectively) have been widely recognized for engineering prowess and technical innovation. Second, even when firms governed by the standard model are clearly more efficient than their nonstandard competitors, the cost-conscious standard-model firms may be forced to abandon particular markets for precisely that reason. Less efficient firms organized under alternative models may overinvest in capacity or accept abnormally low returns on their investments in general, and thereby come to dominate a product market by underpricing their profit-maximizing competitors. But if the competitive advantages of standard-model firms do not necessarily force the displacement of nonstandard firms in established markets, these standard-model firms are likely, for the reasons offered above, to achieve a disproportionate share among start-up firms, in new product markets, and in industries that are in the process of rapid change.[18]

The ability of standard-model firms to expand rapidly in growth industries is magnified, moreover, by access to institutional investors and the international equity markets, which understandably prefer shareholder-oriented governance and are influential advocates of the standard model. Those equity investors, after all, are exclusively interested in maximizing the financial returns on their investments. Over time, then, the standard model is likely to win the competitive struggle on the margins, confining other governance models to older firms and mature product markets. As the pace of technological change continues to quicken, this competitive advantage should continue to increase.

C. THE RISE OF THE SHAREHOLDER CLASS

In tandem with the competitive forces just described, a final source of ideological convergence on the standard model is a fundamental realignment of

---

17. *See, e.g.*, ROMAN FRYDMAN ET AL., WHY OWNERSHIP MATTERS? ENTREPRENEURSHIP AND THE RESTRUCTURING OF ENTERPRISES IN CENTRAL EUROPE (1998) (asserting that firms privatized to outside owners proved superior to state firms and firms privatized to workers or previous managers in new market development).

18. In this regard it should be noted that small- and medium-sized firms in every jurisdiction are organized under legal regimes consistent with the standard model. Thus, shareholders—and shareholders alone—select the members of supervisory boards in the vast majority of (smaller) German and Dutch firms. These jurisdictions impose alternative labor- or manager-oriented regimes only on a minority of comparatively large firms.

452   THE GEORGETOWN LAW JOURNAL   [Vol. 89:439

interest group structures in developed economies. At the center of this realignment is the emergence of a public shareholder class as a broad and powerful interest group in both corporate and political affairs across jurisdictions. There are two elements to this realignment. The first is the rapid expansion of the ownership of equity securities within broad segments of society, creating a coherent interest group that presents an increasingly strong countervailing force to the organized interests of managers, employees, and the state. The second is the shift in power, within this expanding shareholder class, in favor of the interests of minority and noncontrolling shareholders over those of inside or controlling shareholders.

1. The Diffusion of Equity Ownership

Stock ownership is becoming more pervasive everywhere.[19] No longer is it confined to a small group of wealthy citizens. In the United States, this diffusion of share ownership has been underway since the beginning of the twentieth century. In recent years, however, it has accelerated substantially. Since the Second World War, an ever-increasing number of American workers have had their savings invested in corporate equities through pension funds. Over the same period, the mutual fund industry has also expanded rapidly, becoming the repository of an ever-increasing share of nonpension savings for the population at large.[20] We have begun to see parallel developments in Europe and Japan, and to some extent elsewhere, as markets for equity securities have become more developed.[21]

The growing wealth of developed societies is a major factor underlying these changes. Even blue-collar workers now often have sufficient personal savings to justify investment in equity securities. No longer do labor and capital constitute clearly distinct interest groups in society. Workers, through share ownership, increasingly share the economic interests of other equity-holders. Indeed, in the United States, union pension funds are today quite active in pressing the view that companies must be managed in the best interests of their shareholders.[22]

---

19. Stock market capitalization as a percentage of GDP has risen dramatically in virtually every major jurisdiction over the past 20 years. In most European countries, the increase has been by a factor of three or four. *See Schools Brief: Stocks in Trade*, THE ECONOMIST, Nov. 13, 1999, at 85-86.

20. *See generally* THE GLOBAL CORPORATE GOVERNANCE RESEARCH CENTER, THE CONFERENCE BOARD, INSTITUTIONAL INVESTMENT REPORT: PATTERNS OF INSTITUTIONAL INVESTMENT AND CONTROL IN THE UNITED STATES (1997).

21. Latin America offers a telling example. In 1981, Chile became the first country in the region to set up a system of private pension funds. By 1995, Argentina, Colombia, and Peru had done the same. By 1996, a total of $108 billion was under management in Latin American pension funds, which by then had come to play an important role in the development of the local equity markets. In 1997, it was estimated that total assets would grow to $200 billion by 2000 and to $600 billion by 2011. *See A Private Affair*, LATIN FIN., Dec. 1998, at 61; Stephen Fidler, *Chile's Crusader for the Cause*, FIN. TIMES (LONDON), Mar. 14, 1997, at 3; *Save Amigo Save*, THE ECONOMIST, Dec. 9, 1995, at 15.

22. *See* Stewart J. Schwab & Randall S. Thomas, *Realigning Corporate Governance: Shareholder Activism by Labor Unions, in* EMPLOYEE REPRESENTATION IN THE EMERGING WORKPLACE: ALTERNATIVES/SUPPLEMENTS TO COLLECTIVE BARGAINING 341 (S. Estreicher ed., 1998).

2. The Shift in Balance Toward Public Shareholders

As the example of the activist union pension funds suggests, diffusion of share ownership is only one aspect of the rise of the shareholder class. Another aspect is the new prominence of substantial institutions that have interests coincident with those of public shareholders and that are prepared to articulate and defend those interests. Institutional investors, such as pension funds and mutual funds—which are particularly prominent in the U.S. and are now rapidly growing elsewhere as well—are the most conspicuous examples of these institutions. Associations of minority investors in European countries provide another example. These institutions not only give effective voice to shareholder interests, but promote in particular the interests of dispersed public shareholders rather than those of controlling shareholders or corporate insiders. The result is that ownership of equity among the public at large, while broader than ever, is at the same time gaining more effective voice in corporate affairs.

Morever, the new activist shareholder-oriented institutions are today acting increasingly on an international scale. As a consequence, their influence now reaches well beyond their home jurisdictions.[23] We now have not only a common ideology supporting shareholder-oriented corporate law, but also an organized interest group to press that ideology—an interest group that is broad, diverse, and increasingly international in its membership.

In the U.S., the principal effect of the expansion and empowerment of the shareholder class has been to shift interest group power from managers to shareholders. In Europe and Japan, the more important effect has been to shift power away from workers and the state and, increasingly, away from dominant shareholders.[24]

D. WEAK FORCES FOR CONVERGENCE

We have spoken here of a number of forces pressing toward international convergence on a relatively uniform standard model of corporate law. Those forces include the internal logic of efficiency, competition, interest group pressure, imitation, and the need for compatibility. We have largely ignored two other potential forces that might also press toward convergence: explicit efforts at cross-border harmonization, and competition among jurisdictions for corporate charters.

---

23. *See, e.g.,* Greg Steinmetz & Michael R. Sesit, *Rising U.S. Investment in European Equities Galvanizes Old World*, WALL ST. J., Aug. 4, 1999, at A1, A8 (describing U.S. investors as sparking important governance changes in large European companies).

24. Of particular interest are signs of change in the cross-ownership networks among major German and Japanese firms. New legislation proposed by the German government would eliminate the heavy (up to fifty percent) capital gains taxes on corporate sales of stock, which is expected to result in widespread dissolution of block holdings. *See* Haig Simonian, *Germany to End Tax on Sale of Cross-Holdings*, FIN. TIMES (LONDON), Dec. 24, 1999, at 1. In Japan, *keiretsu* structures are beginning to unwind as a result of bank mergers and competitive pressure to seek higher returns on capital. *See* Paul Abrahams & Gillian Tett, *The Circle Is Broken*, FIN. TIMES (LONDON), Nov. 9, 1999, at 18.

454   THE GEORGETOWN LAW JOURNAL   [Vol. 89:439

1. Harmonization

The European Union has been the locus of the most intense efforts to date at self-conscious harmonization of corporate law across jurisdictions. That process, however, has proved a relatively weak force for convergence: Where there exists substantial divergence in corporate law across member states, efforts at harmonization have generally borne little fruit. Moreover, harmonization proposals often have been characterized by an effort to impose throughout the E.U. regulatory measures of questionable efficiency, with the result that harmonization sometimes seems more an effort to avoid the standard model than to further it.

For these reasons, the other pressures toward convergence described above are likely to be much more important forces for convergence than are explicit efforts at harmonization. At most, we expect that, once the consensus for adoption of the standard model has become sufficiently strong, harmonization may serve as a convenient pretext for overriding the objections of entrenched national interest groups that resist reform of corporate law within individual states.

2. Competition for Charters

The American experience of competition among state jurisdictions suggests that cross-border competition for corporate charters can be a powerful force for convergence in corporate law and, in particular, for convergence on an efficient model.[25] It seems quite plausible, however, that the choice of law rules necessary for this form of competition will not be adopted in most jurisdictions until substantial convergence has already taken place. We expect that the most important steps toward convergence can and will be taken with relative rapidity before explicit cross-border competition for charters is permitted in most of the world, and that the latter process will ultimately be used, at most, as a means of working out the fine details of convergence and of ongoing minor experimentation and adjustment thereafter.

IV. CONVERGENCE OF GOVERNANCE PRACTICES

Thus far we have attempted to explain the sources of *ideological* convergence on the standard model of corporate governance. Our principal argument is on this normative level; we make the claim that no important competitors to the standard model of corporate governance remain persuasive today. This claim is consistent with significant differences among jurisdictions in corporate practice and law over the short run; ideological convergence does not necessarily mean rapid convergence in practice. There are many potential obstacles to rapid institutional convergence, even when there is general consensus on what constitutes best practice. Nevertheless, we believe that the developing ideological

---

25. *See generally* ROBERTA ROMANO, THE GENIUS OF AMERICAN CORPORATE LAW (1993).

consensus on the standard model will have important implications for the convergence of practice and law over the long run.

We expect that the reform of corporate governance practices will generally precede the reform of corporate law, for the simple reason that governance practice is largely a matter of private ordering that does not require legislative action. Recent events in most developed jurisdictions—and in many developing ones—bear out this prediction. Under the influence of the ideological and interest group changes discussed above, corporate governance reform has already become the watchword not only in North America but also in Europe and Japan. Corporate actors are themselves implementing structural changes to bring their firms closer to the standard model. In the U.S., these changes include appointment of larger numbers of independent directors to boards of directors, reduction in overall board size, development of powerful board committees dominated by outsiders (such as audit committees, compensation committees, and nominating committees), closer links between management compensation and the value of the firm's equity securities, and strong communication between board members and institutional shareholders. In Europe and Japan, many of the same changes are taking place, though with a lag. Examples range from the OECD's promulgation of new principles of corporate governance, to recent decisions by Japanese companies to reduce board sizes and include nonexecutive directors (following the lead of Sony), to the rapid diffusion of stock option compensation plans for top managers in the U.K. and in the principal commercial jurisdictions of continental Europe.

V. LEGAL CONVERGENCE

Not surprisingly, convergence in the fine structure of corporate law proceeds more slowly than convergence in governance practices. Legal change requires legislative action. Nevertheless, we expect shareholder pressure (and the power of shareholder-oriented ideology) to force gradual legal changes, largely but not entirely in the direction of Anglo-American corporate and securities law. There are already important indications of evolutionary convergence in the realms of board structure, securities regulation, and accounting methodologies, and even in the regulation of takeovers.

A. BOARD STRUCTURE

With respect to board structure, convergence has been in the direction of a legal regime that strongly favors a single-tier board that is relatively small and that contains some insiders as well as a majority of outside directors. Mandatory two-tier board structures seem a thing of the past; the weaker and less responsive boards that they promote are justified principally as a complement to worker codetermination and thus share—indeed, constitute one of—the weaknesses of the latter institution. The declining fortunes of the two-tier board are reflected in the evolution of the European Union's Proposed Regulation on the

Statute for a European Company. When originally drafted in 1970, that Regulation called for a mandatory two-tier board. In 1991, however, the Proposed Regulation was amended to permit member states to prescribe either a two-tier or a single-tier system. Meanwhile, on the practical side, France, which made provision for an optional two-tier board when the concept was more in vogue, has seen few of its corporations adopt the device.[26]

At the same time, jurisdictions that traditionally favored the opposite extreme of insider-dominated, single-tier boards have come to accept a significant complement of outside directors. In the U.S., the New York Stock Exchange listing rules have long mandated that independent directors serve on the important audit committees of listed firms[27] and, more recently, state law doctrine has created a strong role for outside directors in approving transactions where interests might be conflicted.[28] In Japan, a similar evolution may be foreshadowed by the recent movement among Japanese companies, mentioned above, toward smaller boards and independent directors, and by the recent publication of a code of corporate governance principles advocating these reforms by a committee of leading Japanese managers.[29] The result is convergence from both ends toward the middle: while two-tier boards themselves seem to be on the way out, countries with single-tier board structures are incorporating, in their regimes, one of the strengths of the typical two-tier board regime, namely the substantial role it gives to independent (outside) directors.

B. DISCLOSURE AND CAPITAL MARKET REGULATION

Regulation of routine disclosure to shareholders, intended to aid in policing corporate managers, is also converging conspicuously. Without seeking to examine this complex field in detail here, we note that major jurisdictions outside of the United States are reinforcing their disclosure systems, while the U.S. has been retreating from some of the more inexplicably burdensome of its federal regulations, such as the highly restrictive proxy solicitation rules that until recently crippled communication among American institutional investors. Indeed, the subject matter of mandatory disclosure for public companies is startlingly similar across the major commercial jurisdictions today.[30]

---

26. *See* Lauren J. Aste, *Reforming French Corporate Governance: A Return to the Two Tier Board?*, 32 GEO. WASH. J. INT'L L. & ECON. 1, 45 (1999).

27. *See* NEW YORK STOCK EXCHANGE, NYSE LISTED COMPANY MANUAL § 303.00, *available at* http://www.nyse.com/listed/listed.html (last visited Nov. 1, 2000).

28. *See, e.g.*, Weinberger v. UOP, Inc., 457 A.2d 701 (Del. 1983).

29. CORPORATE GOVERNANCE COMM., CORPORATE GOVERNANCE FORUM OF JAPAN, CORPORATE GOVERNANCE PRINCIPLES 48-50 (1998).

30. This can be seen, for example, by comparing the E.U.'s Listing Particulars Directive with the SEC's Form S-1 for the registration of securities under the 1933 Act. If U.S. disclosure requirements remain more aggressive, one must remember that the E.U. Directives establish minimal requirements that member states can and do supplement. *See* John C. Coffee, Jr., *The Future as History: The Prospects for Global Convergence in Corporate Governance and Its Implications*, 93 Nw. U. L. REV. 641, 668-72 (1999). *See generally* Amir N. Licht, *International Diversity in Securities Regulation:*

Similarly, uniform accounting standards are rapidly crystallizing out of the babble of national rules and practices into two well-defined sets of international standards: the GAAP accounting rules administered by the Financial Auditing Standards Board in the U.S. and the International Accounting Standards administered by the International Accounting Standards Committee in London. While important differences remain between the competing sets of international standards, these differences are far smaller than the variations among the national accounting methodologies that preceded GAAP and the new International Standards. The two international standards, moreover, are likely to converge further, if only because of the economic savings that would result from a single set of global accounting standards.[31]

C. SHAREHOLDER SUITS

Suits initiated by shareholders against directors and managers are now being accommodated in countries that had previously rendered them ineffective. Germany recently reduced the ownership threshold that qualifies shareholders to demand legal action (to be brought by the supervisory board or special company representative) against managing directors, dropping that threshold from a ten percent equity stake to the lesser of a five percent stake or a one million *deutsche Mark* stake when there is suspicion of dishonesty or illegality.[32] Japan, in turn, has altered its rules on posting a bond to remove disincentives for litigation. At the same time, U.S. law is moving toward the center from the other direction by beginning to rein in the country's strong incentives for potentially opportunistic litigation. At the federal level, there are recently strengthened pleading requirements upon initiation of shareholder actions, new safe harbors for forward-looking company projections, and recent provision for lead shareholders to take control in class actions. State law rules, meanwhile, are making it easier for a corporation to get a shareholders' suit dismissed.

D. TAKEOVERS

Regulation of takeovers also seems headed for convergence. As it is, current differences in takeover regulation are more apparent than real. Hostile takeovers are rare outside the Anglo-American jurisdictions, principally owing to the more concentrated patterns of shareholdings outside those jurisdictions. As sharehold-

---

Roadblocks on the Way to Convergence, 20 CARDOZO L. REV. 227 (1998) (discussing convergence in disclosure rules, accounting standards, and corporate governance). In addition, a recent survey of the practices of European issuers finds that actual disclosure practices track U.S. and U.K. disclosure standards even more closely than legal disclosure requirements do. *See* HOWELL JACKSON & ERIC PAN, REGULATORY COMPETITION IN INTERNATIONAL SECURITIES MARKETS: EVIDENCE FROM EUROPE IN 1999 34-39 (John M. Olin Center for Law, Econ. & Bus. Working Paper, Sept. 18, 2000).

31. *See, e.g.*, Elizabeth MacDonald, *U.S. Accounting Board Faults Global Rules*, WALL ST. J., Oct. 18, 1999, at A1.

32. *See* THEODOR BAUMS, CORPORATE GOVERNANCE IN GERMANY: SYSTEM AND CURRENT DEVELOPMENTS pt. VIII.1 (Universitat Osnabruck Working Paper, 1999).

ing patterns become more homogeneous (as we expect they will), and as corporate culture everywhere becomes more accommodating of takeovers (as it seems destined to), takeovers presumably will become much more common in Europe, Japan, and elsewhere.[33]

Moreover, where operative legal constraints on takeovers in fact differ, they show signs of convergence. In particular, for several decades the U.S. has been increasing its regulation of takeovers, placing additional constraints both on the ability of acquirers to act opportunistically and on the ability of incumbent managers to entrench themselves or engage in self-dealing. With the widespread diffusion of the "poison pill" defense, and the accompanying limits that courts have placed on the use of that defense, partial hostile tender offers of a coercive character are a thing of the past—a result similar to that which European jurisdictions have accomplished with a "mandatory bid rule," requiring acquirers of control to purchase all shares in their target companies at a single price.

To be sure, jurisdictions diverge in other aspects of takeover law where the points of convergence are still uncertain. For example, American directors enjoy far more latitude to defend against hostile takeovers than do directors in most European jurisdictions. Under current Delaware law, incumbent boards have authority to resist hostile offers, although they remain vulnerable to bids that are tied to proxy fights at shareholder meetings. As the incidence of hostile takeovers increases in Europe, European jurisdictions may incline toward Delaware by permitting additional defensive tactics. Alternatively, given the dangers of managerial entrenchment, Delaware may move toward European norms by limiting defensive tactics more severely. While we cannot predict where the equilibrium point will lie, it is a reasonable conjecture that the law on both sides of the Atlantic will ultimately converge on a single regime.

E. JUDICIAL DISCRETION

There remains one very general aspect of corporate law on which one might feel that convergence will be slow to come: the degree of judicial discretion in ex post resolution of disputes among corporate actors. Such discretion has long been much more conspicuous in the common-law jurisdictions, and particularly in the U.S., than in the civil-law jurisdictions. Even here, though, there is good reason to believe that there will be strong convergence across systems over time. Civil-law jurisdictions, whether in the form of court decisionmaking or

---

33. Already Europe has seen a remarkable wave of takeovers in 1999, culminating in the largest hostile takeover in history: Vodaphone's acquisition of Mannesmann. In addition, many established jurisdictions are adopting rules to regulate tender offers that bear a family resemblance to the Williams Act or to the rules of the London City Code. See, for example, Brazil's tender offer regulations, Secs. Comm'n Ruling 69, Sept. 8. 1987, Arts. 1-4, and Italy's recently adopted reform of takeover regulation, Legislative Decree 58 of February 24, 1998 (the Financial Markets Act or so-called "Draghi Reform"), *cited in* STUDIO LEGALE ABBATESCIANNI: ASSOCIAZIONE PROFESSIONALE DI AVVOCATI E DOTTORI COMMERCIAL-ISTI, *The New Italian Law on Takeovers, at* http://www.sla.it/takeovers.htm (last visited Nov. 1, 2000).

arbitration, seem to be moving toward a more discretionary model.[34] United States securities law is civilian in spirit and elaborated by detailed rules promulgated by the Securities Exchange Commission (SEC). At the same time, there are signs of growing discomfort with the more extreme forms of unpredictable ex post decisionmaking that have sometimes been characteristic of, say, the Delaware courts. Scholars have begun to suspect the open-ended texture of Delware case law,[35] while the American Law Institute has offered a code-like systemization of corporate law in the form of the Corporate Governance Project, which includes even the notoriously vague and open-ended U.S. case law that articulates the fiduciary duties of loyalty and care.

VI. POTENTIAL OBSTACLES TO CONVERGENCE

To be sure, important interests are threatened by movement toward the standard model, and those interests can be expected to serve as a brake on change. We doubt, however, that such interests will be able to stave off for long the reforms called for by the growing ideological consensus focused on the standard model.

To take one example, consider the argument, prominently made by Lucian Bebchuk and Mark Roe,[36] that the private value extracted by corporate controllers (controlling shareholders or powerful managers) will long serve as a barrier to the evolution of efficient ownership structures, governance practices, and corporate law. The essential structure of the Bebchuk and Roe argument is as follows: In jurisdictions lacking strong protection for minority shareholders, controlling shareholders divert to themselves a disproportionate share of corporate cash flows. The controlling shareholders thus have an incentive to avoid any change in their firm's ownership or governance, or in the regulation to which their firm is subject, that would force them to share the corporation's earnings more equitably. Moreover, these corporate insiders have the power in many jurisdictions to prevent such changes. Their position as controlling shareholders permits them to block changes in the firm's ownership structure merely by refusing to sell their shares. Their position also permits them to block changes in governance by selecting the firm's directors. And, in those societies in which—as in most of Europe—closely controlled firms dominate the economy, the wealth and collective political weight of controlling shareholders permits

---

34. *See* The *Holzmüller* decision of the German Federal Court, BGHZ, Zivilsenat, II ZR 174/80 (1982) (German case law extension of shareholder right to vote to all fundamental corporate transactions).

35. *See, e.g.*, Douglas M. Branson, *The Chancellor's Foot in Delaware: Schnell and Its Progeny*, 14 J. CORP. L. 515 (1989); Ehud Kamar, *A Regulatory Competition Theory of Indeterminancy in Corporate Law*, 98 COLUM. L. REV. 1908 (1998); Jonathan R. Macey & Geoffrey P. Miller, *Toward an Interest-Group Theory of Delaware Corporate Law*, 65 TEX. L. REV. 469 (1987).

36. *See* Lucian Bebchuk & Mark Roe, *A Theory of Path Dependence in Corporate Ownership and Governance*, 52 STAN. L. REV. 127 (1999).

them to block legal reforms that would compromise their disproportionate private returns.

This pessimistic view seems unwarranted, though. If, as the developing consensus view holds, the standard shareholder-oriented governance model maximizes corporate value, controlling shareholders who are motivated chiefly by economic considerations may not wish to retain control of their firms. And, even if nonmonetary considerations lead insiders to retain control, the economic significance of firms dominated by these insiders is likely to diminish over time both in their own jurisdictions and in the world market.

A. TRANSACTIONS TO CAPTURE SURPLUS

First, consider the case of controlling shareholders ("controllers") who wish to maximize their financial returns. Suppose that the prevailing legal regime permits controlling shareholders to extract large private benefits from which public shareholders are excluded. Predictably, these controllers will sell their shares only if they receive a premium price that captures the value of their private benefits, and they will reject any corporate governance reform that reduces the value of those returns. That such controllers will prefer to increase their own returns over increasing returns to the corporation does not imply, however, that they will reject governance institutions or ownership structures that maximize firm value. Bebchuk and Roe are too quick to conclude that controllers cannot themselves profit by facilitating efficient governance.

Controllers who extract large private benefits from public companies are likely to indulge in two forms of inefficient management. First, they may select investment projects that maximize their own private returns over returns to the firm. For example, a controller might select a less profitable investment project over a more profitable one precisely because it offers opportunities for lucrative self-dealing. Second, controllers are likely to have a preference for retaining and reinvesting earnings over distributing them, even when it is inefficient to do so. The reason is that formal corporate distributions must be shared with minority shareholders, while earnings reinvested in the firm remain available for subsequent conversion into private benefits—for example, through self-dealing transactions. Moreover, a controller's incentive to engage in both forms of inefficient behavior increases markedly if—as has been common in Europe—she employs devices such as stock pyramids, corporate cross-holdings, and dual-class stock to maintain a lock on voting control while reducing her proportionate equity stake.[37]

Where law enforcement is effective, however, inefficient behavior itself creates strong financial incentives to pursue more efficient ownership and governance structures. When share prices are sufficiently depressed, anyone—

---

37. *See* LUCIAN BEBCHUK ET AL., STOCK PYRAMIDS, CROSS-OWNERSHIP, AND DUAL CLASS EQUITY: THE CREATION AND AGENCY COSTS OF SEPARATING CONTROL FROM CASH FLOW RIGHTS (NBER Working Paper No. 6951, 1999).

including controllers themselves—can generate net gains by introducing more efficient governance structures. It follows that controllers who can capture most or all of the value of these efficiency gains stand to profit privately even more than they profit by extracting non-pro-rata benefits from poorly governed firms. Controllers can capture these efficiency gains, moreover, in at least two ways: (1) by selling out at a premium price reflecting potential efficiency gains to a buyer or group of buyers that is willing and able to operate under nonexploitative governance rules; or (2) by buying up minority shares (at depressed prices) and either managing their firms as sole owners or reselling their entire firms to buyers with efficient ownership structures.

For controllers to extract these efficiency gains, however, efficient restructuring must be legally possible: That is, the legal regime must offer means by which restructured firms can commit to good governance practices. This can be done in several ways without threatening the private returns of controllers who have not yet undertaken to restructure. One solution is an optional corporate and securities law regime that is more dedicated to protecting minority shareholders than the prevailing regime. For example, firms can be permitted to list their shares on foreign exchanges with more rigorous shareholder-protection rules. Another solution is simply to enforce shareholder-protective provisions that are written into a restructured firm's articles of incorporation.

It follows that even financially self-interested controllers have an incentive to promote the creation of legal regimes in which firms at least have a *choice* of forming along efficient lines, which, as we have argued, today means along shareholder-oriented lines. Once such an (optional) efficient regime has been established and many of the existing exploitative firms have taken advantage of the regime to profit from an efficient restructuring, there should be a serious reduction in the size of the interest group that wishes even to maintain as an option the old regime's accommodation of firms that are exploitative toward noncontrolling shareholders.

Bebchuk and Roe appear to assume that such developments will not occur because the law will inhibit controlling shareholders from seeking efficient restructuring by forcing them to share any gains from the restructuring equitably with noncontrolling shareholders. It is more plausible, however, to suppose that the law will allow controlling shareholders to claim the gains associated with an efficient restructuring—by means of techniques such as freezeout mergers and coercive tender offers—in jurisdictions where controllers are able to extract large private benefits from ordinary corporate operations. In short, if current controlling shareholders are interested just in maximizing their financial returns, we can expect substantial pressure toward the adoption of efficient law.

B. CONTROLLERS WHO WISH TO BUILD EMPIRES

Controlling shareholders do not always, however, wish to maximize their financial returns. Rather—and we suspect this is often true in Europe—they may also seek nonpecuniary returns. For example, a controlling shareholder may wish simply to be on top of the largest corporate empire possible, and therefore be prepared to overinvest in building market share by selling at a price too low to maximize returns while reinvesting all available returns in expanded capacity and research and development. Alternatively, a controller may be willing to accept a low financial return in order to indulge a taste for a wide range of other costly practices, from putting incompetent family members in positions of responsibility to preserving quasi-feudal relations with employees and their local communities. Such practices may even be efficient if the controller values his nonpecuniary returns more than he would the monetary returns that are given up. Where the controller shares ownership with noncontrolling shareholders who do not value the nonpecuniary returns, though, there is the risk that the controlling shareholder will exploit the noncontrolling shareholders by refusing to distribute the firm's earnings and instead reinvesting those earnings in low-return projects that are valued principally by the controller.[38]

Efficiency-enhancing control transactions of the type described in the preceding section may have little to offer controlling shareholders of this type, since the restructuring may require that they give up control of the firm, and hence give up not only the nonpecuniary returns they were purchasing for themselves with the noncontrolling shareholders' money, but also the nonpecuniary returns they were purchasing with their own share of the firm's invested capital. Thus, controlling shareholders who value nonpecuniary gains will have less incentive than controllers whose motives are purely financial to favor efficient corporate legal structures.

Moreover, inefficient firms with such controllers may survive quite nicely in competitive markets and, in fact, expand, despite their inefficiencies. For example, if the controllers place value only on the size of the firm they control, they will continue to reinvest in expansion so long as the return offered simply exceeds zero, with the result that they can and will take market share from competing firms that are managed much more efficiently but must pay their shareholders a market rate of return.

Jurisdictions with large numbers of firms dominated by controllers with nonpecuniary motivations will, therefore, feel relatively less pressure than other jurisdictions to adopt standard-model corporate law. Yet even in those jurisdictions—which may include much of Western Europe today—the pressure for moving toward the standard model is likely to grow irresistibly strong in the relatively near future. We briefly explore here several reasons for this.

---

38. This can, of course, happen only where the controllers somehow have been able to mislead the noncontrolling shareholders. If the latter shareholders purchased their shares knowing that they would not have control, and that the controllers would divert a share of returns to themselves through inefficient investments, then they presumably paid a price for the shares that was discounted to reflect this diversion, leaving the noncontrolling shareholders with a market rate of return on their investment.

1. The Insiders' Political Clout Will Be Insufficient to Protect Them

To begin with, the low profitability of firms that pursue nonpecuniary returns is likely to select against their owners as controllers of industry. As long as the owners of these firms subsidize low-productivity practices, they become progressively poorer relative to investors in new businesses and owners of established firms who seek either to enhance shareholder value or to sell out to others who will, with the result that economic and political influence will shift to the latter.

Furthermore, the success of firms following shareholder-oriented governance practices is likely to undermine political support for alternative models of corporate governance for two reasons. First, as we have suggested above, the rise of a shareholder class with growing wealth creates an interest group to press for reform of corporate governance to encourage value-enhancing practices and restrain controlling shareholders from extracting private benefits. Companies, whether domestic or foreign, that attract public shareholders and pension funds by promising a better bottom line also create natural enthusiasts for law reform and the standard model.

The second reason for a decline in the appeal of alternative styles of corporate governance is the broader phenomenon of ideological convergence on the standard model. Where previous ideologies may have celebrated the *noblesse oblige* of quasi-feudal family firms or the industrial prowess of huge conglomerates ruled by insiders, the increasing salience of the standard model makes empire-building and domination suspect, and the extraction of private value at the expense of minority shareholders illegitimate. Costly governance practices therefore become increasingly hard to sustain politically. Viewed through the lens of the new ideology, the old practices are not only inefficient but also unjust, since they deprive ordinary citizens, including pensioners and small investors, of a fair return on their investments. As civil society grows more democratic, the privileged returns of controlling shareholders, leading families, and entrenched managers become increasingly suspect.

Indeed, we expect that the social values that make it so prestigious for families to control corporate empires in many countries will change importantly in the years to come. The essentially feudal norms we now see in many patterns of industrial ownership will be displaced by social values that place greater weight on social egalitarianism and individual entrepreneurship, with the result that there will be an ever-dwindling group of firms dominated by controllers who place great weight on the nonpecuniary returns from presiding personally over a corporate fiefdom.

2. The Insiders Who Preserve Their Firms and Legal Protections Will Become Increasingly Irrelevant

Finally, even if dominant corporate controllers successfully block reform for some period of time in any given jurisdiction, they are likely to become increasingly irrelevant in the domestic economy, the world economy, or both. At home, as we have already noted, the terms on which public equity capital becomes available to finance new firms and new product markets are likely to be dominated by the standard model. Venture capital investments and initial public offerings are unlikely to occur if minority investors are not offered significant protection. This protection can be provided without disturbing the older, established firms by establishing separate standard-model institutions that apply only to new firms. An example of this is the *Neuer Markt* in the Frankfurt Stock Exchange, which provides the additional protection of enhanced disclosure and GAAP accounting standards for investors in start-up companies in search of equity capital, while leaving the less rigorous older rules in place for already established firms.

Moreover, to the extent that domestic law or domestic firms fail to provide adequate protections for public shareholders, other jurisdictions can supply the protection of the standard model. Investment capital can flow to other countries and to foreign firms that do business in the home jurisdiction. Alternatively, domestic companies may be able to reincorporate in foreign jurisdictions or bind themselves to comply with the shareholder protections offered by foreign law by listing on a foreign exchange (as some Israeli firms now do by listing on NASDAQ).[39]

Through devices such as these that effectively permit new firms to adopt a model that differs from that applicable to old firms, the national law and governance practices that protect controlling insiders in established firms can be maintained without crippling the national economy. The result is to partition off, and grandfather in, the older family-controlled or manager-dominated firms, whose costly governance practices will make them increasingly irrelevant to economic activity even within their local jurisdictions.

VII. EFFICIENT NON-CONVERGENCE

Not all divergence among corporate law regimes reflects inefficiency. Efficient divergence can arise either through adaptation to local social structures or through fortuity. Neither logic nor competition is likely to create strong pressure for this form of divergence to disappear. Consequently, it could survive for a considerable period of time. Still, though the rate of change may be slower, there is good reason to believe that even the extent of efficient divergence, like the extent of inefficient divergence, will continue to decrease relatively quickly.

A. DIFFERENCES IN INSTITUTIONAL CONTEXT

Sometimes jurisdictions choose alternative forms of corporate law because those alternatives complement other national differences in, for example, forms of shareholdings, means for enforcing the law, or related bodies of law such as bankruptcy. A case in point is the new Russian corporation statute, which

---

39. *See, e.g.*, Coffee, *supra* note 30, at 674-76; EDWARD ROCK, MANDATORY DISCLOSURE AS CREDIBLE COMMITMENT: GOING PUBLIC, OPTING IN, OPTING OUT, AND GLOBALIZATION (University of Pennsylvania Institute for Law and Economics Working Paper, 1998).

deviates self-consciously from the type of statute that the standard model would call for in more developed economies. To take just one example, the Russian statute imposes cumulative voting on all corporations as a mandatory rule, in strong contrast to the corporate law of most developed countries. The reason for this approach was largely to ensure some degree of shareholder influence and access to information in the context of the peculiar pattern of shareholdings that has become commonplace in Russia as a result of that country's unique process of mass privatization.[40]

Nevertheless, the efficient degree of divergence in corporate law appears much smaller than the divergence in the other institutions in which corporate activity is embedded. For example, efficient divergence in creditor protection devices is probably much narrower than observed differences in the sources and structure of corporate credit. Similarly, the efficient array of mechanisms for protecting shareholders from managerial opportunism appears much narrower than the observed variety across jurisdictions in patterns of shareholdings.

Moreover, the economic institutions and legal structures in which corporate law must operate are themselves becoming more uniform across jurisdictions. This is conspicuously true, for example, of patterns of shareholdings. All countries are beginning to face, or need to face, the same varied types of shareholders, from controlling blockholders to mutual funds to highly dispersed individual shareholders. Some of this is driven by the converging forces of internal economic development. Thus, privatization of enterprise, increases in personal wealth, and the need for start-up finance (which is aided by a public market that offers an exit for the initial private investors) all promote an increasing incidence of small shareholdings and a consequent need for strong protection for minority shareholders. The globalization of capital markets presses to the same end. Hence Russia, to return to our earlier example, will presumably evolve over time toward the patterns of shareholdings typical of developed economies, and it will ultimately feel the need to conform its shareholder voting rules more closely to the rules found in those economies.

B. HARMLESS MUTATIONS

In various cases we anticipate that there will be little or no efficiency difference among multiple alternative corporate law rules. In these cases, the pressures for convergence are lessened, although not entirely eliminated (since we still expect global investors to exert pressure to standardize).[41] Accounting

---

40. Following Russian voucher privatization in 1993, managers and other employees typically held a majority of shares in large companies. Publicly held shares were mostly widely dispersed, but there was often at least one substantial outside shareholder with sufficient holdings to exploit a cumulative voting rule to obtain board representation. *See* Bernard Black & Reinier Kraakman, *A Self-Enforcing Model of Corporate Law*, 109 HARV. L. REV. 1911, 1922-23 (1996).

41. Ronald Gilson refers to processes in which facially different governance structures or legal rules develop to solve the same underlying functional problem as "functional convergence." RONALD J. GILSON, GLOBALIZING CORPORATE GOVERNANCE: CONVERGENCE OF FORM OR FUNCTION (Columbia Law

standards offer an example. As we noted earlier, there are currently two different accounting methodologies that have achieved prominence among developed nations: the American GAAP and the European-inspired International Accounting Standards. Because these two sets of standards evolved separately, they differ in many significant details. From the best current evidence, however, neither obviously dominates the other in terms of efficiency.

If the economies involved were entirely autarchic, both accounting standards might well survive indefinitely with no sacrifice in efficiency. The increasing globalization of the capital markets, however, imposes strong pressure on all countries not only to adopt one or the other of these regimes but also to select a single common accounting regime. Over time, then, the network efficiencies of a common standard form in global markets are likely to eliminate even this and other forms of fortuitous divergence in corporate law.

VIII. INEFFICIENT CONVERGENCE

Having just recognized that efficiency does not always dictate convergence in corporate law, we must also recognize that the reverse can be true as well: A high degree of convergence need not always reflect efficiency. The most likely sources of such inefficient convergence are flaws in markets or in political institutions that are widely shared by modern economies and that are reinforced rather than mitigated by cross-border competition.

A. THIRD-PARTY COSTS: CORPORATE TORTS

Perhaps the most conspicuous example of inefficient convergence is the rule—already universal, with only minor variations from one jurisdiction to the next—that limits shareholder liability for corporate torts. This rule induces inefficient risk-taking and excessive levels of risky activities—inefficiencies that appear to outweigh by far any offsetting benefits, such as reduced costs of litigation or the smoother functioning of the securities markets. As we have argued elsewhere, a general rule of unlimited pro rata shareholder liability for corporate torts appears to offer far greater overall efficiencies.[42]

Why, then, has there been universal convergence on an inefficient rule? The obvious answer is that neither markets nor politics works well to represent the

---

School, Center for Law and Economics Working Paper No. 174, 2000). On the assumption that formal law and governance practices are embedded in larger institutional contexts that change only slowly, Gilson conjectures that functional convergence is likely to outpace formal convergence. Such functional convergence, when it occurs, is what we term harmless mutation. In contrast to Gilson, however, we believe that formal law and governance structures are less contextual and more malleable than is often assumed, once the norm of shareholder primacy is accepted. Functional convergence—rather than straightforward imitation—is thus less necessary than Gilson supposes. We also suspect that close substitutes among alternative governance structures and legal rules are less widespread than Gilson implies.

42. *See* Henry Hansmann & Reinier Kraakman, *Toward Unlimited Shareholder Liability for Corporate Torts*, 100 YALE L.J. 1879, 1882-83 (1991).

interests of the persons who bear the direct costs of the rule, namely tort victims. Since, by definition, torts involve injuries to third parties, the parties affected by the rule—corporations and their potential tort victims—cannot contract around the rule to capture and share the gains from its alteration. At the same time, owing to the highly stochastic nature of most corporate torts, tort victims—and particularly the very large class of *potential* tort victims—do not constitute an easily organized political interest group.[43] Moreover, even if a given jurisdiction were to adopt a rule of shareholder liability for corporate torts, difficulties in enforcement would arise from the ease with which shareholdings or incorporation can today be shifted to other jurisdictions that retain the rule of limited liability.

B. MANAGERIALISM

A second example of inefficient convergence, arguably, is the considerable freedom enjoyed by managers in almost all jurisdictions to protect their prerogatives in cases when they might conflict with those of shareholders, particularly including managers' ability to defend their positions against hostile takeover attempts. Again, political and market failures seem responsible. Dispersed public shareholders, who are the persons most likely to be disadvantaged by the power of entrenched managers, face potentially serious problems of collective action in making their voice felt. Managers, whose positions make them a powerful and influential interest group everywhere, can use their political influence to keep the costs of collective action high—for example, by making it hard for a hostile acquirer to purchase an effective control block of shares from current shareholders. Corporate law might therefore converge, not precisely to the shareholder-oriented standard model that represents the ideological consensus, but rather to a variant of that model that has a slight managerialist tilt.

C. HOW BIG A PROBLEM?

The problem of inefficient convergence in corporate law appears to be a relatively limited one, however. Tort victims aside, the relations among virtually all actors directly affected by the corporation are heavily contractual, which tends to give those actors a common interest in establishing efficient law. Moreover, as our earlier discussion has emphasized, shareholders, managers, workers, and voluntary creditors either have acquired or are acquiring a powerful interest in efficient corporate law. Indeed, limited liability in tort arguably should not be considered a rule of corporate law at all, but instead should be viewed as a rule of tort law. And even limited liability in tort may come to be abandoned as large-scale tort damage becomes more common and, consequently, of greater political concern. We already see some movement in this

---

43. By way of contrast, the largely *non*stochastic tort of environmental pollution has made an easier focus for political organizing in the United States and, as noted in the text below, has led to strong legislation that partially pierces the corporate veil for firms that pollute.

direction in U.S. environmental law, which pushes aside the corporate veil to a startling degree in particular circumstances.

CONCLUSION

The triumph of the shareholder-oriented model of the corporation over its principal competitors is now assured, even if it was problematic as recently as twenty-five years ago. Logic alone did not establish the superiority of this standard model or of the prescriptive rules that it implies, which establish a strong corporate management with duties to serve the interests of shareholders alone, as well as strong minority shareholder protections. Rather, the standard model earned its position as the dominant model of the large corporation the hard way, by out-competing during the post-World War II period the three alternative models of corporate governance: the managerialist model, the labor-oriented model, and the state-oriented model.

If the failure of the principal alternatives has established the ideological hegemony of the standard model, though, perhaps this should not come as a complete surprise. The standard model has never been questioned for the vast majority of corporations. It dominates the law and governance of closely held corporations in every jurisdiction. Most German companies do not participate in the codetermination regime, and most Dutch companies are not regulated by the managerialist "structure" regime. Similarly, the standard model of shareholder primacy has always been the dominant legal model in the two jurisdictions where the choice of models might be expected to matter most: the U.S. and the U.K. The choice of models matters in these jurisdictions because large companies often have highly fragmented ownership structures. In continental Europe, where most large companies are controlled by large shareholders,[44] the interests of controlling shareholders traditionally dominate corporate policy no matter what the prevailing ideology of the corporate form.

We predict, therefore, that as equity markets evolve in Europe and throughout the developed world, the ideological and competitive attractions of the standard model will become indisputable, even among legal academics. And as the goal of shareholder primacy becomes second nature even to politicians, convergence in most aspects of the law and practice of corporate governance is sure to follow.

---

44. *See* Rafael La Porta et al., *Corporate Ownership Around the World*, 54 J. FIN. 471, 505 (1999) (stating that large firms tend to have controlling shareholders in all but common-law jurisdictions).

[6]

Explaining Western Securities Markets

MARK J. ROE

Introduction

How important is corporate law—and its capacity to protect minority stockholders from insider machinations—in building securities markets and separating ownership from corporate control? Quite important, according to most recent analyses, and maybe central. Without strong corporate law protections, securities markets, it is said, will not arise. And if corporate law is good enough in technologically advanced nations, ownership will be diffused away from concentrated ownership into dispersed stock markets.

This new perspective contributes to understanding the fragility of capital markets in transition and Third-World economies, chiefly where even basic contract and property rights are weak. But it has been used—and I argue here it has been overused—to explain primarily the persistence of dominant stockholders and fragile securities markets in many of the world's richest nations in Europe and Asia. I say 'overused' because there is too much that is critical to ownership separation that corporate law *does not even seek to reach* in the world's richest, most advanced nations.

Two conceptual problems afflict the idea that corporate law is primary. Each is sufficient to render the corporate law argument, while still relevant, secondary, not primary.

First, current academic thinking lumps together costly opportunism due to a controller's self-dealing and costly decision-making that inflicts losses on the owners. The former—self-dealing—corporate law seeks to control directly. The latter—bad decision-making that damages shareholders—it does not. Other institutions control the latter, and their strength varies from firm to firm and from nation to nation. Yet owners tend to stay as block-holders—and ownership does not become diffuse, and securities markets remain weak—if stockholders expect that managerial agency costs to shareholders would be very high if ownership were fully separated.

Second, the focus on legal families is probably over-sold. Civil law systems are said to over-regulate, while common law systems, operating through

I make arguments similar to some of those I make here in Roe (2002; 2003*b*). Thanks for comments on the draft of this chapter go to Margaret Blair and Anna Grandori.

wise judges, do not. The theoretical difficulty with this perspective is that American regulatory agencies (such as the Securities and Exchange Commission) arose because common law institutions were thought to insufficiently regulate securities markets.

To recast our angle of vision from a national overview of the system to a micro-perspective, if ownership did not separate from control in a nation (or a firm), we cannot know whether separation was aborted because block-holder rampages are uncontrolled or because *managerial agency costs* would be far too high if ownership were separated. *Either* could have prevented separation. Or one alone could have, with the other not standing in the way. And the first is closely and directly affected by corporate law; the second is not.

Managerial agency costs come in two 'flavors', only one of which corporate law tightly controls. One flavor—machinations that transfer value to the controllers and managers, or 'stealing'—corporate law seeks to control. But the other—'shirking', or pursuing goals other than shareholder value— corporate law largely leaves alone. If underlying economic, social, or political conditions make managerial agency costs very high, and if those costs are best contained by a controlling shareholder, *then concentrated ownership persists whatever the state of corporate law in checking block-holder misdeeds.*

I speculate on what underlying economic, political, and social conditions could make managerial agency costs persistently high. I also speculate on how a shrinking of these agency costs, plausibly now going on in continental Europe, could raise the demand to build legal institutions that facilitate separation. First, for ownership to be separated in the modern economy, distant shareholders seem to need, or at least do better if they have, some pro-stockholder institutions, such as a few of transparent securities markets, aligning compensation systems, intermittent takeovers or other means to control managers, and shareholder primacy norms. (Enron and WorldCom failures show us how fragile these can be even in a nation, like the United States, that favors such institutions.) But some polities, unlike America's, have been hostile to pro-shareholder institutions and don't support them.

Second, some polities further open up the gap between managers and shareholders by encouraging managers to expand, to go slow in down-sizing, to give employees more rights against firms that can be best mitigated for shareholders via concentrated ownership, and so on. When those pressures are strong, dominant stockholders stay in place to resist them. Some nations have pursued a vision of what makes for a just society in ways different from how they have been pursued in the United States. And, hence, it's no surprise that their corporate systems differ.

Third, in corporatist polities, owners and stakeholders have protected themselves by being concentrated enough to be national political players, because that's where the economic pie is divided up (Faccio 2002; Roe 2000).

Some of these pressures are in flux today, but their historical reality is quite concrete. The relationships fit some types of industrial production, especially where soft commitments and close working relationships between owners and workers are critical.

* * *

High-quality, protective corporate law is a good institution for a society to have. It lowers the costs of building strong, large business enterprises. It can prevent or minimize diversions engineered by dominant stockholders, and some institution that minimizes these is a necessary condition for separation to stay stable. It, or a substitute such as reputational intermediaries (DeLong 1991; Miwa and Ramseyer 2000) or stock exchange rules (Mahoney 1997; Roe 2000; Coffee 2001), lowers the cost of ownership separation and seems to precede, or shortly follow after, ownership separation. But, among the world's wealthier nations, corporate law does not primarily determine whether it is worthwhile to build those enterprises and their supporting institutions. It is only a tool, not the foundation. With labor and political institutions in mind, we can better explain why some nations have deep separation and strong stock markets while others, about equally wealthy, do not.

The Argument: Corporate Law as Propelling Diffuse Ownership

Today's dominant academic and policy explanation of why continental Europe lacks deep and rich securities markets is the purportedly weak role of corporate and securities law in protecting minority stockholders, a weakness that is said to contrast with America's strong protections of minority stockholders. A major European-wide research network, leading financial economists, and increasingly legal commentators have stated so (La Porta *et al.* 1998: 1136–7; Bebchuk 1999; Coffee 1999; Becht and Röell 1999).

Leading economists showed that deep securities markets correlate with an index of basic shareholder legal protections. And 'protection of shareholders ... by the legal system *is central* to understanding the patterns of corporate finance in different countries. Investor protection [is] *crucial* because, in many countries, expropriation of minority shareholders ... by the controlling shareholders is extensive' (La Porta *et al.* 2000: 4, emphasis added). According to Modigliani and Perotti (1998: 5), nations with deficient legal regimes cannot get good stock markets and, hence, 'the provision of funding shifts from dispersed risk capital [via the stock market] ... to debt, and from [stock and bond] markets to institutions, i.e., towards intermediated credit'. And legal origin (civil law vs. common law) is said to load the dice in the results.

282   MARK ROE

While the academics are developing a theory and gathering data, international agencies such as the IMF and the World Bank have admirably promoted corporate law reform, especially that which would protect minority stockholders (Iskander *et al.* 1999). The OECD and the World Bank have had major initiatives to improve corporate governance, both in the developing and the developed world (OECD 1999; Nestor 2000; Witherell 2000).

These efforts by the international agencies are valuable at some level. They could well contribute to reaching their goals of more stable enterprises and better economic performance, especially in transition nations. But corporate law, and the reach of government policy-makers through corporate law reform, has limits. And those limits are much closer than the policy-makers and academic theory now discern. Here I demarcate those limits in the world's richest nations beyond which corporate law ceases to be primary. If the limits are close, and the cost of constructing corporate law high, then other development strategies may be seen as even more valuable.[1]

Protecting Minority Stockholders

The basic law-driven story is straightforward. Imagine a nation whose law badly protects minority stockholders against a block-holder extracting value from small minority stockholders. A potential buyer fears that the majority stockholder would later shift value to itself, away from the buyer. So fearing, the prospective minority stockholder does not pay pro rata value for the stock. If the discount is deep enough and cannot be accurately priced (or if the transfer diminishes firm value), then the majority stockholder decides not to sell, concentrated ownership persists, and stock markets do not develop.

To approach the problem from the owner's perspective, posit large private benefits of control. The most obvious benefits that law can affect are those that the controller can derive from diverting value from the firm to himself. The owner might own 51 per cent of the firm's stock but retain 75 per cent of the firm's value if the owner can over-pay himself in salary, pad the company's payroll with no-show relatives, use the firm's funds to pay private expenses, or divert value by having the 51 per cent-controlled firm

---

[1] I do not address here *how* valuable those corporate law initiatives are. That is, if the advantages of securities markets can be cheaply achieved through other means, then those substitutes might make securities markets development of secondary importance to general economic development. It is plausible that well-developed securities markets *reflect* economic development and only secondarily help induce it. The development agencies are pursuing securities market development as, one assumes, a means to general economic development, in the belief that it is a strong cause, not a minor reflection. But if it is a reflection, then the agencies' efforts might go better into building the underlying foundations. (And the effort here in this chapter becomes one of explaining why we see, or don't see, strong securities markets, not in planning how to get them.)

overpay for goods and services obtained from a company totally owned by the controller. Strong fiduciary duties, strong doctrines attacking unfair interested-party transactions, effective disclosure laws that unveil these transactions, and a capable judiciary or other enforcement institution can reduce these kinds of private benefits of control.[2] The owner considers whether to sell to diffuse stockholders. With no controller to divert value, the stock price could reflect the firm's underlying value. But the rational buyers believe, so the theory runs, that the diffuse ownership structure would be unstable, that an outside raider would buy up 51 per cent of the firm and divert value, and that the remaining minority stockholders would be hurt. Hence, they would not pay full pro rata value to the owner wishing to sell; and the owner wishing to sell would find that the sales price to be less than the value of the block if retained (or if sold intact) (La Porta *et al.* 1997, 1998; Bebchuk 1999; Modigliani and Perotti 1997, 1998).

Hence, the block persists. The controller refuses to leave control 'up for grabs' because, if it dips below 51 per cent control, an outsider could grab control and reap the private benefits.

The Attractions of a Technical Corporate Law Theory

The quality-of-corporate-law argument is appealing. Technical institutions are to blame, for example, for Russia's and the transition nations' economic problems. The fixes, if technical, are within our grasp. Humans can shape the results. Progress is possible, one could believe, if we just can get the technical institutions right. And, one might further believe, if we make these technical fixes, economic development will follow. And, as a descriptive matter, if we don't see ownership separation in Germany, France, and Scandinavia, it must be because a technical fix is missing, one we can provide as easily as downloading a computer program across the Atlantic Ocean. But if it turns out that deeper features of society—industrial organization and competition, politics, conditions of social regularity, or norms that support shareholder value—are more fundamental to inducing securities markets, we would feel ill at ease because these institutions are much harder for policy-makers to control.[3] These institutions might change over time (and seem to have been changing in Europe), but they are not in the hands of a technocrat drafting corporate law reform.

---

[2] Private benefits also arise from pride in running and controlling one's own, or one's family's, enterprise. On this, corporate law has little direct impact.

[3] To be clear, I am not speaking simply of corporate law but also of securities law, and of the quality of regulators and judges, of the efficiency, accuracy, and honesty of the regulators and the judiciary, of the capacity of the stock exchanges to stymie the most egregious diversions, and so on. Cf. Black (2000).

As self-contained academic theory, there is little to quarrel with in the quality-of-corporate-law argument. It is sparse and appealing. Good corporate law lowers the costs of operating a large firm; it is good for a nation to have it because it seems to cost so little. But we need *more* to understand why ownership is not separate from control *even where core corporate law is good enough*. Where managerial agency costs due to potential dissipation are substantial, concentrated ownership persists *even if conventional corporate law quality is high*.

Given the facts that we shall develop in the third section—there are too many wealthy, high quality corporate law countries *without* much separation—the quality-of-corporate-law theory needs to be further refined or replaced. This we do next in the second section of the chapter.

Corporate Law's Limits

How Managerial Agency Costs Impede Separation

Managers would run some firms badly if ownership were separated from control. Effective corporate laws constrain managers' *overreaching* but do much less to directly make them operate their firms well. A related-party transaction can be attacked or prevented where corporate law is good; judges examine these transactions and remedy them. But judges leave unprofitable transactions untouched, with managers—when untainted by self-dealing—able to invoke corporate law's business judgment rule to deflect direct legal scrutiny.

Consider a society (or a firm) in which managerial agency costs from dissipating shareholder value would be high if ownership were separated but low if it were not, because a controlling shareholder can contain those costs. When high but containable by concentration, concentrated shareholding ought to persist *even if corporate law fully protects minority stockholders from insiders' overreaching*. Block-holders would weigh their costs in maintaining control (in lost liquidity and diversification) against what they would lose if managerial agency costs were high. Control would persist even if corporate law were good.[4]

This is a basic but important point, and it is needed to explain the data that we look at in the next section.

Improving Corporate Law Without Increasing Separation

The basic but often missed argument in the prior section—that variance in managerial agency costs can drive ownership structure, and that managerial agency costs can vary greatly *even if conventional corporate law is quite good*—can

---

[4] This section and its brief model draw on Roe (2002).

be stated formally in a simple model. High managerial agency costs can preclude separation *even if there is high-quality conventional corporate law*.

Let:

A_M = the managerial agency costs to shareholders from managers' dissipating shareholder value, to the extent avoidable via concentrated ownership.

C_{CS} = the costs to the concentrated shareholder in holding a block and monitoring (that is, the costs in lost liquidity, lost diversification, expended energy, and, perhaps, error).

When A_M is high, ownership concentration persists whether or not law successfully controls the private benefits that a controlling shareholder can siphon off from the firm. Further, let

V = value of the firm when ownership is concentrated.

B_{CS} = the private benefits of control, containable by corporate law.

Consider the firm worth V when ownership is concentrated. Posit first that managerial agency costs are trivial even if the firm is fully public. As such, the private benefits of control, a characteristic legally malleable and reducible with protective corporate law, can determine whether ownership separates from control. Consider the controller who owns 50 per cent of the firm's stock. As such she obtains one-half of V plus her net benefits of control. (In this simple first model, the value of the firm remains unchanged whether it has a controlling stockholder or is fully public.) She retains control when the following inequality is true:

$$V/2 + B_{CS} - C_{CS} > V/2. \qquad (1)$$

The left side is the value to the controlling stockholder of the control block: half the firm's cash flow plus the private benefits diverted from minority stockholders minus the costs of maintaining the block (in lost diversification and liquidity). The right side is the value she obtains from selling the block to the public. Equation (1) states that, as long as the private benefits of control exceed the costs of control, then concentrated ownership persists. Because corporate law can dramatically shrink the private benefits, B_{CS}, corporate law matters quite a bit in equation (1). This is the current theory[5] that we next amend.

We amend by introducing A_M, managerial agency costs from dissipating shareholder value in ways that a controlling shareholder would avoid. If those managerial agency costs are non-trivial, then the controller's proceeds from selling into the stock market would be $(V - A_M)/2$. Concentration

---

[5] See Bebchuk (1999), who models the problem; see also Coffee (2001); La Porta, Lopez-de-Silanes, and Shleifer (1999); La Porta *et al.* (1997; 1998).

persists if and only if

$$V/2 + B_{CS} - C_{CS} > (V - A_M)/2. \tag{2}$$

To rearrange: concentration persists if the net benefits of control $(B_{CS} - C_{CS})$ are more than the controller's costs of diffusion $(A_M/2)$:

$$B_{CS} - C_{CS} > -A_M/2. \tag{3}$$

Or, further re-arranging, concentration persists if:

$$B_{CS} + A_M/2 > C_{CS}. \tag{4}$$

Quality-of-corporate-law theory predicts that diffusion fails to occur when $B_{CS} > C_{CS}$, with corporate law the means of containing B_{CS}. That is correct but incomplete. Where A_M is high, diffusion does not occur *even if B_{CS} is zero and corporate law perfect, because A_M could take over and drive the separation decision.* B_{CS}, the controlling shareholder's private benefits, are relatively unimportant if A_M is very high. Only when $A_M \to 0$ do legally malleable private benefits determine diffusion.[6]

These simple relations adapt to much complexity here. For instance, if the controller can no longer manage well then the sign on agency costs, A_M, changes. Similarly, the relationships can absorb uncertainty. That is, most business decisions are made under uncertainty. The billion-dollar factory that turns out to have been a bad investment is not, if the decision to build was made by agents, necessarily an agency cost. Mistakes are not necessarily agency costs. Rather, if the agent was more likely than a sole owner to overestimate the probabilities of success (because the agent benefited even from moderately unprofitable expansion), then this 'extra' portion of mis-estimate (the *increased* probability of taking on the project, the increased investment in the project once started, and so on) becomes the agency cost that (astute) close ownership would reduce. According to Levinthal (1988: 182), 'It is not the industriousness of top management that is the issue, but the qualitative nature of the decisions they make.'

Corporate Law's Limited Capacity to Reduce Agency Costs

One might reply that core corporate law when improved reduces *both* the controlling stockholder's private benefits (B_{CS}, by reducing the controller's capacity to siphon off value) *and* managerial agency costs (A_M, by reducing

---

[6] The best-developed model of the corporate law problem begins by assuming a population of firms that is more valuable when diffusely owned than when privately-owned (see Bebchuk 1999). As such, its author does not have to address managerial agency costs, since these are assumed away as central for the population under discussion. But it is here where the critical calculus can occur whether firms go public. (Not all other analyses of the relationship between corporate law and ownership diffusion confine their inquiry so adroitly.)

the managers' capacity to siphon off benefits for themselves). And it does so, one might mistakenly then argue, about equally.

1. The Business Judgment Rule.   This criticism, however, fails to reflect what American corporate law really does. Managerial agency costs are the sum of managers' overreaching (unjustifiably high salaries, self-dealing transactions, and so on) *and* their mismanagement (that is, the part of their mismanagement that a stronger owner would avoid). Economic analyses typically lump these two together and call them 'agency costs'. But agency costs come from stealing *and* from shirking. It is correct to lump them together in economic analyses *as a cost to shareholders* because both costs are visited upon shareholders. For example, Fama (1980) notes that agency costs come from 'shirking, perquisites or incompetence'. But it is incorrect to think that *law* (especially American corporate law) minimizes each cost to shareholders equally well.

The standard that corporate law applies to managerial decisions is, realistically, no liability at all for mistakes, absent fraud, or conflict of interest (Dooley and Veasey 1989: 521; Bishop 1968; 1095). *But this is where the big costs to shareholders of having managerial agents lie, exactly where law falls silent.*

Conventional corporate law—the law of corporate fiduciary duties, which common law is said to be particular adept at—does little or nothing to directly reduce shirking, mistakes, and bad business decisions that squander shareholder value. The business judgment rule is, absent fraud or conflict of interest, nearly insurmountable in America. It insulates directors and managers from the judge, removing them from legal scrutiny. Most American analysts think that one wouldn't want the judge second-guessing managers on a regular basis.

2. Controlling Shareholders.   One might refine this analysis by accounting for controlling shareholder error. But the costs of these errors are usually thought to be smaller than legally uncontrollable managerial error. True, similar legal doctrines (the business judgment rule) shield the controlling shareholder from lawsuits for a non-conflicted mistake. But, because the controlling stockholder owns a big block of the company's stock, it internalizes much of the cost of any mistake (unlike the unconstrained managers). A controller has some incentive to turn the firm over to professional managers if he realizes they would make the firm more profitable. (And, as I mentioned, in those settings where the controller would overall be worse than unconstrained managers, we then should get diffusion. A_M's sign flips.)

Even if Law Critically Affects Both

Still, one might reject the proposition that law is secondary in inducing good management for shareholders. Law affects those other institutions that indirectly control managerial agency costs (competition, compensation, takeovers, transparency, and so on), and one might believe *these* laws to be central to whether public firms can arise and whether ownership can be separated from control.

But, even so, the structure of my argument—of *corporate* law's limits—persists. The institutions and law that affect managerial agency costs of running the firm differ from the institutions and laws that affect insider machinations. The two sets are *not* identical. If one society does better with one set than with the other, then the degree of diffusion should be deeply affected. Corporate law might minimize insider transactions in both nations, but the other laws in one might fail to reduce managerial agency costs from running the firm, or even increase them.

That is, assume arguendo that corporate law, broadly defined, can, if 'unleashed', affect both private benefits and managerial agency costs. But, if other institutions *also* affect managerial agency costs, then corporate law could be perfect but these *other* institutions would determine the degree of ownership separation through their effect on managerial agency costs from running the firm. These other institutions might vary across nations and systematically determine, or affect, the degree of ownership separation across nations.

The Difficulty of Seeing Legal Origins as Causal

Moreover, a theory based primarily on legal origins is weakened by the means of regulation in the United States. America uses a regulatory agency, the Security and Exchange Commission (SEC), as the primary regulator of stock markets. This agency, though, is not a common law mechanism. As such, it is unclear where the *legal* advantage, if it has any, arose for the United States as compared with continental European civil law nations. Perhaps civil law nations have to regulate less than they usually might, so as to be effective in securities market. But common law has to regulate more. (And the impression one has is that civil law nations actually regulate securities markets *less* than their emblematic level.) Civil law nations may simply have decided for reasons exogenous to the legal system—more about that in the next subsection—*not* to regulate securities markets, because for some reason—say, political—making good security markets was not a national priority.

The Tight Limits to the Purely Legal Theory

Thus, the basic theory I propose here is that, first, if one observes persistent block-holding, one cannot a priori know whether the blocks persist because minority stockholders fear the controller or because they fear the *managers*, who might dissipate shareholder value if the controlling stockholder disappears. Even if better corporate law usually increases diffusion in rich nations with adequate but not outstanding corporate law (a proposition open to theoretical challenge, see Roe 2003*a*: 181[7]), concentration might be due to high managerial agency costs in running the firm and have little to do with core corporate law's constraints on insider machinations.

If distant shareholders fear unrestrained managers, the controller cannot sell stock at a high enough price and thus she keeps control to monitor managers or to run the firm.

Second, stock markets are regulated, not left to the unadorned common law. This is so even in common law nations. Indeed, common law nations may regulate stock markets more than civil law nations do. As such, a theory based on legal origins—that civil law regulates, while common law judges— is not prima facie convincing. Even today, when corporate structures go awry—think of Enron—and fiduciary duties fail, the systemic reaction, even in a common law nation like the US, is to regulate—think of Sarbanes-Oxley of 2002—*not* to rely primarily on judge-made common law fiduciary duties.

Data: Political Variables as the Strongest Predictor of Ownership Separation

If a society's institutions do not promote shareholder value, or if a society adds institutions that raise managerial agency costs (because it wants managers loyal to a wider spectrum of interests than elsewhere), then ownership separation ought to be narrower than elsewhere.

Politics Can Increase Managerial Agency Costs

In nations where labor institutions—whether via social democracy or corporatist power-sharing or other cooperative arrangements—are strong, one would expect managerial agency costs to shareholders to often be higher in firms that had ownership and control divided than in nations where such labor institutions were weaker.

Two channels would be in play, one through the firm and the other through institution-building: First, through the firm, the polity would tend to promote non-profit-maximizing expansion (and make it even harder to contract when firms' capabilities are misaligned with markets). And there would be more bargaining over the surplus, with some of that bargaining at the national political level and some inside the firm. Concentrated owners could often bargain better in such polities. Second, nations in which labor or the left held significant political power could be unwilling to build the institutions that facilitate distant shareholding, such as building good securities regulation, promoting profit-building institutions, facilitating shareholder

---

[7] The idea is that when corporate law is 'passable'—neither excellent nor atrocious— then improving it could make distant shareholders *more* comfortable with a controller, and therefore *more* willing to buy minority stock. See also Roe (2000; 2002).

control over (or influence on) managers, and enhancing shareholder primacy norms that induce managers to align themselves with stockholders, even those stockholders that cannot control the managers day-to-day.

If this is right, and one or both of these channels is strong, then one could hypothesize a basic model with testable implications. Greater labor protection should predict weaker ownership separation. Consider the results in Table 12.1 and Fig. 12.1 from OECD data indexing the level of job protection in the OECD.

With a small sample like, this multiple controls are hard, and the small 'n' makes the econometric behavior here tricky. But consider the results in Table 12.2 when we control for two measures of corporate law, one the well-known La Porta *et al.* (1998) index and a less well-known measure of the control premium in the world's richer nations from Dyck and Zingales (2002). Each legal measure standing alone predicts separation. But look at what happens when we combine the legal measures with the political one.

The bottom-line: employment protection *strongly dominates the two measures of corporate law*.[8] Roughly, these results suggest that controlling insider

TABLE 12.1   *Employment protection and ownership separation*

Country	Employment protection	Widely-held at 20% for medium-sized corporations (med 20)
Australia	4	0.30
Austria	16	0.00
Belgium	17	0.20
Canada	3	0.60
Denmark	5	0.30
Finland	10	0.20
France	14	0.00
Germany	15	0.10
Italy	21	0.00
Japan	8	0.30
Netherlands	9	0.10
Norway	11	0.20
Sweden	13	0.10
Switzerland	6	0.50
United Kingdom	7	0.60
United States	1	0.90

Note: Employment protection measures how strongly a nation's law protects employees from being fired. (It is an inverse, relative measurement: a value of 1 means the employees are relatively unprotected; 17 means that they are well protected.) It aggregates specific employment rules in each nation in the OECD (OECD 1994). Widely-held at 20% measures the dispersion of stock in public companies. It is a nation-by-nation index, compiled by La Porta, Lopez-de-Silanes, and Shleifer (1999), of the portion of companies that are widely-held in a slice of mid-sized firms in each nation. A company was classified as not being wide-held if it has a stockholder owning 20% or more of the firm's stock.

[8] Indeed, it is robust even to "throwing" both legal indicators at it, as a commentator suggested.

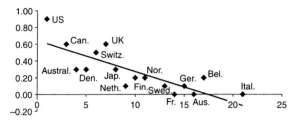

Technical data: Separation (med 20) v. employment protection

Regression	S = −0.04EmpPro + 0.65
Adj R-Sq	0.64
t-stat	−5.24***

FIGURE 12.1 *Employment protection as predicting mid-sized firms' separation.*
*** Significant at the 0.0005 level.
Source: The x-axis is an index of employment protection compiled by the OECD (1994); the y-axis is an index of ownership concentration in mid-sized public companies, compiled by La Porta, Lopez-de-Silanes, and Shleifer (1999). The data for both items are arrayed in Table 12.1.

TABLE 12.2 *Employment protection vs. corporate law in predicting separation*

	Dependent variable: ownership separation in mid-cap companies				
Corp. law : La Porta	0.14 (3.69***)			−0.03 (−0.57)	
Corp. law : control premium		−1.07 (−1.94*)			0.43 (0.87)
Employment protection			**−0.04 (−5.24***)**	**−0.03 (−2.62**)**	**−0.05 (−4.39***)**
R^2	0.53	0.18	0.64	0.71	0.72

Note: This table shows how well two determinants of ownership separation predict the dispersion results in Table 12.1. The dependent variable is the degree of ownership dispersion in the mid-cap companies in each nation, as listed in Table 12.1. The independent variables are employment protection and the quality of corporate law.

The third data column shows the labor index of employment protection (from Table 12.1) nicely predicting ownership dispersion. The labor predictor is robust to two measures of corporate law quality, one from La Porta, Lopez-de-Silanes, and Shleifer (1999: 492) and the other from Dyck and Zingales (2002). The first index of corporate law quality, from La Porta, indexes corporate law features that are thought to protect outside shareholders from insider over-reaching; the second measures the premium paid for a control block above the trading value of minority stock. (A high premium suggests small shareholders are poorly protected; a low premium, well-protected.) The two indices of corporate law quality predict ownership separation in these rich nations, but they are not robust to adding the employment protection index. The latter strongly dominates corporate law in predicting the degree of ownership separation in the OECD, as is indicated in the third, bold-faced, row.

overreaching—the type of costs of public firms that law can reach—gets us at most (only) half-way to making public firms viable. If the political environment impedes manager-shareholder alliances, the second type of agency costs to shareholders would rise, and ownership could not easily be separated from control, *even if controller machinations are contained.* In fact, in most of these 'models' law doesn't significantly increase the predictive power of left-right politics alone.[9]

Do Block-holders Increase or Decrease Value?

A pure law-driven theory would predict that increasing block-holding would decrease the value of minority shares. A pure managerial agency cost theory would predict the opposite. An integrative theory would look for both.

But bigger block-holders in many countries *increase* the value of minority stockholders' shares (Roe 2003*b*). This is not a relationship consistent with the legal theory. But it is one consistent with a managerial agency cost theory, that block-holders restrain managerial agency costs. And it is a result that fits with the political theory I have advanced, because for these countries in particular political and employment pressures are strong, and it is plausible that dominant stockholders are able to create more value for shareholders than do managers acting alone.[10] Overall, there are mixed results, some studies finding block-holders demeaning minority shareholder value, some showing them enhancing it, others showing offsetting effects. These overall results suggest that the legal theory again is insufficient in explaining the strength of ownership separation. Both effects—diversionary and agency cost—seem to be in play.

[9] See Roe (2003*a*). Surely the correlation here does not prove the theory. And, even if the basic theory—a relationship between labor and ownership concentration—is right, other channels linking the two are possible. Visible ownership concentration might have provoked labor protection. Or the two may work hand in hand: high human capital industries might dominate in some nations, and they may fit well with concentrated owners (who can make soft deals better than can distant stockholders). The commonality between the footnoted relationships and the textually-noted ones is that institutional protection of minority stockholders plays a secondary role in determining whether ownership is separated or stays close.

[10] Reality is more complex. First, distant shareholders might suffer through two channels. They might suffer the controllers' machinations, but the agency cost minimization may be so great that it exceeds the controllers' diversions of private benefits. Second, endogeneity might lead the low private benefits companies to have dominant stockholders, while the high private benefits companies build barriers to keep controllers out or they never go public. Nevertheless, the dominant observable effect is hard to reconcile with weak law primarily determining separation as opposed to being a secondary factor.

And the Not-So-Rich Nations?

One might observe that many poorer nations have decrepit corporate law institutions. This is true, and possibly weak corporate law is holding them back, but the coincidence of bad law and a bad economy does not tell us enough. To learn that, say, Afghanistan has poor corporate law does not tell us whether its weak economy and low degree of ownership separation are primarily due to its weak corporate law or to its *other* weak institutions. If the other institutions, particularly the other property rights institutions, are decrepit, *these* may be the critical debilities preventing Afghanistan from developing wealth and complex private institutions that get it ready for public firms and ownership diffusion. Only then, when it gets that far, will we be able to tell whether weak corporate law holds it back. The omitted variable might be weak property rights institutions generally, with weak corporate law institutions just a visible and perhaps minor surface manifestation of the deeper weakness.

In any case, we are here focusing on the world's richer nations, not its poorer nations. Even if corporate law is the institution holding back the transition and developing nations—an unlikely hypothesis—the data indicate that it is not holding back every one of the richer nations from getting stronger securities markets and sharper ownership separation. Something else is.

Other data are consistent. There are too many studies showing that increasing block-holders in many countries *increase* the value of minority stockholders.

Conclusion: Politics and Corporate Law as Explanations for Securities Markets

We should be skeptical about a pure, or even a primarily, law-based theory or legal-origins theory for predicting ownership separation and stock market strength in the wealthy West. True, strong corporate law that protects distant stockholders is good to have. It is useful in building efficacious business enterprises and has utility in explaining some key aspects of corporate differences around the world, especially in transition and developing nations. For deep securities markets and strong ownership separation, nations probably need it or a substitute.

But the quality-of-corporate-law argument has limits, and these limits are probably much closer than is commonly thought. High-quality corporate law is insufficient to induce ownership to separate from control in the world's richest, most economically advanced nations. Technologically advanced nations in the wealthy West can have the potential for fine corporate law in theory, and several have it in practice, but ownership would *not* become separated from control wherever managerial agency costs are high. And managerial agency costs, unlike insider self-dealing, are *not* closely connected with corporate law. Indeed, American corporate law's business judgment rule has corporate law *avoid* dealing with managerial agency costs.

By examining a restricted sample of the world's richest nations, we can move towards two conclusions, one strong and the other weak. The strong one focuses on the richer nations in the wealthy West: studies that examine corporate law worldwide tend to over-predict the importance of corporate law in the world's richest nations. It seems almost intuitive that these nations—where contract can usually be nicely enforced—shouldn't have much technical trouble developing satisfactory corporate law or good substitutes. Some, by measurement, already have. If ownership still hasn't separated widely, then other institutional explanations are probably in play. The weak conclusion focuses on the world's transition and developing nations. We cannot conclude that improving corporate law is irrelevant there (because we have examined here only the restricted set of the world's richest nations). But we can offer the weak conclusion that the development agencies may do everything right in getting the corporate law institutions of these nations ready for ownership separation, and it is at least possible that no one comes to the party.

The quality of conventional corporate law does not fully explain why and when ownership concentration persists in the wealthy West, because core *corporate law does not even try to directly prevent managerial agency costs from dissipating a firm's value.* The American business judgment rule keeps courts and law out of basic business decisions and that is where managers can lose, or make, the really big money for shareholders. Non-legal institutions control these costs. In nations where those *other* institutions, such as product competition or incentive compensation, fail or do less well, managerial dissipation would be higher and ownership cannot as easily become separate from control as it can where dissipation is lower. Corporate-law quality can be high, private benefits of control low, but if managerial agency costs from dissipation are high, separation will not proceed. Even if we believed law to be critical to building these *other* institutions, the analysis would persist because *different* laws support the agency cost controlling institutions (antitrust and product market competition; tax law and incentive compensation; and so on).

Moreover, the regulatory character of the means by which securities law is made seems to run counter to the strengths of the common law system—it operates through rules and regulations, not common law, judge-made fiduciary duties. The SEC's regulatory character thus casts some doubt on the primacy of legal origins, that is, the idea that legal origins heavily affect the ability to protect minority stockholders.

Variation in other institutions could explain why managerial agency costs are not low enough. If other institutions induce managers, if untethered, to stray from shareholder profit-making, then shareholders would be less likely to untether the managers. When those other institutions are strongly in play, then corporate law—even corporate law writ large—no longer primarily determines the degree of separation.

A nation need not control insider machinations and motivate managers equally well; and, to the extent it does one better than the other, concentration and diffusion are deeply affected. The diffusion decision is based on the *sum* of private benefits of control and managerial agency costs. Even if traditional corporate law drives private benefits to zero, concentration should persist if managerial agency costs are high.

Data are consistent. Several nations have, by measurement, good corporate law, but not much diffusion and hardly any separation. These nations also have a potential for high managerial agency costs if ownership and control were separated: relatively weaker product market competition and relatively stronger political pressures on managers to disadvantage shareholders. Political variables predict separation well, and they dominate corporate law quality in predicting separation in the wealthy West.

The quality of a nation's corporate law cannot be the only explanation of why diffuse Berle-Means firms grow and dominate. Perhaps, for some countries at some times, it is not even the principal one.

References

Bebchuk, L. (1999). *A Rent-Protection Theory of Corporate Ownership and Control* (Law and Economics Working Paper). Cambridge, MA: Harvard University (Discussion Paper No. 260).

Becht, M. and Röell, A. (1999). 'Blockholdings in Europe: An International Comparison', *European Economic Review*, 43: 1049–56.

Bishop, J. Jr. (1968). 'Sitting Ducks and Decoy Ducks: New Trends in the Indemnification of Corporate Directors and Officers', *Yale Law Journal*, 77: 1078–103.

Black, B. (2000). 'The Core Institutions That Support Strong Securities Markets', *Business Lawyer*, 55: 1565–607.

Coffee, J. (1999). 'The Future as History: The Prospects for Global Convergence in Corporate Governance and Its Implications', *Northwestern University Law Review*, 93: 641–707.

—— (2001). 'The Rise of Dispersed Ownership: Theories of Law and the State in the Separation of Ownership and Control', *Yale Law Journal*, 111: 1–82.

DeLong, B. (1991). 'Did J.P. Morgan's Men Add Value?', in P. Temin (ed.), *Inside the Business Enterprise: Historical Perspectives on the Use of Information*. Chicago: University of Chicago Press.

Dooley, M. and Veasey, E. (1989). 'The Role of the Board in Derivative Litigation: Delaware Law and the Current ALI Proposals Compared', *Business Lawyer*, 44: 503.

296   MARK ROE

Dyck, A. and Zingales, L. (2002). 'Why are Private Benefits of Control so Large in Certain Countries and What Effect does this Have on their Financial Development?'. Working paper, Chicago: University of Chicago, January (forthcoming, *Journal of Finance*).

Faccio, M. (2002). 'Politically-connected Firms: Can they Squeeze the State?' Social Science Research Network working paper.

Fama, E. (1980). 'Agency Problems and the Theory of the Firm', *Journal of Political Economy*, 88: 288–307.

Iskander, M., Meyerman, G., Gray, D., and Hagan, S. (1999). 'Corporate Restructuring and Governance in East Asia', *Finance and Development*, 36: 42–5.

La Porta, R., Lopez-de-Silanes, F., and Shleifer, A. (1999). 'Corporate Ownership Around the World', *Journal of Finance*, 54: 471–517.

La Porta, R., Lopez-de-Silanes, F., Shleifer, A., and Vishny, R. (1997). 'Legal Determinants of External Finance', *Journal of Finance*, 52: 1131–55.

——————————(1998). 'Law and Finance', *Journal of Political Economy*, 106: 1113–50.

—————— (2000). 'Investor Protection and Corporate Governance', *Journal of Financial Economics*, 58: 3–27.

Levinthal, D. (1988). 'A Survey of Agency Models of Organizations', *Journal of Economic Behavior and Organization*, 9: 153, 182.

Mahoney, P. (1997). 'The Exchange as Regulator', *Virginia Law Review*, 83: 1453–500.

Miwa, Y. and Ramseyer, M. (2000). 'Corporate Governance in Transitional Economies: Lessons from the Pre-War Japanese Cotton Textile Industry', *Journal of Legal Studies*, 29: 171–203.

Modigliani, F. and Perotti, E. (1997). 'Protection of Minority Interest and the Development of Security Markets', *Managerial and Decision Economics*, 18: 519–28.

—— (1998). 'Security Versus Bank Finance: The Importance of a Proper Enforcement of Legal Rules'. Unpublished manuscript. Cambridge, MA: MIT Sloan School of Management.

Nestor, S. (2000). *Corporate Governance Trends in the OECD Area: Where Do We Go From Here?* (Working paper). Paris: OECD.

OECD (Organization for Economic Cooperation and Development) (1994). *The OECD Jobs Study: Evidence and Explanations—Part II—The Adjustment Potential of the Labour Market*. Paris: OECD.

—— (1999). *Principles of Corporate Governance*. Paris: OECD.

Roe, M. (2000). 'Political Preconditions to Separating Ownership from Corporate Control', *Stanford Law Review*, 53: 539–606.

—— (2002). 'Corporate Law's Limits', *Journal of Legal Studies*, 31: 233–71.

—— (2003*a*). *Political Determinants of Corporate Governance*. Oxford: Oxford University Press.

—— (2003*b*). 'Institutional Foundations of Ownership Separation in the West.' Working paper.

Witherell, W. (2000). 'Corporate Governance: A Basic Foundation for the Global Economy', *The OECD Observer*, Summer: 24–6.

Name Index